# Directory of Classic Sports and Grand Touring Cars

# Directory of Classic Prototypes and Grand Touring Cars

## Anthony Pritchard

**Aston Publications**

Published in 1988 by Aston Publications
Limited
Bourne End House, Harvest Hill,
Bourne End, Bucks, SL8 5JJ

© Aston Publications Limited 1988

This book is copyrighted under the
Berne Convention. All rights reserved.
Apart from any fair dealing for the
purpose of private study, research,
criticism or review, as permitted under
the Copyright Act 1956, no part of this
publication may be reproduced, stored
in a retrieval system, or transmitted in
any form or by any means, electronic,
electrical, chemical, mechanical, optical,
photocopying, recording or otherwise
without prior written permission. All
enquiries should be addressed to the
publishers.

ISBN 0 946627 29 0


Designed by Chris Hand


Photoset and printed in England by
Redwood Burn Limited,
Trowbridge, Wiltshire


Sole distributors to the
U.K. book trade,
Springfield Books Limited,
Norman Road, Denby Dale,
Huddersfield, West Yorkshire,
HD8 8TH


Sole distributors for the USA,
Motorbooks International,
Osceola, Wisconsin 54020,
United States

# Contents

# Introduction

For me it has been a great pleasure writing this book. So many memories (mainly happy) were brought back as I referred to race reports and my notes of the period, and researched through Nigel Snowdon's photographs (which now belong to Aston Publications). During the years covered by this book I attended many of the European races, very often with Nigel, who attempted, without a great deal of success, to teach me the rudiments of motor racing photography.

It was an era that was dominated by three makes, Ferrari, Ford and Porsche. By the time that Matra achieved domination in 1973–74, the excitement was over and Endurance racing was dieing, partly because the constant changes in the racing regulations deterred serious constructors from incurring the vast costs of design and development for a category that could be changed at short notice and partly because racing of such excitement and sheer quality can only be sustained for a limited period.

Mainly because of lack of opposition, Ferrari had dominated Prototype racing during its first couple of years, 1962–63. When Ford entered the arena, it was clear that the American effort would be a serious threat or a farce. Ferrari's reaction was slow and guarded. The 250P V-12 Prototype of 1963 was a beautifully balanced and, for its time, technically advanced and sophisticated car that the then meagre opposition, with one exception, could not oppose. That exception was Porsche, who by 1963 had accumulated more class wins in post-war days than any other manufacturer, and did represent a serious threat to Ferrari on such slower, difficult circuits as the Nürburgring and the Little Madonie, used for the Targa Florio road race.

Ford failed in both 1964 and 1965, not exactly surprising with a radical new design, and I remember the excitement we all felt when privately entered but works-supported Ferrari 250LMs took first two places at Le Mans in 1965, but the Dearborn Company, through buying expertise in the shape of Holman and Moody and Shelby-American, broke through to eventual success at Le Mans and elsewhere with the enormously powerful 7-litre Mk 2 and Mk 4 cars. From Ferrari came a muted reaction in 1966 with the 4-litre P3 cars, strongly trying to give the impression that Maranello represented but a tiny, enthusiastic team, struggling on limited means against the mighty American sledgehammer. At some races he entered only one car, he missed the Le Mans Test Weekend and the Ferraris were trounced in the 24 Hours race. Ferrari escaped with his reputation untarnished,

*Unusual contender – the McLaren M8C Can-Am car with Ford-Cosworth DFV V–8 engine driven by Chris Craft/Trevor Taylor in the 1970 BOAC 500 Miles race at Brands Hatch.* (Nigel Snowdon)

save only for the unpleasant altercation at Le Mans, where Surtees withdrew from the team because of Ferrari internal politics, and with the universal recognition that to compete in both Formula 1 and Prototype racing threw an impossible burden on any racing organization.

Ferrari fought back in 1967 with the magnificent P4 cars, 4-litre V-12s again, technically sophisticated, highly competitive, superbly styled – the epitome of the competition Prototype of the 1960s – and with a great deal of mechanical design in common with Ferrari Formula 1 cars. As mentioned above, Ford won again at Le Mans, and although the Ferraris were beaten into second and third places, it was a shameless defeat; to many it seemed a near-miracle of technical engineering that such highly developed cars could last 24 hours, and (because the Mirage victory at Spa counted marks separately from Ford) won the Prototype Championship. One of the great sights of 1967 was the Chaparral 2F, 'the great white whale', with towering rear aerofoil that eventually justified its creators' and General Motors' confidence by winning the BOAC 500 Miles race at Brands Hatch. Everyone liked Jim Hall and the Chaparral team because they were such thoroughly nice people.

With the imposition of a 3-litre-capacity limit for Prototypes and a 5-litre limit for Competition Sports Cars for 1968, the face of endurance racing changed; Ferrari withdrew, as did the Chaparral and works Ford teams. For two years racing was fought out between Porsche and the superbly prepared and carefully developed 4.7-litre Ford GT40s of John Wyer's Gulf-sponsored team. During this period, Alfa Romeo, Ferrari and Matra all raced 3-litre Prototypes (the Italian teams from 1969 only), but they achieved no real success. The Ferrari 312P, little more than a Formula 1 car with full-width aerodynamic bodywork, was one of the prettiest cars raced. The quality of racing was not high in 1968–69, but the Le Mans race in 1969 provided one of the closest finishes in the history of the 24 Hours race with the GT40 of Jacky Ickx leading the Porsche 908 of Hans Herrmann across the finishing line with a lead of only one hundred or so yards. Although the 4.5-litre Porsche 917 appeared during 1969, few of us appreciated either its implications or its potential.

For those who follow motor racing closely, factory visits are essential to obtain first-hand information and material (at a race, unless you had very close connections with the team and drivers, no one had time to tell you anything). At Matra in October 1969 I was entertained by Gérard Ducarouge and I was impressed by not only the determination of Matra to succeed, but by the superb food – and the quality of the wine – in the Directors dining room at Vélizy. A few days later I was

*One of the fastest contenders in 1971 was the Roger Penske-developed Sunoco-Ferrari 512M. It was driven at Le Mans by Mark Donohue/David Hobbs, but it retired with engine problems.* (Nigel Snowdon)

with Autodelta at Settimo Milanese. The facilities were impressive, as was the team's dedication, despite an appallingly unsuccessful season, and the *Spaghetti Carbonara* in the local *trattoria* in the company of Roberto Bussinello and Ignazio Giunti (and his fianceé) was superb. Sadly, Giunti was killed in the Buenos Aires 1000 km race less than three months later. Almost equally sad was the fact that Carlo Chiti, at Autodelta and later with his own Motori Moderni organisation, consistently failed to achieve real success.

The decision of both Porsche and Ferrari to build 5-litre Competition Sports Cars for 1970 (in fact the 917 Porsche was originally 4.5 litres) not only frustrated the intention of the FIA to restrict the speed of Prototypes (for they tended to make Formula 1 cars appear slow) but provided two years of the most exciting racing ever seen. In 1970 Ferrari battled with Porsche and in 1971 Porsche team battled with Porsche team, but 1970 was the really great year. Porsche were dominant, because the 917 cars were lighter and less complex, they were better prepared and, in the main, they were better driven. The sheer eclat, bravado, car control and skill of Jo Siffert and Pedro Rodriguez of the Gulf 917 team was astounding. Their driving was exciting – and immensely satisfying to watch – and the spectacle was heightened by the close rivalry that existed between them. The sight of a 917 at full bore through the sweeps of Spa or on the Mulsanne straight at Le Mans was not just exciting – it was awe-inspiring and almost frightening.

So much in 1970 depended on Le Mans. That year Nigel Snowdon and I were able to accompany the Gulf team and stay with them at the Hôtel de France at La Chartre. Through Wyer's patronage with Aston Martin, Ford and Gulf teams, the hotel became renowned throughout the motor racing world and its cuisine is superb. The Gulf team was relaxed, confident in the knowledge that they were 'the favourites', with the cars superbly prepared for battle. On the eve of the race the

*Lack of adequate finance cramped the style of John Wyer's team in the 1970s. At Spa in 1974 Derek Bell/Mike Hailwood finished second with the Gulf GR7.* (Nigel Snowdon)

mechanics worked on the 917s, putting the finishing touches to final preparations, in an almost lighthearted manner. In the Ferrari garage, however, Mauro Forghieri brooded over a gloomy atmosphere; it was as if Ferrari knew that, whilst they had to win the race, they were going to lose. In fact both the Ferrari and Gulf entries failed and victory went to a Martini-entered 917. So successful was the Gulf team overall in 1970, so good were relations within the team, that even on the day after the Le Mans débâcle when three cars had retired, everyone was still smiling – with the exception of John Wyer – and relaxed as ever. John Wyer's austere manner was superbly balanced within the team by David Yorke's ability to communicate so well, to attend to minor details and to act as a superb on-the-spot manager.

At the end of 1970, Ferrari withdrew from racing the big 5-litre Competition Sports Cars and concentrated on development of the 3-litre 312P Prototype for 1972, when the 5-litre cars would be banned. The result was a battle in 1971 between the 917s of the Wyer team and the similar cars from the Martini team. However, throughout the year the 917s displayed a surprising lack of reliability and in this one year, while the Ferrari was not only very much under development, but suffering from more than its fair share of bad luck, Autodelta enjoyed a tremendous run of success with the now sorted Tipo 33 winning outright three races and the Prototype class in every event except the Nürburgring 1000 km race, where the Porsche 908/03s, specially built for this race and the Targa Florio, were the winners, and Le Mans, which the team did not enter.

*Throughout the years 1967–76 Autodelta entered works Alfa Romeos in long-distance events, but, overall, achieved little success. Arturo Merzario/Brian Redman were holding second place with this T33 TT12 car in the 1974 Nürburgring 1000 Km race, but retired because of a broken oil cooler. (Nigel Snowdon)*

With the imposition of the 3-litre capacity limit in 1972, Ferrari enjoyed a season of outright success, almost completely unchallenged, except for Le Mans, which Maranello did not enter, and where Matras took the first two places. For 1972 Ferrari had managed to get the ingredients just right, a superbly, well-balanced car closely related to the team's Formula 1 cars in design, very high standards of preparation, largely due to Ermanno Cuoghi, formerly with the Gulf team, but by then joint chief mechanic at Ferrari, excellent team management by former driver Peter Schetty and some of the world's best drivers in the team, including Jacky Ickx, Clay Regazzoni, Ronnie Peterson and Brian Redman. One race that Ferrari did not enter was Le Mans and here again the Matras took the first two places. By 1973 Matra development had been substantial and the cars were vastly improved. Throughout the year the French cars gave Maranello a good run for its money and Ferrari withdrew from the category at the end of the year. The result was that Matra was unopposed in 1974, apart from its own occasional weaknesses, and completely dominated the year's racing. When Matra withdrew from racing at the end of 1974, it meant the death of Endurance racing, although that death was to prove a long drawn out and rather boring affair. For some years long-distance racing languished in the doldrums, proving a largely Porsche benefit, but happily, since the reappearance of the Jaguars, it has vastly revived over the last few years and we are now seeing yet again a golden era in long-distance racing.

In this book I have been somewhat selective about the makes included and I have not religiously included every make that appeared in Championship races. Instead I have concentrated on the more important marques and those of special interest, but occasionally allowed myself the indulgence of including a relatively unimportant car of personal interest. One result of this approach has been that I have tended to pay little attention to the small-capacity French cars, as I think that the interest in these is very parochial.

# Races and Regulations

The Commission Sportive Internationale of the Féderation Internationale De l'Automobile decided to abolish the World Sports Car Championship for 1962. The reason for this was that Ferrari had been dominating racing year in and year out with only occasional challenges from the Maserati 'Bird-cage' cars and by the German Porsche entries. In its place there was to be a Grand Touring Car Championship, divided into three classes up to 1000 cc, 1001–2000 cc and over 2000 cc. However, the Automobile Club de l'Ouest, organisers of the Le Mans 24 Hours race, believed that an event for GT cars only would result in a major fall-off in attendances. They announced that they would include a class for 'Experimental' Prototype cars of up to 4 litres, in addition to GT cars. After negotiations, the organisers of the Sebring, Targa Florio and Nürburgring 1000 km races also decided to include Prototypes. There was to be a new championship, the Challenge Mondial de Vitesse. Points were to be awarded to makes that were represented only in *all* the qualifying rounds. Grand Touring cars could also score in this Championship, but not Sports Cars, which the organisers of the Sebring, Targa Florio and Nürburgring races had decided to permit in their events. Ferrari won the Challenge Mondial de Vitesse from Porsche and Alfa Romeo and these were the only makes that competed in all four rounds of the new Championship. In the Grand Touring Championship the winners in the respective classes were Fiat-Abarth, Porsche and Ferrari.

So far as Grand Touring Prototypes were concerned, these rules carried on through 1963, with the exception that from 1963 onwards there was no 4-litre-capacity limit. The Grand Touring Car Championship also continued, but the rules had become even more complicated and the Championship now included rallies and hill climbs. The Grand Touring Prototype category remained unchanged until the end of 1967, by when Ford and Chaparral were both racing 7-litre cars. So far as the Grand Touring category was concerned, it became more and more of a farce, as both the Ferrari 250GTO and the racing Cobras were homologated as Grand Touring cars even though far fewer than 100 had been built. In both cases the argument was that they were modified versions of production cars, but the differences were so vast that they were in reality completely different designs. This caused a major problem when Ferrari tried to homologate the 250LM, his production mid-engined car in 1964, and was turned down because nothing like the 100 had been built. The Grand Touring category was amended for

*At the end of 1967 unlimited-capacity Prototypes were banned. These are the three works Ferrari P4s at the 1967 BOAC 500 Miles race at Brands Hatch. To the left are two Lotus 47s and behind the Ferraris is Sid Taylor's Chevrolet-powered Lola T70 Mk 3.* (Nigel Snowdon)

1966, when it became known as the Group 4 Sports Car category, of which 50 identical units had to be produced, and accordingly both the Ferrari 250LM and the Ford GT40 in 4.7-litre form were admitted to the category. The Grand Touring Prototypes were now known as Group 6 Prototypes.

A further change was made to the regulations for 1968, when the CSI announced that there would be a new Sports Car Manufacturers Championship, the proper title of which was le Championnat Internationale des Marques. This imposed a maximum capacity limit of 3 litres for Group 6 Sports Prototypes, ie, the one-off 2-seater cars such as the Matras and Alpines. In addition there would be the category for Group 4 Competition Sports Cars, of which not fewer than 50 examples had been built. These would be allowed to compete alongside the Prototypes, provided the engine capacity did not exceed 5 litres. This was intended as a concession to small manufacturers such as Lola and to their owners and for homologation purposes manufacturers were allowed to include in their total cars with engines of both greater and less capacity than 5 litres, but, of course only cars up to 5 litres could be raced in Championship events. For 1979 the CSI again changed the rules, and reduced the number of cars needed to be built to secure homologation as a Group 4 Competition Sports Car to 25. The whole *raison d'être* of the CSI rules was thrown out of the window by first Porsche in 1969, with their 4.5-litre flat-12 917 cars, and then by Ferrari in 1970, with their 5-litre V-12 512S. In addition there were still categories for Grand Touring cars proper, these being on the basis of a minimum production of 500. These larger-production Grand Touring cars have little part to play in the story in this book. In addition there was inaugurated in 1970 the European 2-litre Constructors Championship. This was open to a wide range of cars and many of those that were eligible and complied with the detailed regulations also took part in endurance races.

At the end of 1971 the rules were changed yet again and the 5-litre Competition

13

By building 25 examples both Porsche and Ferrari circumvented the ban on large-capacity cars. This is the line-up of 25 917s for inspection by the Commission Sportive Internationale in 1969. (The Author's Collection)

With the introduction of a 3000 cc limit, Ferrari dominated the 1972 season with his flat-12 312P cars. In the 1972 BOAC 1000 Km race Tim Schenken (co-driving with Ronnie Peterson) with his 312P leads the similar car of Regazzoni/Redman. The race was won by another Ferrari driven by Ickx/Andretti. (Nigel Snowdon)

Sports Cars were banned. From 1972 racing was limited to 3-litre Group 5 Sports Cars (that is the former Protoypes), together with Group 4 Grand Touring Cars. Because there had been so many changes in the rules, already Sports Car racing was losing interest and support and the entry lists had frequently to be made up by 2-litre sports cars, Group 4 Grand Touring cars and sometimes even Group 2 saloons. Ferrari in 1972 won ten out of ten races entered and completely dominated the World Championship of Makes with a total of 140 points, to the 63 of the second-place make Alfa Romeo.

*When Jarier/Beltoise drove this Matra MS670C to a win in the 1974 British Airways 1000 Km race at Brands Hatch and clinched the World Championship of Makes for the French team, it meant the real end of this class of racing, although it was to linger on for another couple of years.* (Nigel Snowdon)

In 1975 the Le Mans 24-Hours race was not part of the World Championship for Makes, because the Automobile Club de l'Ouest decided to introduce a fuel consumption limit with a view to publicising the economy of racing cars! The figures needed to be achieved approached something in the order of 50 per cent better than the Matras had been achieving in 1974 and this was one of the real reasons why Matra withdrew from endurance racing after dominating the 1974 season. By 1977, which marks the end of the period covered by this book, the FIA had introduced a second Championship. The existing World Championship of Makes for Sports Cars up to 3 litres was now known as The World Championship for Sports Cars, the cars were in the category known as Group 6 and the races had a maximum duration of four hours. In addition there was a new World Championship of Makes, the so-called Silhouette Formula, whereby the cars were to be similar in silhouette to actual production cars of a country where 400 had been produced in two years. These cars, categorized in Group 5, would run in races with a race distance of a minimum of six hours. Le Mans did not qualify in either category in 1976, because the organisers had decided to go their own way once again, admitting Touring cars, Grand Touring cars, Silhouette Formula cars and Sports-Racing cars in addition to American Stock Cars. This situation prevailed throughout 1977, by when the traditional sports cars were almost completely dead and the Group 6 races were totally dominated by Alfa Romeo. At the end of 1977, the World Championship for Sports Cars disappeared and was replaced for 1978 by a rather parochial European Sports Car Championship, which was very poorly supported. By 1979 international sports car racing had disappeared.

# Abarth (Italy)

The history of Carlo Abarth and Abarth cars is long and confused (and told as well as it can be told in *Abarth* by Pat Braden and Greg Schmidt, Osprey Publishing, 1983). Austrian-born Abarth became in post-war days technical and racing director of the Italian Cisitalia concern, financed by industrialist Piero Dusio, and when the Cisitalia firm folded in 1949 because of Dusio's financial difficulties, Abarth set up his own Scuderia Abarth. In the 1950s the small company concentrated on development and modification of the 1100 cc Fiat engine, and, from 1956, a long series of cars based on the Fiat 600. The most famous of these cars was the Fiat-Abarth 750 Zagato *Bialbero*, characterised by the double-bubble roof; there were also a number of Zagato aluminium coupés without the double-bubble. In 1958 Abarth introduced a version of the 600-based engine with twin-cam cylinder head. When Fiat produced an 850 cc car, Abarth produced 1000 cc derivatives of this. In addition Abarth produced a whole range of cars based on larger-capacity Fiat chassis, in the main with Allemano bodywork, but also displayed at various shows cars based on Ferrari, Alfa Romeo and Renault chassis. One of the most successful of these early Abarth designs was the strikingly and dramatically styled Porsche Carrera Abarth, lighter than the works Carreras and considerably more potent.

*This Simca-Abarth OT1300 driven by Martin/Messange finished 16th and last at Le Mans in 1967.* (Nigel Snowdon)

In 1962 Abarth entered into an arrangement with the French Simca company whereby Abarth produced high-performance derivatives of the Simca 1000 rear-engined saloon. The most successful derivative was the Simca-Abarth coupé, based on the Simca's platform chassis, and front and rear suspension and steering, but with Abarth's own engine of 1288 cc (76 × 71 mm); most engines featured twin overhead camshafts and two valves per cylinder (although a four-valve per cylinder head was offered, as was a version with single overhead camshaft), the crankshaft

*This Abarth 2000 Prototype with wedge-shaped bodywork and the engine mounted at the extreme rear of the car was driven in the 1969 BOAC 500 Miles race by Hezemans/van Lennep, but was eliminated by engine failure.* (Nigel Snowdon)

ran in three main bearings, twin Weber 45DCOE carburettors were fitted and power output was 147 bhp at 8800 rpm. Later there followed other engine variations, including 1600 cc and 1000 and 2000 cc. Generally these engines followed the design of the earlier units, but with the 2000 cc engine the crankshaft ran in five main bearings.

During 1963 these cars enjoyed an immense run of success in the Grand Touring category, including wins in the 1300 cc class at Sebring by Guichet/Noblet, with a similar car in third place in the class (but the cars failed in both the Targa Florio and at the Nürburgring), together with a large number of successes in Italian events. It was much the same story in 1964, with strong entries, but overall little was achieved in major events. The three cars entered in the Targa Florio failed, but at the Nürburgring Abarth/Simca 1300s took the first three places in the up to 1300 cc class for Grand Touring cars, with Herrmann/Jüttner winning the class. There were no cars entered at Le Mans, and following the take-over of Simca by Chrysler in 1965, the Simca-Abarth line came to an end.

From 1963 onwards, Abarth had produced a production run of 100 of a 2-litre Simca-Abarth to qualify for homologation as a Grand Touring car. This engine was destined to power the Fiat-Abarth 236B sports-racing car, which appeared in 1968. This new car, which featured a multi-tubular space-frame with stressed skinning on the sills, had front suspension by double wishbones and coil spring/damper units, while at the rear there were lower links, radius arms and coil spring/damper units. The engine, as raced in this car, had a capacity of 1946 cc (88 × 80 mm) with twin overhead camshafts, two twin-choke Weber carburettors, two valves per cylinder, a compression ratio of 11.5:1 and a power output of 250 bhp at 8000 rpm. This 4-cylinder engine was mounted behind the rear axle line of the new car and in unit with a 5-speed gearbox. The body, constructed in glass-fibre, featured detachable front and rear panels, wedge-shaped nose, and very large perspex windscreen. Later in 1968 a 3-litre V-8 Abarth Prototype, distinguished by having the oil radiator mounted high above the tail, appeared, and Peter Schetty won races with it at Aspen and Innsbruck, both of a very minor nature, but during the year the 2-litre cars achieved nothing in the way of success.

However, in 1969 to 1970, and 1971 Austrian driver Johannes Ortner with a works car dominated the Competition Sports Car class of the European Mountain Championship, and Abarth continued to race the cars, primarily in Italian events and the 2-litre European Sports Car Championship with developments of the car, featuring minor modifications. In 1970 Abarth contracted with his dealer in Turin,

*Two views of the very fast 2-litre Abarth driven by Merzario/Hezemans in the 1972 BOAC 1000 Km race at Brands Hatch. It retired early in the race because of valve spring failure.* (Nigel Snowdon)

Enzo Osella, to operate the works cars on behalf of the company, and six racing mechanics were assigned on a full-time basis to Osella. By 1970 the Abarth had the engine moved ahead of the rear axle line and the wedge-shaped body was more aerodynamic. Nothing much was gained that year, but in the 2-litre Championship Casoni was fourth at the Paul Ricard circuit, Swart finished fourth in Finland in a very poorly supported race (there were no other finishers running), Ortner was third at the Salzburgring and at Anderstorp in Sweden, Swart was fifth at Hockenheim and Merzario led home two other Abarths driven by Kinnunen and van Lennep in the Circuit of Mugello in Italy. Merzario and Kinnunen were second and third in the Nürburgring 500 km race and in the Championship Abarth finished third behind Lola and Chevron.

In 1970 two 3-litre Abarths were entered in the Targa Florio for Jonathan Williams/Casner and Ortner/Merzario. Casoni crashed in practice, wrecking the suspension, so only one car started; this was eliminated by gearbox failure.

It was much the same story in 1971, when the team raced the improved *Cuneo* car, with Merzario taking second place at the Salzburgring and finishing third at Hockenheim, whilst Jabouille was second at Bologne, Merzario won at Vallelunga at Rome and Abarth took third place in the Championship. For 1972 the cars were much improved, with a redeveloped engine claimed to develop 270 bhp, improved rear suspension, redesigned body and lower weight. The cars were now more than a match for the Lola and Chevron opposition and during the year Hezemans won the Ignazio Giunti Trophy at Vallelunga, Merzario won at Dijon, Silverstone and Enna, also finishing third at Barcelona, whilst 'Nanni' Galli finished second at Jarama in Spain; the result was that Abarth won the Championship by a small margin from Chevron. In 1971 Abarth had been absorbed into the Fiat organisation and the Turin Company decided that Abarth should discontinue its racing activities at the end of 1972. Henceforth Abarth's main function, apart from the production of exhaust systems and the use of the name on certain high-performance Fiats, was to prepare works Fiat rally cars. Enzo Osella continued to race cars, but these now carried his own name and were developed by him, and Osella survives, just about, as an entrant in Formula 1.

# *Alfa Romeo (Italy)*

Until Alfa Romeo finally withdrew from serious racing at the end of the 1953 season, they had a reputation second to none as one of the world's leading manufacturers of racing cars and also as one of the world's most successful motor racing contenders. The company built its reputation in the 1920s, setting a pattern that was followed through the thirties and continued into post-war years with the Tipo 158 and 1959 Alfettas. After Alfa Romeo withdrew from Grand Prix racing at the end of 1951, they spent two seasons devoted to sports car racing with the unsuccessful *Disco Volante* sports car. After the failure of this promising design, the company did not again enter motor racing seriously, despite laying down designs for a new contender for the 2500 cc Grand Prix formula of 1954 onwards and building competition cars based on production models.

In 1964 the directors decided that it was now time that Alfa Romeo should return to motor racing and in December they founded the Autodelta concern with a capital of five million lire with premises in the village of Settimo Milanese, some distance from the centre of Milan. The new company was a reorganisation of the Udine company, a very small concern set up in 1962 by Carlo Chiti, former Ferrari and A.T.S. technical chief. Chiti became general manager of Autodelta and he was assisted as Sports Manager by Roberto Bussinello. The excessively fat and genial Chiti has earned something of a poor reputation over the years, because of the continued failure of the cars built under his direction. His engineering ability and astuteness are without doubt, but every project that he has been involved with has suffered from bad organization and administration and Autodelta revealed this in all its forms. Throughout its years its success was minimal and its outgoings vast. Its whole history ran in parallel with the general decline of Alfa Romeo and its loss of repute and reliability.

Although Autodelta did achieve success over a six-year period with competition versions of production Alfa Romeo cars, the pure competition cars, the subject of this book, in the main proved dismal failures.

## Tipo 33, 1967

For 1967, Chiti produced the Tipo 33 with a 1995 cc (78 × 52.2 mm) 90-degree V-8 engine designed by Alfa Romeo engineers Orazio Satta and Giuseppe Busso. This engine was of light alloy construction throughout, with twin overhead cam-shafts per bank of cylinders, Lucas fuel injection and a power output of 260 bhp at 9000 rpm, a very competitive figure for the period. Transmission was by a 6-speed

*The Tipo 33 driven by Zeccoli on its debut in the Fléron Hill Climb in Belgium in 1967. On this occasion the car looks very spruce, which is more than can be said for its surroundings!* (Alfa Romeo)

gearbox. The most unusual feature of the car was the design of the chassis, consisting of two large-section light alloy main side-members, of cylindrical shape, linked by a similar main cross-member running across the car at the rear of the cockpit area. These three main members also served as fuel tanks. An intricate magnesium-alloy casting at the front of the car provided additional cross-bracing and the attachments for the steering and front suspension. The engine was mounted at the rear between two projecting magnesium-alloy members linked by a fabricated sheet-steel metal section that carried the rear suspension. Wishbones and links were used at the front, with a similar layout incorporating radius rods at the rear. Ventilated disc brakes were fitted front and rear, with those at the rear mounted inboard. Heavily louvred 13 in. magnesium-alloy wheels were used. The body was a chunky, glass-fibre design, with an enormous windscreen and with a large forward-facing duct for the fuel injection mounted on the right-hand side of the rear panel of the car. A very dark red colour finish was adopted, set off by silver-painted wheels.

That, within its class, the 33 was a car of immense potential was beyond doubt, but throughout 1967 the cars were turned out in the most scruffy, appalling condition, two drivers Jean Rolland and Leo Cella were killed whilst testing, and the team not only missed races while it tried to sort out its reliability problems, but when it did race, the cars were hopelessly unreliable. For some reason that has never been explained, the Tipo 33 made its debut driven by Teodoro Zeccoli in the Fléron hill climb in Belgium, an event of absolutely no importance, where Zeccoli set fastest time of the day without difficulty. The team next entered the Sebring 12 Hours race and the Targa Florio (where four cars were entered) and all were eliminated. In practice for the Sicilian race, the cars were so plagued by a tendency for the front suspension to break, with the result that a wheel and hub parted company, that Chiti was forced to improvise a wire-cable device that offered some safety by preventing the hub from detaching itself completely. Two of the three cars retired at the Nürburgring, with the survivor fifth, and the 33s were not raced again until the Circuit of Mugello in late July. Here the cars looked scruffier than ever, with the rear intakes removed and the holes in the bodywork roughly patched over. Once again all three cars retired. During the year the team's only success with the 33 was a win in the very unimportant Bettojia Trophy race on the Vallelunga circuit at Rome.

## Tipo 33/2, 1968

It was clear to Chiti that there was nothing basically wrong with the engine design of the Tipo 33, the basic chassis concept or the transmission layout. Accordingly for 1968 he concentrated on the development of a new car round these basic components. At the front stronger suspension was fitted, and both front and rear track were increased. The water-cooling arrangements were redesigned so that they were now radiators, these days known as hip radiators, either side of the car just ahead of the rear wheels. There was now a new and attractive fibre-glass coupé body of sleek but conventional styling. The 33/2, as the new model was known, could be raced with both long and short tails and with or without the roof section in place. In addition the team also produced an enlarged 2.5-litre engine (78 × 64.4 mm) with a power output of 315 bhp at 8800 rpm and this was used in a few races. The cars were also sold to private teams and during the year a total of 28 of these cars was built so that they could become homologated as Competition Sports Cars for 1969. Although the 33/2 was always known at the works as the *Daytona*, because it was first raced at that circuit, it was in fact homologated as the *'33*

*Typical Italian road race: the Circuit of Mugello. In the 1968 race Autodelta made a very determined effort to win with an entry of four cars, but three, including this 33/2 driven by Casoni/Dini, retired.* (Alfa Romeo)

*At Le Mans in 1968 the Tipo 33/2s with long-tail bodywork finished fourth, fifth and sixth overall. Here the Vaccarella/Baghetti car (which retired) leads the Casoni/Biscaldi car, which finished sixth.* (Nigel Snowdon)

*Spyder'*. This engine was sold for use in Tasman racing, in which it enjoyed a fair measure of success.

In the Daytona 24 Hours race in February 1968, Autodelta fielded three 33/2s and they ran surprisingly well to finish fifth, sixth and seventh overall and take first three places in the 2000 cc class. Two of the three entries retired in the BOAC '500' race at Brands Hatch and the only finisher took a poor 14th place. A near miss followed in the Targa Florio, where Schütz crashed when in second place, but the 2-litre car of Galli and Giunti led at one stage in the race and took second place overall, with other 33/2s in third, fifth and sixth places. At the Nürburgring 1000 km race Galli/Giunti again upheld the team's reputation by finishing fifth overall and winning their class. The 2500 cc car driven by Schütz/Bianchi challenged the Porsche opposition until delayed by a broken alternator belt and finished seventh.

Autodelta were almost desperate to win the Circuit of Mugello and a full month was spent in training and preparation work. Even so three of the four 33/2s retired and the survivor, shared by Bianchi, Vaccarella and Giunti, only won after a mix-up in the pit of the leading Porsche driven by Siffert and Steinemann. In the absence of opposition, other than private Porsche 910s, Autodelta took the first three places in the Shell Cup at Imola over 500 km. The last race of the season for the team was Le Mans, postponed until the end of September, in which the team ran four cars with long aerodynamic tails with tail fins. In contrast to some of the team's efforts earlier in the season, the cars were superbly prepared and there had been careful attention to detail. The 33/2s took fourth, fifth and sixth places overall and the first three places in the 2000 cc class.

# The 33/3, 1969

For 1969, the 33/2 was homologated in Group 4 as a Competition Sports Car. Autodelta, however, had turned their attention to a larger-capacity car, which bore only the barest resemblance to its predecessors. The H-section chassis had been replaced by a more conventional monocoque constructed from sheet-alloy and tubing, with large side-boxes containing the foam-filled rubber fuel bags. Although the layout of the suspension was generally similar to that of the 2-litre cars, it was largely constructed from titanium, as were many other components of the new 33/3, and Autodelta had their own sophisticated titanium welding facilities.

*The Tipo 33/3 3-litre cars made their debut at Sebring in 1969, but they were untested and hopelessly unreliable.* (Alfa Romeo)

For the 33/3, Autodelta had developed a 90-degree V-8 engine of 2993 cc (86 × 64.4 mm), with light alloy construction throughout, twin overhead camshafts per bank of cylinders, four valves per cylinder, Lucas fuel injection and a claimed power output of 390/395 bhp at 9000 rpm. Although this 3-litre engine had been installed in a Cooper Formula 1 chassis in 1968 and had been extensively tested, it in fact proved to be one of the most unreliable features of this car that was notoriously unreliable during its first couple of seasons.

A 6-speed gearbox was used in the early part of the 1969 season, but later in the year Autodelta substituted a 5-speed gearbox. There were twin water radiators just ahead of the rear wheels, the rear disc brakes were again mounted inboard and the open glass-fibre bodywork was made by Autodelta themselves. In all, six of these cars were constructed during 1969.

Although the model made its competition debut with a great flourish and indeed some degree of conflict at Sebring, they arrived looking tatty and badly prepared and proved hopelessly unreliable. The conflict lay over John Surtees, who had contracted to drive for Alfa Romeo only to find that it conflicted with his fuel contract with another company and he was obliged to withdraw from the team. All three cars retired early in the race because of failure of the glue-assembled radiators. There were more problems at the Le Mans Test Weekend, when Lucien Bianchi, at the wheel of a new car with a longer and more aerodynamic tail, crashed with fatal results.

For much of the remainder of the year Autodelta concentrated on development work and the cars were rarely seen. After 33/2s had been run in the Targa Florio, the Martini Meeting at Silverstone and the Nürburgring 1000 km race, the 33/3 reappeared at the minor German Norisring event at Nuremberg. By this time the 33/3 had been fitted with a larger radiator and there had been a change of glue! Giunti retired with engine trouble, but the following month at Hockenheim Vaccarella, with a new fixed-head coupé version, and Giunti took third and sixth places. At long last the Tipo 33/3 scored a win in the inaugural meeting on the new Österreichring circuit in Austria, but it was something of a shameful victory. De Adamich finished second with his 33/3, but Chiti lodged an objection against the winner, Masten Gregory, with a private 908 Porsche, which had been pushed across the line by another Porsche after its engine had blown. Another failure followed in the Austrian Grand Prix on the same circuit a fortnight later, but at Enna Vaccarella won with the 3-litre coupé. In their final race of the year, at Imola, Giunti took second place for Autodelta behind the Gulf-Mirage of Jacky Ickx.

## *The Tipo 33, 1970*

By the start of the 1970 season, Chiti believed that most of the problems with the 33/3 had been resolved. The bodywork had been 'cleaned up' and he was looking forward to a season of reasonable success, notwithstanding the fact that the prospects of competing on even terms with the 5-litre Porsche 917 and Ferrari 512S opposition was slim. Autodelta had a strong team of drivers, that included Formula 1 drivers Piers Courage and Rolf Stommelen.

At the beginning of the year there were two non-Championship races held in the Argentine, an event over 1000 km, in which Autodelta achieved no success, but the following weekend there was a 200-mile race, run in two heats, in which Courage and de Adamich scored an encouraging victory over a works Matra and a number of private Porsche 908s. At Sebring in March all three Tipo 33/3s were plagued by mechanical troubles, but they finished and the highest placed car, driven by Masten Gregory and Toine Hezemans, took third place. For some reason not sensibly explained, only a single 33/3 with short tail was entered for Courage/de Adamich in the BOAC 1000 km race at Brands Hatch and it was crashed twice, by each driver, and damaged so badly that it had to be withdrawn. Four cars were entered at Monza, but on this high-speed circuit they were no match for the larger-capacity opposition and the highest placed Autodelta finisher was Galli/Stommelen in second place. All three entries crashed in the Targa Florio, a race in which they proved no match in terms of either speed or handling for the German opposition, the Porsche 908/03s.

By the Nürburgring 1000 km race, Autodelta had developed an improved version of the 33/3, with much more extensive use of titanium for engine and chassis components, revised steering geometry and new and lighter wheels. It was driven by Stommelen/Courage, but retired with rear suspension failure. At Le Mans Autodelta entered four cars with long tails and small rear vertical fins, and all to the specification of the cars raced at the Nürburgring. All four cars were eliminated, two of them with engine problems. In the non-Championship 500 km race at Imola, an Alfa driven by Galli/de Adamich finished second, three laps behind the winning Porsche 917. Autodelta's last race of the year was the Austrian 1000 km race at the Österreichring, where the cars had modified front suspension and were running on smaller 13 in. wheels. Once again three of the four cars were eliminated, but the survivor, driven by de Adamich/Pescarolo took second place. In fact the use of the term 'survivor' is a misnomer, because it finished the race in the pits with a blown engine three laps before the chequered flag after a frantic chase of the leading Porsche 917 driven by Siffert/Redman.

*In the pits at the 1970 BOAC 1000 Km race at Brands Hatch is the 33/3 driven by de Adamich/Courage. It was the only Autodelta entry, but retired after two off-course excursions. The 33/3s were now lighter and with more compact bodywork.* (Nigel Snowdon)

*For Le Mans in 1970 Chiti prepared a team of four 33/3s with long-tail bodywork surmounted by small tail fins, but all retired. This is the car driven by de Adamich/Courage which retired early in the race with engine problems.* (Nigel Snowdon)

## The Tipo 33/3 and 33/3 TT, 1971

The 33/3s had by 1971 improved substantially in terms of both performance and reliability and Chiti seemed at long last to have sorted out the team management. At the beginning of the year in the Buenos Aires 1000 km race, which was now a round in the championship, the team took third and fourth places behind two JW-entered Porsche 917s. It was much the same story at Sebring, where a Martini-entered 917 was the winner but 33/3s were second and third. At long last outright victory came the team's way at Brands Hatch, in the BOAC 1000 km race. After the Porsche 917s ran into problems, de Adamich/Pescarolo were the outright winners. At Monza de Adamich/Pescarolo took third place, with two other 33/3s in fourth and fifth places. Yet another third place followed at Spa in the 1000 km race. However, the team's finest victory of the year was in the Targa Florio in Sicily. Not only were the Alfas as fast with as good handling as the Porsche 908/03 opposition, but all three of the German cars were eliminated in accidents and the 33/3s of Vaccarella/Hezemans and de Adamich/van Lennep took first and second places.

At the Targa Florio Autodelta produced the 33/3 TT car, clearly inspired by the design of the Porsche 908/03, with central monocoque box-section and light alloy tubular framework. It was narrower, shorter, lower and lighter than the ordinary 33/3 and had superbly simple and attractive lines. It also weighed 50 kg less than the usual 33/3. As on the Porsche 908/03, a lighter gearbox was mounted ahead of the rear axle. The TT stood for 'telaio tubolare' or 'tubular chassis', but it was nicknamed the 'Tipo Tedesco' (German type) because of its lack of originality. Although tested during the year and appearing at several races, this model was not in fact raced until 1972.

*This 33/3 driven by de Adamich/Pescarolo won the 1971 BOAC 1000 Km race. The 1971 season brought Autodelta an exceptional run of successes.* (Nigel Snowdon)

*Alfa Romeo took the first two places in the 1971 Targa Florio, following the failure of the Porsche 908/3s. This is the second-place car of de Adamich/van Lennep.* (Nigel Snowdon)

On the strength of their win in the difficult Targa Florio road race, Autodelta were optimistic of success at the Nürburgring, but the Alfa Romeos proved no match for the Porsche opposition and de Adamich/Pescarolo trailed home fourth behind a trio of the 908/03s, with Hezemans/Vaccarella fifth.

Chiti had already missed the Daytona race and now missed Le Mans, because he took the view that special cars were needed for these high-speed events. Accordingly the next Championship race for the Alfas was in Austria at the end of June. A Porsche 917 won, but Hezemans/Vaccarella took second place. Yet another outright win followed for the team at Watkins Glen, where Peterson/de Adamich were the winners.

Despite the strength of the 5-litre Porsche opposition, Autodelta had achieved remarkable success in 1971 and their prospects in 1972, when racing was limited to 3-litre cars, were exceptionally good. However, success was to elude them.

## The Tipo 33/3 TT, 1972

Although Autodelta had been working on the development of their own flat-12 engine, which would be much more powerful, this was not ready for the start of the 1972 season and the team was forced to use the new 33/3 TT with the V-8 unit. Since 1971, a heavier steel tubular space-frame had been adopted, together with front and rear sub-frames, suspension, engine connecting rods and steering column all constructed in titanium. Early in the season the cars were fitted with Chiti's fireproof fuel tanks, for which much had been claimed. These were based on an independent series of thin, hollow layers intermeshing to provide alternative horizontal chambers, the one series containing petrol and the other an extinguishing liquid. In an accident the separation between the layers broke to produce a mixture of fuel and extinguishing liquid which would not ignite. As each of the two tanks fitted to the 33/3 TT weighed 52 lb more than the conventional system, the arrangement was soon abandoned.

What ruined Alfa Romeo's prospects of success in 1972 was a full team of flat-12 Tipo 312P cars entered by Ferrari and these dominated the year's racing. Throughout the year the Alfa Romeos trailed home behind the opposition from Maranello.

In Buenos Aires the highest placed Alfa finisher, in third place, was the 33/3 of Alberti/Facetti, a private but works-supported car. Despite Chiti's comments about Daytona in 1971, a team of 33/3 TTs cars was entered and Elford/Marko finished third behind a brace of Ferraris. This performance was repeated at Sebring, where Hezemans/Vaccarella finished third behind the Ferraris, and at Brands Hatch in the BOAC 1000 km race, where Revson/Stommelen finished third with team-mates de Adamich/Elford fourth, again with Ferraris in the first two places. Autodelta missed both the Monza and Spa races to concentrate on a victory in the Targa Florio. Four cars ran, and although two finished, they were in second and third places behind the solo Ferrari entered for Merzario/Munari. By entering only one car, Ferrari had managed to manoeuvre Autodelta into the position where they were on to a hiding to nothing. If they had won, everyone would have said so they should have done, and as they lost, they were almost disgraced. It was third place again at the Nürburgring, for de Adamich/Marko behind the Ferraris. Autodelta entered two cars at Le Mans, and, remarkably, one survived the 24 hours to finish fourth in the hands of de Adamich/Vaccarella, but was trounced by the Matras, which took the first two places, and an old Porsche 908 *Lang* which had been refurbished at Stuttgart. After this series of failures, Autodelta withdrew from the last two rounds of the Championship to concentrate on development work

*An unusual view of the 33/3 TT of Stommelen/Revson in the pits at the 1972 BOAC 1000 Km race at Brands Hatch. It finished third, no match for the Ferrari opposition.* (Nigel Snowdon)

*At Le Mans in 1972 this 33/3 TT driven by de Adamich/Vaccarella finished fourth, but the race was Matra-dominated.* (Nigel Snowdon)

for 1973. They did, however, run at the non-Championship Imola race in September, where de Adamich took third place.

## The 33/3 TT and 33 TT 12, 1973

Development of the flat-12 engine was taking much longer than expected and the 33 TT 12 car did not appear until mid-season. For much of the year, therefore, Autodelta was forced to rely on the now outdated V-8. When the flat-12 cars did appear, they were beset by engine problems, particularly with the lubrication system, and engine failure succeeded engine failure. The sensation of the year, however, was the Matra team, which substantially dominated the year's racing at the expense of both Ferrari and Autodelta. At the end of the year Autodelta had nothing to look back on with satisfaction apart from some fast times in practice and a second place in a non-Championship race at the end of the year.

## The 33 TT 12, 1974

By 1974, Autodelta had the 2995 cc (77 × 53.6 mm) flat-12 engine, which developed around 500 bhp at 11,000 rpm largely sorted and it proved to be the best part of the 1974 cars. The real problem now with Autodelta was that the chassis was too heavy, the cars still lacked reliability and team management was deficient. Ferrari had now withdrawn to concentrate on Formula 1, so the opposition in strength was limited to Matra-Simca.

The opening round of the World Championship was at Monza in April and after the failure of the Matras, Autodelta enjoyed a clean sweep with Merzario, partnered by Mario Andretti, winning from Stommelen/Ickx and Facetti/de Adamich.

*A broken oil cooler eliminated this 33 TT 12 driven by Arturo Merzario (seen here at the wheel) and Brian Redman when holding second place in the 1974 Nürburgring 1000 km race.* (Nigel Snowdon)

Because the Spa race was held only ten days later, Autodelta could not be ready in time and were forced to give this a miss. They were, however, strong contenders at the next round of the Championship at the Nürburgring later in May. A Matra won, but the Alfa Romeos of Stommelen/Reutemann and Facetti/de Adamich took second and third places. It was the same story at Imola in June, where Matra was again the winner and the same Alfa driver pairings settled for second and third places. Chiti was always wary of Le Mans, knowing his cars lacked the stamina for this race, and Autodelta once again withdrew in 1974, claiming they had done insufficient endurance testing. The Alfa Romeos were back in the fray in Austria at the end of June, but again were beaten by Matra, and Facetti/de Adamich and Ickx/Merzario finished in second and fifth places. Autodelta sent two cars to Watkins Glen in July, but one was written off in practice because of tyre failure and the other was eventually disqualified after never having been in the running. Beaten and demoralized, Autodelta withdrew from endurance racing for the rest of the year.

*Work in the pits in the 1974 Nürburgring 1000 km race on the 33 TT 12 of de Adamich/Facetti which took third place.* (Nigel Snowdon)

## The 33 TT 12, 1975

In 1975 there was virtually no opposition to the Alfa Romeos, for Matra had now withdrawn and Alfa Romeo continued to run two cars, occasionally three, entered in the name of Willibert Kauhsen, a wealthy German private entrant. The Sports Car class at Daytona was cancelled for lack of entries so the team's first race was at Mugello in March. Here the turbocharged Alpine-Renault of Larrousse/Jabouille, running for the first time, scored a totally unexpected victory when the Alfa Romeos were delayed. The Autodelta cars of Merzario/Ickx and Pescarolo/Brambilla finished second and fourth. However, the Kauhsen team pulled itself together and scored victories at Dijon, Monza, Spa, Pergusa (the Coppa Florio) and the Nürburgring. There were no Alfa Romeos at Le Mans, which was not a round in the Championship, and the team rounded off the season with wins in Austria and at Watkins Glen. It was a very hollow Championship victory.

## Postscript

By 1976 Sports Car racing was at its nadir and soon to disappear altogether. Autodelta, having at long last won the Championship, turned their attention to other matters. A new monocoque car, the 33 TS 12, made but three appearances. In the hands of Merzario and Brambilla it finished second at Imola to the Porsche 936 of Ickx/Mass, it was third fastest in practice at Pergusa, but failed to finish and was fastest in practice at the Salzburgring, but again failed to finish. In 1977 Alfa Romeo, sponsored by Fernet Tonic, returned to Sports Car racing with the 33 SC 12s, improved versions of the 1975 cars, and won all eight rounds of the Championship at Dijon, Monza, Vallelunga, Enna, Estoril, Paul Ricard, Imola and the Salzburgring. In Austria the team had fielded one of the cars with the 2134 cc (77 × 38.2 mm) turbocharged engine and said to develop 640 bhp at 11,000 rpm. The turbocharged Alfa Romeo had appeared at the Salzburgring in 1976 and at the same circuit in 1977 Merzario, despite brake and tyre problems, took second place behind team-mate Brambilla. Already Autodelta were supplying engines to the Brabham Formula 1 team, and in 1979 entered Formula 1 with their own cars. Alfa Romeo's Formula 1 racing career was to be as chequered as that in sports car racing. Alfa Romeo finally lost patience with Autodelta and wound the team up.

## The Grand Touring Cars

Back in 1954 Alfa Romeo had introduced the 1290 cc (74 × 75 mm) Giulietta, initially as the Sprint coupé, but followed a year later at the Turin Motor Show by a saloon version. This model, with jewel-like twin-cam engine, delightful road handling and, in coupé form, with superbly styled Bertone body, became the definitive Alfa Romeo production car. From it was developed a whole range of Giulietta variations. In 1962 there followed the Giulia, with engine capacity enlarged to 1570 cc (78 × 82 mm).

It was from this long line of production cars that there grew Alfa Romeo's return to racing. In 1957 there had appeared the Giulietta Sprint Speciale, with 100 bhp engine and very slippery bodywork, featuring a sharply sloping roof line with Kamm cut-off tail and pronouncedly curved wing line. It was, however, a car for Sorrento or Sunset Boulevard, rather than competition work. Zagato was requested to develop the car and the result was the much more powerful Sprint Zagato built in the Zagato works, and with a total production run of 210 including the Prototype car. Of these 210, the last 30 featured Kamm tails, sharply cut off, and with this and other aerodynamic improvements top speed was around 140 mph.

The next stage in development was the production of a pure competition car, now based on the 1570 cc Giulia engine developing 112 bhp at 6500 rpm. This car was known as the TZ ('Tubolare Zagato') and the basis was a new multi-tubular space-frame design by Edo Mazoni. This extremely rigid frame weighed only 88 lb, including the mounting points for the front and rear suspension. At the rear there was independent suspension and the body was a very light Zagato design, again with Kamm cut-off tail, and of similar basic concept to the body of the later SZ cars. The chassis was constructed by Zagato and the cars were assembled by Alfa Romeo dealers, Chizzola Brothers, in Udine to the north of Venice. Their assembly company was known as Delta, but the name was changed to Autodelta when Carlo Chiti joined the firm, and the organisation was subsequently transferred to the outskirts of Milan. In all 120 of the cars were built, so that they could be homologated, and they were raced by Italian teams, including Scuderia Sant' Ambroeus and The Jolly Club.

The cars were first raced late in the 1963 season, scoring a class win at Monza and were very widely raced in 1964. In the Sebring 12 Hours race a car shared by Stoddart/Kaser/Elio Zagato (of the coach-building family) finished 13th overall and won its class. The Targa Florio road race in Sicily brought the TZ more success, with the cars of Bussinello/Todaro and 'Kim'/Thiele in third and fourth places behind a brace of Porsche 904s. Another success followed in the Nürburg-

*The Alfa Romeo Giulia SZ of Sala/Rossi in the pits at Le Mans in 1963. It retired because of transmission problems.* (Nigel Snowdon)

ring 1000 km race, where Biscaldi/Furtmayr and Bussinello/Pianto finished 13th and 14th, taking the first two places in the 1600 cc GT class. At Le Mans Bussinello/Deserti finished 13th, but as there was no 1600 cc class at this race they were classified fifth in the 2000 cc GT category. The cars also performed well during the year in rallies and wins were scored in the Coupe des Alpes and the Tour de Corse in Corsica.

*Boley Pittard with the Walker-Day Alfa Romeo TZ1 in the Martini Trophy at Silverstone in 1965.* (Guy Griffiths)

*A view of the Autodelta works at Settimo Milanese. The car being worked on is a TZ2.*
(Alfa Romeo)

At Autodelta work was proceeding on an even higher-performance version of the Tubolare Zagato, to be known as the TZ2. Only 12 of these cars were built, exclusively for the use of Autodelta, and none was sold. The main difference was much lower, lighter, glass-fibre body work. By this stage the Giulia engine had been developed, with 11.4:1 compression ratio and twin-plug ignition to produce 170 bhp at 7500 rpm. It is perhaps irrelevant to comment of a competition car that the TZ2 had vastly inferior looks to its immediate predecessor, but it was immensely more potent and enjoyed a very successful run of success in 1965.

At Sebring the TZ of Rolland/Constan finished 16th, well down the field, but it won the 1600 cc GT class. At the Targa Florio Autodelta was still racing the original TZ and Lucien Bianchi/Jean Rolland finished seventh overall with their TZ, winning the 1600 cc GT class. Alan Day, the Alfa Romeo dealers in the Finchley Road in London, had been running a team of TZs in collaboration with Ian Walker, and these were entered in the Spa 500 km race. The Walker/Day car of Boley Pittard won the 1600 cc class at 113.77 mph, but apparently something broke on Hegbourne's car on the Masta straight when he was travelling at around 125 mph, and the car flipped end over end, finishing well off the track. Sadly the driver suffered fatal injuries. At the Nürburgring, de Adamich/'Geki' with a TZ won the 1600 cc GT class, with the similar car of Bussinello/Zuccoli in third place in the class. It was in this race that the TZ2 was raced for the first time and Furtmayr/Schultz finished 19th overall. At Le Mans four GTZ2s were entered, three in the name of Autodelta, but although works owned, the fourth entry ran in the name of the Équipe Grande Ducale Luxembourgeoise. All four cars were accepted in the GT category. Unfortunately three cars retired with engine failure, but the Zec-

*The TZ2 of Zuccoli/'Geki' at Le Mans in 1965. It retired because of loss of engine oil.*
(Ford of Britain)

coli/Rosinski entry was eliminated when Zeccoli rammed the sandbanks at Mulsanne corner. In addition of course the cars scored many minor successes in Italian events, and elsewhere Bussinello was third in the 35-mile Prix du Tyrol at Innsbruck and Pittard with the surviving Walker-Day car took a second place at the Crystal Palace.

For 1966 the Autodelta team developed the GTA version of the Giulia intended primarily for saloon car racing and this model was to enjoy an immense run of success, with wins in the European Touring Car Championship in 1966, 1967 and 1968. The result was that the TZ2 now tended to take something of a back seat. However, a reasonable amount of success was gained. At Sebring, Bussinello/de Adamich won their class with their TZ2, but it was a victory made all the more remarkable by the fact that Bussinello had overturned the car in practice and a great deal of panel-beating had been needed to get it to the starting line. At Monza de Adamich/Zeccoli won their class and in the Targa Florio Pinto/Todaro finished fourth overall and won their class. Another class win followed for Bianchi/Schültze at the Nürburgring. There were no entries at Le Mans, and although the outings for the TZ2 had been somewhat limited, it had been yet another successful season.

By 1967 Autodelta were struggling to solve their many problems with the new Tipo 33 cars, and the days of the TZ2 were over. The one area in which Carlo Chiti achieved real progress at Autodelta was with modified versions of Alfa Romeo production cars and these did enjoy immense success. However, it must be remembered that instead of creating new cars from scratch, much of the development work had been done before Chiti came on the scene and he was working with already well-established and developed designs.

# Alpine (France)

The Alpine concern of Dieppe was sponsored by Renault, eventually being taken over by the main Renault company, and used engines designed by Amédée Gordini, who had raced his own Formula 1 and 2 and sports cars up until 1957, when he himself had joined the Renault concern. Alpine had first fielded Prototypes of up to 1500 cc since 1963 and had enjoyed a good measure of success. However, the decision was made to move up into the larger-capacity class with a new model known as the A-211, which first appeared at Montlhéry in 1967. The chassis design of the older 1500 cc A-210 was used, but it had heavier-gauge chassis tubing. This chassis had been designed by freelance designer Len Terry. It was a multi-tubular space-frame, based on a large number of fully triangulated small-diameter tubes. Suspension design was virtually identical front and rear, by wide-based double wishbones with coil spring/damper units. It was already outdated when the decision to use it for the 3-litre car was made.

The Gordini-designed power unit was a 2986 cc (85 × 66 mm) V-8 based on two of the 1500 cc sets of cylinders on a common crankcase, with twin chain-driven overhead cam shafts per bank of cylinders. At the time there was talk of a power output of around 320 bhp, but in fact the output was well under 300 bhp. Alpine adopted a 5-speed ZF gearbox. Perhaps the best feature of the Alpine was the low, sleek, very aerodynamic body, which had done much to help the smaller-capacity cars achieve success in their class. There was no way, however, that it was going to compensate for the substantial lack of bhp suffered by the 3-litre engine and in real terms the prospects of any sort of success were slim indeed.

*Alpine had a long history of success in the 1500 cc class, but they were unlucky at Le Mans in 1963. This is the M63 coupé of Boyer/Verrier that retired only a couple of hours before the finish because of a broken connecting rod. (Nigel Snowdon)*

The A-211 was first raced in the Paris 1000 km race at Montlhéry in 1967 and its seventh place proved sufficiently encouraging for Alpine to decide to press on with a full team of 3-litre cars in 1968.

## The A-220, 1968

For the 1968 season Alpine produced an improved version of the previous year's prototype, the A-220, which featured strengthened suspension, larger ventilated disc brakes and larger radiators mounted on either side of the car ahead of the rear wheels. The A-220 first appeared at the Le Mans Test Weekend, but arrived late on the Sunday after an earlier testing accident in which it had lost its engine cover. It was first raced at the Monza 1000 km race, together with the original A-211.

*The 3-litre Alpine A-220 of Vinatier/de Cortanze which finished eighth at Le Mans in 1968. It was the sole survivor of four 3-litre entries.* (Nigel Snowdon)

Although the new car retired with handling problems, following an accident in practice, the long list of retirements in this race enabled Patrick Depailler and Alain de Cortanze to drive the older car into third place overall, three laps in arrears at the finish. Alpine, wisely, missed the Targa Florio and next appeared with a new A-220 and the older A-211 at the Nürburgring. During practice Henri Grandsire had a particularly horrific accident with the latest A-220, which was launched into the air by a bad bump, smashed itself to pieces on landing, and spread its wreckage for some one hundred yards down the track. Miraculously the driver was uninjured apart from cuts on the arms and legs. The A-211 driven by Larrousse and Depailler finished well down the field in ninth place. By the Spa race Alpine were able to field only the A-211 driven by Bianchi and Grandsire, but it was never in the running. Alpine missed the Watkins Glen race and next ran at Zeltweg, where a single A-220 was driven by Bianchi, but this was eliminated by a leaking oil union.

For the Le Mans 24 Hours race, postponed until the end of September, Alpine made a very special effort with a total of four A-220 cars, three of which ran in the name of Société des Automobiles Alpines and one in the name of Ecurie Savin Calberson, a team sponsored by a major French haulage concern of that name. Of the four entries, one retired and two crashed and that of Mauro Bianchi was particularly spectacular; he lost the brakes on the run down to the Esses, hit the bank and the car exploded in a cloud of flames and black smoke. Quite remarkably the driver suffered only minor injuries. The surviving car of de Cortanze/Vinatier finished well down the field in eighth place.

## A-220, 1969

Following the failures of 1968, the Alpine concern continued to race the 3-litre cars on a very half-hearted basis in 1969. At the Le Mans Test Weekend three A-220 cars appeared. One of these featured radiators at the rear, incorporated in the spoiler. During testing the team had also tried a high-mounted aerofoil, but this was not raced following the ban on moveable aerodynamic devices imposed at the Monaco Grand Prix in May. Three A-220 cars were entered at Monza, but they were even less competitive than in 1968, although thanks to retirements the car of Depailler/Jabouille finished sixth. The Alpines were completely out of the picture on the fast Spa circuit, where three were entered in the 1000 km race, and then four cars, three of them the 1969 version with tail-mounted radiators, appeared at Le Mans. The race proved a complete débâcle for the team and all four cars retired. The writer, who left the race early on this occasion, recalls overtaking the Alpine transporters, already on their way back to Dieppe long before the race was over, tails metaphorically between their legs. After Le Mans the V-8 cars were not again raced.

## Postscript

Alpine returned to racing with turbocharged cars in 1974 with the A441 and won all seven rounds of the European 2-litre Sports Car Championship. In 1976 Renault re-entered Sports Car racing, with the turbocharged Alpine A442, with iron-block 24-valve 1997 cc 90-degree V-6 engine, said to develop 500–510 bhp at 9400–10,500 rpm. Unfortunately the Alpines, under the management of André de Cortanze, proved hopelessly unreliable and their best performances during the year were second places at Monza (Pescarolo/Jarier), and Dijon (Depailler/Lafitte

*At Spa in 1969 this Alpine A-220 with tail-mounted radiators was driven by Jabouille/Grandsire, but after mechanical problems it finished at the tail of the field.* (Nigel Snowdon)

with Jabouille/Jarier in third place). In 1977 Alpine-Renault limited themselves to an entry at Le Mans with four A442 cars, but all four retired.

Renault returned to Le Mans in 1978 with extensively modified cars and after very extensive testing sessions. Aerodynamic changes had been made to the bodywork, the cars were now designated A442As or A442Bs and three were entered. In addition there was a fourth car, the new A443, with larger 2140 cc engine, longer wheelbase, wider front wheels, longer-tail bodywork section, semi-enclosed cockpit with Plexiglas cowling and driven by Jabouille/Depailler. In a poorly supported race, Pironi/Jaussaud were the winners, from two Porsche entries, with another Alpine driven by Frequelin/Ragnotti/Dolhem/Jabouille in fourth place. By this time Renault were competing in Formula 1 as the pioneer entrant of turbocharged cars and they maintained a consistent, but not particularly successful, Formula 1 programme until they finally withdrew at the end of 1985, never having won the World Championship.

# Aston Martin (United Kingdom)

Following the team's win in the Sports Car Championship in 1959, Aston Martin had withdrawn from sports car racing and entered on their second disastrous season of Formula 1 in 1960. After yet another failure in that year's Grands Prix, the team withdrew from racing altogether.

Aston Martins, however, continued to appear in Grand Touring events and as early as the international meeting at Silverstone in May 1959, the team had entered Stirling Moss in the GT race with the yet as unhomologated DB4GT and at Le Mans had fielded the same DB4GT, but fitted with the experimental DBR3 engine as raced at Silverstone in 1958. This car had won at Silverstone, but was an early retirement at Le Mans. Thereafter, Aston Martin's racing reputation was maintained by private teams, notably the Essex Racing Team, with both the ordinary version of the DB4GT and the DB4GTZ with Zagato bodywork. Some measure of success was achieved, but the cars were no match for the Ferrari opposition.

In late 1961, partially as a result of pressure from their agents throughout the world, Aston Martin decided to return to racing and in two more seasons the cars were again seen on the race tracks before David Brown finally withdrew.

41

## DP212

For 1962 the team decided to build a Prototype to comply with the 4000 cc limit for 'Experimental' cars imposed at Le Mans in 1962. This was a much developed version of the DB4GT with the wheelbase of the platform chassis increased by one inch from 7 ft 9 in. to 7 ft 10 in., but with the same front and rear track of 4 ft 6 in. The front suspension, by unequal-length double wishbones and coil springs, was broadly similar to that of the DB4GT, but at the rear a de Dion axle suspended on torsion bars replaced the live axle and coil springs of the DB4GT. Girling disc brakes were fitted front and rear, together with Borrani 16 in. wire wheels and triple-eared hub caps.

The new car was powered by a development of the aluminium-block DB4GT engine linered out to 96 mm (compared with the standard 92 mm), but retaining the stroke of 92 mm and giving a capacity of 3996 cc. With three Weber 50 DCO carburettors and a compression ratio of 9:1 the power output in Le Mans form was 327 bhp at 6000 rpm. This compared with the 345 bhp claimed in the team's press statement and the 314 bhp of the DB4GT. Transmission was by a 5-speed S532 gearbox with synchromesh on the upper four ratios, a developed version of the gearbox used in the 1957–58 DBR2, whereas the DB4GT was fitted with a 4-speed all-synchromesh gearbox. The body of the DP212, constructed from magnesium-aluminium alloy, was superbly sleek and shapely and it was probably the best-looking competition car Aston Martin ever built.

At Le Mans the drivers were Graham Hill and Richie Ginther. At the start Hill led away, and was in second place at the end of the first hour, but there were delays because of problems with the dynamo, and after six hours' racing the 212 was retired with piston failure. Although the car was somewhat on the heavy side, it was clearly very competitive and the only problem experienced was aerodynamic lift at high speed.

New cars were planned for 1963 and the 212 acted as the test-bed for these. As a result of somewhat belated wind-tunnel tests, a new shape tail with flat rear panel and spoiler were adopted and this cured the aerodynamic problems. The DP212 was not raced again, but it ran at the Le Mans Test Weekend in 1963.

*The Aston DP212 of Graham Hill and Richie Ginther at Le Mans in 1962. It retired because of piston failure after six hours' racing. (Geoffrey Goddard)*

## DP214 and DP215

For 1963 three cars were built, two to run in the Grand Touring class, the DP214s, and the DP215 prototype, of which only the one was built.

All three 1963 cars featured light, heavily drilled and substantially cross-braced girder-section chassis frames. In fact, because the 214s were supposed to be the DB4GT modified within the permitted limits and homologated as GT cars, this did not comply with the rules. Whilst the DP214s retained suspension similar to that of the DB4GT production cars, there was independent rear suspension on the DP215. The DP215 had a power unit similar to that of the 1962 car, but to improve weight distribution, the team used the CG537 5-speed gearbox in unit with the final drive, as on the sports-racing DBR1s. It was a particularly odd choice, bearing in mind the many problems that the team had experienced with this gearbox during 1957–59. On the DP214s, the DB4GT engine was bored out to 93 mm, giving a capacity of 3750 cc. With triple Weber 50 DCO carburettors, 9.1:1 compression ratio and special exhaust valves and crankshaft, the power output was 317 bhp at 6000 rpm, only slightly more than that of the production cars, but for competition purposes with a much improved power range.

The three cars had new, lower, longer 20-gauge magnesium alloy bodywork, but because of their wet-sump engines, the 214s had a slightly higher bonnet line.

All three cars were entered at Le Mans, but the team was very much out of luck. The DP215, driven by Phil Hill/Lucien Bianchi, retired after only two hours with transmission problems. Both the DP214s suffered piston problems. The McLaren/ Ireland car blew its engine at close to 180 mph on the Mulsanne straight, liberally coating the road with oil, which resulted in several crashes, including the death of Bino Heinz (Alpine). The second DP214, driven by Kimberly/Schlesser, retired on the Sunday morning when in third place.

Another failure followed in the Prototype and GT race at Reims at the end of

*The DP215 in the pits at Le Mans at 1963, when the car was about to be withdrawn because of transmission problems. On the pit counter Lucien Bianchi and Phil Hill discuss the problems and to their left is John Wyer. (Nigel Snowdon)*

*The DP214 of McLaren/Ireland at full chat at Le Mans in 1963. When the engine of this car blew at the kink on the Mulsanne Straight, it deposited oil all over the track and triggered off a series of accidents. (David Phipps)*

June, when only the DP215 was entered. Schlesser retired this early in the race with valve problems. In the Guards Trophy at Brands Hatch on Bank Holiday Monday, Kimberly spun his DP214 and retired, but, despite poor handling, Ireland brought his car home in sixth place. DP215 was not entered.

In the Tourist Trophy at Goodwood in August, the team ran into immense problems in scrutineering. The DP214s had run throughout the year on 6.5 in. rims, but the RAC scrutineer had realised that the cars had been homologated with 5.5 in. rims and they had to be raced in this form. As a result handling was appalling. Ireland drove the race in almost a frenzy, with the DP214 travelling sideways, and spinning frequently, for much of the time. He eventually finished seventh, two laps in arrears, whilst McLaren, who had driven a much steadier race, to rise to third place, dropped back with engine problems and retired.

Despite this bad record during the early part of the year, Aston Martin were very successful in the last two races of the season. In September the team entered the two DP214s in the Coppa Inter-Europa three-hour race for GT cars at Monza. For this race Roy Salvadori, who had driven for Aston Martin since 1953, was brought

*Bruce McLaren with his DP214 leads an E-type Jaguar and two Ferrari 250GT0s through the chicane in the 1963 Tourist Trophy at Goodwood. The New Zealander retired because of engine problems. (Nigel Snowdon)*

back into the team and the second car was driven by Lucien Bianchi. For much of the race Salvadori battled with Mike Parkes at the wheel of a Ferrari 250GTO and won by the narrowest of margins, with Bianchi in third place. John Wyer had left Aston Martin at the end of September to run the Ford GT40 project and the cars ran in only two more races. With the DP214s entered by the French distributor Le Guezec and Dewez were first and second in the Coupe de Paris at Montlhéry and Schlesses and Le Guezec were first and fifth in the Coupe de Salon.

With the departure of John Wyer, the team's impetus and will also departed and it was another 25 years before a works Aston Martin was again planned.

# Astra (Costin-Nathan) (United Kingdom)

A bright light that shone in racing in the late 1960s, but soon faded, the Astra, originally known as the Costin-Nathan, was the result of collaboration between aerodynamicist Frank Costin and racing driver Roger Nathan. Nathan had raced Lotus Elites and a Brabham BT8 sports-racing car and had build up a business in Brixton selling tuning kits for Hillman Imp cars. When he decided to build his own competition car he approached Frank Costin, designer of bodies for Vanwall, Lotus and Lister cars, creator of the original Marcos of wood construction, and with many original ideas.

Costin drew up a monocoque centre-section built of resin-bonded plywood with front and rear end-frames constructed from 20-gauge round and square-section of tubing. Suspension was conventional, by double wishbones and coil spring/damper units at the front and, at the rear, by links, radius arms and coil spring/damper units. Power unit was the Hillman Imp engine, set in the chassis at an angle of 54 degrees to the right to reduce overall height and with an extensively modified lubrication system and the Imp gearbox mounted upside down and fitted with close-ratio gears. The gear-change was on the right-hand side of the cockpit and linked to the gearbox by flexible cable. In the nose of the car were the radiator and spare wheel, while fuel was carried in a 6-gallon tank on the left of the car with the filler just ahead of the windscreen. Although the car originally had Lotus 13 in. wheels, Minilite wheels were later substituted and there were 9.5 in. disc brakes front and rear. The body, constructed in aluminium, was a low, open two-seater with small air intake and full-width perspex screen. Later cars had glass-fibre panels.

By the time the first car was raced, Nathan had moved his premises to Fortis Green in North London and with the Costin-Nathan painted in distinctive blue and gold colours, enjoyed a successful season in British events, scoring five wins and a second out of six events entered, including a win at Montlhéry against fairly strong Abarth opposition.

By 1967, Nathan and Costin had developed a new GT version, weighing some 220 lb more than the open sports car, and intended primarily for Le Mans. Apart from a glass-fibre cockpit top section, incorporating a glued-in windscreen and recessed rain channels above the waistline, which was strapped and bolted to the centre-section of the hull, other changes were steel fuel tanks, extra cladding and a quick-release filler, and although this was done so as to avoid ballasting and to make the additional weight required to comply with the regulations, it served a useful purpose, but when the car was weighed at Le Mans it was nearly 100 lb over the minimum limit. With Le Mans gearing, top speed was around 155 mph. At Le

Mans the car was driven by Nathan and Mike Beckwith, but retired during the fifth hour because of an electrical fault.

John Blunsden, track-tested the Costin-Nathan GT for *Motor Racing* magazine and commented, 'The GT did not appear to handle as consistently through the corners, and would tend to flick into an oversteer through all the right-handers, whereas fundamentally the Costin-Nathan [i.e. the open car] is an understeering car. The result was some rather untidy and inconsistent cornering, usually terminating in excessive understeer which was scrubbing off speed just when it was most needed . . . The small GT felt a very pleasant car to drive, even though I found the cockpit room restricted, particularly around the pedals. The interior is fully trimmed and well padded, and there is a profusion of dials and switches including fuel pressure, ammeter, gearbox oil pressure, water temperature, engine oil pressure and temperature gauges and a tachometer . . . The gear shift has very short, quick movements, neutral into second being so short that you cannot feel any engagement. A second gear stick on the left of the centre tunnel was a reverse selector for when the 5-speed box was fitted for Le Mans . . . The Stage 4 "plus" Nathan engine which produces 102 bhp, has been used up to 9000 rpm in a race, although we restrained ourselves to 8000 rpm . . . Remember, too, that this one is a Le Mans "heavyweight" and that future GTs will be 100 lb lighter. Then they should *really* go!' By this time three GTs and five sports cars had been built.

Throughout 1967 and 1968 the Costin-Nathans continued to perform well and in 1968 they were raced with B.M.W. and Ford SCA engines, winning a total of 21 races out of 27 starts, and in addition taking four second places and setting ten class records. In 1968 one of the GTs, masquerading as a Moynet-Simca XS with 1204 cc Simca engine, was driven by Max/Ligonnet at Le Mans but retired in the second hour with oil pump failure.

From 1968 the cars became known as the Astra and Nathan announced the new RNR1 (Roger Nathan Racing) open car to comply with the latest Prototype regulations. When it first appeared the RNR1 was powered by the 2-litre Coventry Climax engine, but later the Cosworth-Ford 1600 cc twin-cam engine was substituted and this was used in conjunction with the 5-speed Hewland FT200 gerabox/final drive unit, as was usually fitted to Formula 2 cars at the time. Once the Cosworth engine had been installed, Nathan enjoyed an immensely successful run of success, including a third place overall in a Prototype GT race at Nogaro in France and a seventh place overall (second in his class to Brian Redman's Chevron) in the Nürburgring 500 km race.

For 1970, Nathan standardised on the Cosworth FVC engine in 1800 cc form and the cars were raced throughout the year. The real problem was that although they were well engineered and well developed, they were in reality no match for contemporary Chevrons, and by the end of the year had largely disappeared from the racing scene. In all some forty cars of all types were built.

*Roger Nathan entered this Astra RNR1 for himself and Clive Baker in the 1969 BOAC 500 Miles race at Brands Hatch, but it non-started after a practice crash.* (LAT)

# Chaparral (United States)

Between 1961 and 1970 these Texan-built cars, named after the 'road runner', a member of the cuckoo family and familiar through TV cartoons, were the most innovative and technically advanced of American competition cars. Built by Jim Hall and Hap Sharp in Midland, Texas, in functional but exceptionally well-equipped workshop premises alongside Rattlesnake Raceway, they were financed substantially by General Motors.

All Chaparrals were powered by the same 'small-block' Chevrolet engine, and featured a chassis structure of glass-fibre reinforced plastic, not entirely original as the same idea had been seen on the Lotus Elite, and Hall forged a relationship with General Motors Tech Center at Warren near Detroit, which led to General Motors-backed development of experimental automatic transmissions in racing and the supply of aluminium block engines through Roger Penske. In fact although the automatic transmisson was to become a characteristic feature of Chaparrals, it was not raced until May 1964, whereas the Chaparrals themselves first appeared in late 1963. In 1965 Hall and Sharp scored a totally unexpected victory with the Chaparral 2 in the Sebring 12 Hours race and that year Jim Hall won the United States Road Racing Championship. This led directly to the development of a car for European endurance racing.

## The 2D, 1966

The car that appeared in Endurance racing in 1966 was known as the 2D and was a logical continuation of the existing Chaparral design practice. Again the glass-fibre chassis was used, but it should be stressed that metal was used throughout to take localised loadings. At the front suspension was by double wishbones and coil spring/damper units, while at the rear there were two trailing links, single top transfer links and reversed lower wishbones. The power unit was the 5360 cc (102 × 83 mm) V-8 Chevrolet fitted with four carburettors of Weber type, but Chevrolet manufacture, and there was a separate exhaust system for each bank of cylinders. It was claimed that the power output was limited to 425 bhp in the interest of reliability.

Inevitably the most interesting feature of the car was the transmission, not strictly an 'automatic transmission', but it has perhaps more accurately been described as a fluid-clutch transmission. There were three gears, with a hydraulic coupling and a torque converter. The straight-cut spur gears were engaged by sliding dog clutches. The driver changed gear by easing his throttle foot, which took the loading off the dogs, and then quickly moved the gear lever.

The 2D was striking in appearance, with coupé glass-fibre body featuring gull-wing doors, and after its first race a very prominent air scoop on the top of the roof to draw air into the carburettors. At its first race, the 2D also had a 'flipper' tail, but this was replaced by a simple spoiler by Sebring. One of the interesting features of the Chaparral was the split-rim wheels, which enabled a choice of rim widths to be selected.

During 1966 the 2D was raced in four events and retired in all but one. Steering problems eliminated Bonnier/Phill Hill at Daytona and at Sebring, where two cars were entered, both were eliminated by what was believed to be the voracious thirst for oil of the automatic transmission. The team missed the races earlier in the European season and first appeared at the Nürburgring for the 1000 km race in June. The drivers were again Bonnier and Hill. They were second fastest in

*The winning Chaparral 2D of Joakim Bonnier and Phil Hill in the 1966 Nürburgring 1000 Km race.* (Nigel Snowdon)

practice and took the lead, once Surtees' Ferrari had retired with damper failure. When rain began to fall, the Chaparral, running on dry tyres, became almost uncontrollable. Hill stopped at the pits for a specially cut set of rain tyres to be fitted, rejoined the race on a track that stayed wet and went on to win by a minute from the second-place Ferrari Dino. It was a quite unexpected success. The only other outing for the 2D in 1966 was at Le Mans, and in the face of an overwhelmingly strong entry of Ferraris and Fords, the Chaparral never rose above seventh place and retired on the Saturday evening with electrical problems.

## The 2D and 2F, 1967

The first Chaparral development seen in 1967 was the installation of a 7000 cc (108 × 95.3 mm) Chevrolet engine, developing 575 bhp at 7500 rpm. This car appeared in two races, at Daytona, where it was driven by Johnson/Jennings, and at Sebring, with the same drivers, but failed to finish on either occasion because of transmission problems.

The main Chaparral thrust in 1967, however, was the new 2F car, of which two were built, a magnificent-looking competition car, not entirely dissimilar to the Ford 'J-Car' in appearance but built to the highest possible standards of quality and with every effort made to reduce weight. In appearance this new coupé was dominated by a large aerofoil mounted above body turbulence on tall struts bolted to the suspension uprights, a feature first seen on Chaparral's 1966 Can-Am cars. This was hydraulically operated from a foot pedal so that when the pedal was depressed by the driver's left foot, the aerofoil pivoted to a virtually flat position for minimum drag on the straights, but when pressure was released it would move into the maximum downforce position.

Despite all the careful development work that had gone into the evolution of this superb-looking car, its major weakness lay in the transmission. Instead of evolving a new gearbox to handle the power of the 7-litre engine, General Motors had satisfied themselves with strengthening the existing box and this was to prove the Achilles' heel of the Chaparral in 1967.

48

*Phil Hill with the Chaparral 2F at Le Mans in 1967. Note the angle of the aerofoil. The car retired with transmission problems.* (Nigel Snowdon)

In all the 2Fs ran in eight races in 1967, but once again it was a series of retirements with just one win in the year. At Daytona, where the car ran with fixed aerofoil, it was eliminated by damage caused as a result of driver error. At Sebring Spence brought the Chaparral through into the lead, but transmission problems caused its retirement. The Chaparral team then moved to Europe, and Spence was fastest in practice at Monza and his team-mate Phil Hill was fastest at Spa, but in both races transmission problems caused retirement. Then, with one of the most unsuitable cars ever seen in the race, Chaparral entered the Targa Florio. Here the drivers were Phil Hill and Hap Sharp and by hard driving they managed to work their way up to fourth place, only to retire when a tyre punctured and the engine heat had made the spare unusable. It also retired at the Nürburgring.

At Le Mans the team entered two cars for Spence/Hill, who were second fastest in practice, and Johnson/Jennings. Spence held fourth place after the first hour, rising to second place after two hours, but the car was delayed in the pits with transmission problems. In the meantime the other 2F had retired with electrical problems and despite a change of gearbox the Spence/Hill car was also retired.

For the BOAC 500 Miles race at Brands Hatch, Chaparral entered only a single car for Spence/Hill. Initially the race was led by the Lola of Denis Hulme, but this retired with engine problems and Spence/Hill assumed the lead, dropping to third after a pit stop, but regaining the lead from the Ferrari of Stewart/Amon and winning by a small margin.

## Postscript

Brands Hatch was the last appearance of the 2F because, from 1968, Prototypes were limited to 3 litres and Chaparral had neither the ability nor the willingness to build enough cars to qualify for the 3-litre category. Chaparral continued to race in Can-Am events until 1970, and in that year Chaparral introduced their revolutionary 2J with 7.6-litre Chevrolet engine and twin rear-mounted high-velocity fans, two feet in diameter, driven by a twin-cylinder two-stroke engine. The purpose of these was to suck the air from underneath the car and keep it close to the

49

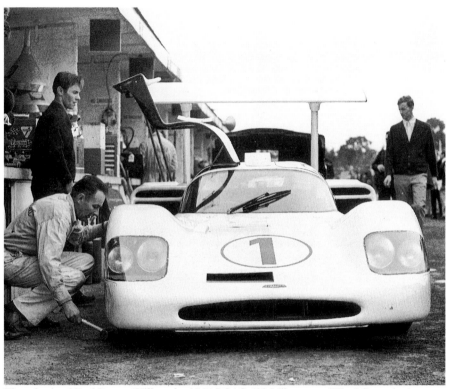

*The winning 2F of Spence/Hill at the 1967 BOAC 500 Miles race.* (Nigel Snowdon)

ground, instead of using an aerofoil. The car was very much in the testing stage during 1970, but at the end of the season the Chaparral 'ground effect' system was banned and Chaparral withdrew from racing altogether. In the few years that they had competed in North American and European events, their high standard of preparation, their technical innovation, their enthusiasm and their sheer ability had brought a breath of fresh air to motor racing.

# *Chevron (United Kingdom)*

Chevron was the creation of Derek Bennett, a Manchester enthusiast who was also a very able driver and soon proved himself to be a designer of outstanding ability. He had built a number of Austin 750 Specials for customers to race in 750 Motor Club events. In 1956 he built two rear-engined 'Specials' with J.A.P. 500 cc engines for Midget speedway racing and subsequently built his own Special, initially as a 750 Formula car, but later fitted with a Ford 1172 cc engine, for the category of racing for cars powered by that engine organised by the 750 Motor Club. There followed a front-engined Ford-powered Formula Junior car, and subsequently Bennett raced a Lotus Elite and Gemini Formula Junior and Brabham Formula 3 cars. While he was racing the Brabham, he started construction of two cars to comply with the Clubmen's Formula, and these were eventually finished in 1965, one to be raced by himself and the other by Brian Classic. These were the first cars to bear the name Chevron and were later retrospectively typed the B1. Four more Clubmen's cars followed in 1966 and these were typed the B2.

As his business prospered, Bennett acquired premises in Bolton that were part of a former cotton mill, and set up the company known as Derek Bennett Engineering Limited. From these humble beginnings there grew a major force in international motor racing.

## B3

For 1966, Bennett embarked on what at the time seemed a most ambitious project, a mid-engined Grand Touring coupé, a very sophisticated design, and, as events were to prove, of immense potential. Bennett drew up a multi-tubular space-frame constructed from 16- to 20-gauge 1 in. to 1.5 in. square and round tubing with the tubes running up the windscreen pillars to the roof area, with stiffening by monocoque steel sills, two bulkheads and a stressed full-length dural undertray. Front suspension was by wide-angled double wishbones, coil spring/damper units and an anti-roll bar. At the rear there were wide-based lower wishbones, single top links, twin radius rods and coil spring/damper units. At the front the anti-roll bar operated on the upper wishbone and at the rear on the bottom wishbone. Modified Triumph suspension uprights were used at the front, but the rear uprights were machined from magnesium castings. Steering was Triumph rack-and-pinion, there were magnesium wheels machined from castings and Girling disc brakes mounted outboard front and rear. A 12-gallon fuel tank was mounted transversely behind the cockpit (but there was space for an additional 6- or 8-gallon tank in the nose), the water radiator was at the front of the car, but the oil tank was rear-mounted. The oil and water pipes passed through the sills of the chassis.

The first car built for Digby Martland was powered by a Ford-Cosworth twin-cam, 1598 cc engine, developing approximately 155 bhp at 7800 rpm. Transmission was through a twin-plate clutch and Hewland HD 5-speed gearbox/final drive unit, although on later cars the Hewland FT200 Formula 2 gearbox/final drive unit was substituted. The engine was angled in the chassis at 17 degrees, which lowered the centre of gravity, kept the rear decking as low as possible and improved water circulation.

Although later Chevron designs were to make it look very dated, it was in fact a superb-looking coupé, in glass-fibre with conventional doors and lightweight Plexiglas windows, and with detachable nose and tail sections with quick-release fittings.

Martland soon fulfilled the B3's potential by winning on its debut at Oulton Park and finishing a close second shortly afterwards to Piper's Ferrari at the Crystal Palace. Many more successes in British events were to follow during the year. Only one other B3 was constructed.

## B4

Parallel with the construction of the Cosworth-powered car, Bennett developed a B.M.W.-engined version known as the B4. The B.M.W. 2000 T1 engine of 1900 cc (89 × 79.9 mm) with two valves per cylinder, 11:1 compression ratio, Schnitzer or Kugelfisher fuel injection (or with twin Weber carburettors) was modified by Chevron to develop 195 bhp at 7300 rpm by 1969. This engine had already been used in racing, but had been regarded as unreliable. Working in close collaboration with the B.M.W. factory in Munich, Bennett was able to put in hand a development programme which ironed out most of the problems with these engines. Once again the Hewland transmission was used and, engine apart, there were few differences between the B4 and the B3.

The first B4 was raced by Bennett, but achieved its greatest success with John Lepp at the wheel. In the Paris 1000 km race at Montlhéry in October 1966, Lepp and Peter Gethin finished eighth overall and second in their class.

## B5, 1966–67

David Bridges acquired a Chevron fitted with a 2-litre V-8 B.R.M. engine and Hewland 5-speed gearbox in 1966 and this was given the designation B5. The car was not a great success, mainly because the transmission was not suitable, but it did score a remarkable victory in the hands of Brian Redman at the Crystal Palace in 1967. Subsequently the car passed to Willie Green and with a B.R.M. 2-litre engine of the later centre-exhaust type and with 6-speed B.R.M. gearbox, enjoyed a good run of success in albeit minor British events.

## B6, 1967

The designation B6 was used for all production cars in 1967, regardless of the type of engine installed. In all eight were produced, most with B.M.W. engines, but other cars were also built with Ford twin-cam, Cosworth FVA and Coventry Climax 2-litre engines. Apart from an enlarged air intake to improve the cooling, there were few changes. Production had now been streamlined by having the chassis frames supplied direct by Arch Motors and the bodywork was manufactured, to a much high standard than previously, by Specialised Mouldings. The great run of successes in British events continued, but the cars had still to make their mark on the international scene.

## B8, 1968–69

For 1968 a number of modifications were made to the car, including the bonding of the undertray to the chassis frame, larger radiators, oil pipes and tanks and an adjustable front anti-roll bar (described by Bennett as 'a psychological modification') and sufficient cars were built during the year so that the B8, as the slightly improved model was known, became homologated as a Competition Sports Car (minimum production of 50) and by the end of the year a total of 68 B6 and B8 cars had been constructed.

International appearances by the B8s were rare during 1968, but towards the end of the year Brian Redman drove a car in the Springbok Series in Africa. The range of African countries in which these races took part are indicative of the much more relaxed political atmosphere of the period. In the Kyalami 9 Hours race two works-entered B8s appeared, and Redman/Schenken finished fourth behind a 5.7-litre Mirage, a Ferrari Dino and a P4 Ferrari. In seventh place came the second works car driven by Digby Martland and Derek Bennett. Redman was a sole driver in the Cape International 3 Hours race at Kilarney in Cape Province a couple of weeks later, but here he was delayed by oil scavenge pump problems and finished

*This Chevron B8–B.M.W. was entered by Chevron Cars for Brian Classic/Digby Martland in the 1968 BOAC 500 Miles race at Brands Hatch and finished eighth overall.* (Nigel Snowdon)

well down the field in 14th place. Next came the Rhodesian Grand Prix, a race for single-seaters, but there were also two short 25- and 15-lap races for sports cars, and Redman finished fourth in the 25-lap and third in the 15-lap. The teams then moved on to Lourenço Marques in Mozambique for the 3 Hours race and there Brian Redman finished third behind the 5.7-litre Mirage and the Ferrari P4. The final round in the Springbok Championship was the Pietermaritzburg 3 Hours race on Boxing Day, but unfortunately Redman was unable to take part in this because of a minor operation on his arm.

B8s were seen much more frequently in international events in 1969 and in the Daytona Continental 24 Hours race in February the car driven by Kleinpeter/ Gun/Beatty finished sixth overall and won its class. In the BOAC 500 race at Brands Hatch in April a B8 driven by Wisell/Hine finished seventh overall, winning its class, and defeating some formidable Alfa Romeo and Porsche opposition. Cars ran at Spa, the Nürburgring and Le Mans, but no success was gained mainly because of lack of reliability in longer events. However, the cars still continued to do immensely well in British races and John Lepp, with the works/Red Rose Racing car, won the RAC British Sports Car Championship in 1969, a success repeated in 1970 with a car driven by Trevor Thwaites.

## The Gropa MCM

In 1969 a Group 6 Prototype body conversion for the Chevron B8 was announced. The Gropa MCM (the word Gropa stood for Graphics Racing Organisation for Prototype Automobiles) was marketed by Andrew Mylius and designed by Nomad designer Bob Curl. The conversion, which cost only £500, was approved by Derek Bennett and took about two weeks to carry out. Quite a number of B6 and B8 cars were converted during 1970–71 and thus their racing life was extended.

53

## B12

In 1968 John Woolfe commissioned from Chevron a Prototype Group 6 car, designated the B12, broadly similar to the B8, but with wheelbase increased by 2.5 in. so as to lengthen the engine bay. The engine was the Australian-built Repco 90-degree V-8 2996 cc (89 × 60 mm) with single overhead camshaft per bank of cylinders, Lucas fuel injection and a power output of 330 bhp at 8800 rpm. This engine had been used by Brabham in their 1966–67 Formula 1 cars, but was now redundant and examples were available at very low cost. The only other real difference between the B12 and the production B8 was the use of 15 in. Brabham wheels. The car ran with some success in minor British events, but it proved hopeless in long-distance events. At Watkins Glen it was driven by Woolfe and David Piper, but retired after pumping out all its water through a blown cylinder head gasket. At Le Mans, where the co-driver was Digby Marland, the Chevron-Repco was eliminated after two hours with the same problem. Woolfe did not persevere with the car, and sadly he was killed in the first-lap accident at Le Mans in 1969 with his new Porsche 917.

## B16, 1969–70

In August 1969 Derek Bennett revealed the new B16 car, with dramatic new styling and considerably enhanced performance. The centre-section of the B16 was now a true monocoque, made up of a number of separate box-type structures with front and rear space-frames carrying the suspension and engine/gearbox assembly. The suspension layout was similar to that of the B8, but there were detail changes.

*Chevron B16 entered by Digby Martland for himself and Charles Lucas in the 1970 BOAC 500 Miles race; it retired with ignition trouble.* (Nigel Snowdon)

Although the car was given its shakedown tests at Aintree and Croft with a 2-litre B.M.W. engine, the normal power unit was to be the Ford-Cosworth FCV 1790 cc developing 245 bhp. Cars were, however, raced with B.M.W. engines and there was also a version that raced with a Mazda Rotary engine. The Hewland FT200 gearbox/final drive unit was fitted. The superbly styled bodywork, with graceful curving lines and cut-off tail, had clearly been inspired by the P4 Ferrari. This body was again the work of Specialised Mouldings. The car was offered at a price of around £5,500 with Cosworth engine and Hewland gearbox (compared to the original price of the B8 of £1,800).

Brian Redman drove the prototype in the Nürburgring 500 km race in September 1969, but here it was fitted with the smaller Ford-Cosworth FVA 1.6-litre engine because the new FCV was not ready. Once handling problems had been solved, Redman took pole position in practice and despite agreeing to drive a cautious race, went straight into the lead and won by a substantial margin from the

*Seen in the pits at the 1971 BOAC 1000 Km race is the Chevron B19 of John Miles/Graham Birrell which finished ninth overall and led the 2-litre Prototype class from start to finish.* (Nigel Snowdon)

Abarth opposition. For 1970 this car was homologated in Group 5 as a Competition Sports Car (minimum production now reduced to 25).

In 1970 cars ran at Daytona, Sebring and in the BOAC race at Brands Hatch without success, mainly because of minor reliability problems, and at Spa the Mazda 2 litre-powered car of Deprez/Vernaeve made its debut; incredibly noisy but not spectacularly fast, this car finished right down the field in 15th place. It appeared again at the Nürburgring, where it was tenth. Two B16s, including the Mazda-powered car, ran at Le Mans, but both were eliminated. Chevron's real success, however, came in the European Constructors Championship for Group 5 and 6 cars under 2 litres. Thanks mainly to superb driving by Brian Redman, who won at the Paul Ricard circuit in April, was second at Anderstorp, second at Hockenheim, third at Enna, and won at Spa, Chevron won the Championship by one point from Lola. Other wins were by John Burton at Hameenlinna in Finland and by Vic Elford at the Nürburgring. Redman's win at Spa was with the new B16s Spyder.

## B19, 1971

Although Chevrons continued to appear in World Championship races, nothing was gained, apart from a class win in Group 5 at Spa by Birchenhough/Joscelyne with a B8, and in the main Chevron concentrated on the European 2-litre Constructors Championship and British events. At the Nürburgring in 1970, the team had revealed the new B16S Spyder and with this Brian Redman had set fastest lap. The slightly improved version of this marketed and raced in 1971 was the B19 Spyder; it represented steady and progressive development by Chevron, and there were no radical changes apart from the open body. The 2-litre Championship was won by Lola, with a margin of 11 points from Chevron, but the Chevrons were well to the fore throughout the year. At the Paul Ricard circuit in April Miles/Hezemans took third place, Niki Lauda won at the Salzburgring, Hezemans was again the winner at the Martini race at Silverstone, Chris Craft with a works car was second at the Nürburgring in the 500 km race and John Hine won from Swart at Zandvoort.

## B21, 1972

In 1972, a B19 driven by Hine/Juncadella finished fifth and won its class in the Buenos Aires 1000 km race, a new addition to the Championship year, and in addition an eighth place by Bamford/McInerney (second in class) in the BOAC race at Brands Hatch, sixth by Tonadelli/Formento (and second in class) at Monza, and third overall by Hine/Bridges at Spa were gained in the early races of the Championship. A total of nine Chevrons, all B19s or 21s (some of the 21s being updated versions of the 19), had run at Spa and the third-place car ran with an Alan Smith-developed 1.9-litre Cosworth FVC engine, whilst the remainder had the more usual 1.8-litre engines. Fifth place for Hine/Bridges with the B21 followed at the Nürburgring and Stommelen/Hezemans with a B21 were fifth in the Austrian race ahead of the similar car of Juncadella/Bridges. It was in fact Chevron's most successful year in World Championship racing.

However, the team concentrated again on the European 2-litre Constructors Championship and, as mentioned, the 1972 car was the B21 Spyder, a slightly improved version of the previous year's car. There were three principal teams competing, the Red Rose Racing/Tergal team running cars for Juncadella, Bosch and Hine; the Cannon Camera-sponsored team for John Burton and Bob Wollek; and later in the season the Red Rose Team with a car using a Chevrolet Vega-based 2-litre Cosworth engine. In addition Dieter Quester raced a B21 powered by a B.M.W. 2-litre engine. In 1972 Abarth won the Championship by a margin of three points from Chevron and out of nine races in the series Chevron won two, at the Salzburgring, where Quester was first, and Barcelona, where Burton was the winner. In addition Chevron took five second places and five third places during the year.

## B23, 1973

Nothing worth mentioning was gained in the World Championships in 1973 and again Chevron's efforts were concentrated on the European 2-litre Sports Car Championship with the updated B23 car still powered by the Ford-Cosworth FVC engine. Again Lola was the winner, but Chevron took second place and enjoyed some notable successes, including the first two places at the Paul Ricard circuit, a second at Santa Monica in Italy, and other seconds at Imola and at Clermont-Ferrand, the Nürburgring, the Österreichring and at Barcelona. The latest Chevrons were simply not quick enough to beat the Lola T292 opposition.

## B26, 1974

*With this works-entered Chevron B26, Brian Redman/Peter Gethin finished fourth overall in the 1974 British Airways 1000 Km race at Brands Hatch.* (Nigel Snowdon)

Already the European 2-litre Sports Car Championship was diminishing in importance and interest and in 1974 it was reduced to seven races and the winner was Alpine-Renault with Chevron second. The updated Chevron B26 engine with Ford BDA did not achieve much in the way of success during the year, although Lepp was third at the Paul Ricard circuit and at Clermont-Ferrand and took second place at Hockenheim.

### Postscript

By 1975 the European 2-litre Sports Car Championship had sunk to a mere two rounds and was no longer recognised by the FIA. That year Chevron continued to offer the B26 as a rolling chassis with gearbox for £6,500. The following year there appeared the B31 sports car, now priced at £7,250 for a rolling chassis, and 80 per cent of Chevron production, mainly single-seaters, was being exported to the United States. As Chevron had grown over the years, Bennett was joined by John Bridges as joint managing director and he also provided considerable finance for the company. The racing manager was Paul Owens, who had been with Derek Bennett since the very early days. The company seemed set for a strong healthy future as a manufacturer of Competition cars, but sadly, in 1978, Derek Bennett was killed in a hang-gliding accident. It soon became evident just how much the company depended on him and it was not long before liquidation took place. Derek Bennett was a great loss to motor racing, not only as an inspired and able designer who had learnt the hard way, but for his charming and entertaining personality. Later the Chevron name was revived by a new company which supplied parts for the earlier Chevrons as well as initiating new designs.

# Cobra (United States)

Whilst the Cobra was very much the concept of American Carroll Shelby and the name is a registered trademark of the Ford Motor Company, the origins of the Cobra were historically very British. The car resulted from the collaboration of Shelby, former racing driver and occasional member of the works Aston Martin team, who was looking for a suitable sports car to market in the United States, and the traditional A.C. Cars Limited of Thames Ditton. Since late 1953 A.C. had been marketing the Ace, with twin-tubular chassis frame, simple independent suspension front and rear by lower wishbones and transverse leaf spring, and with a very elegant open two-seater body based on Superleggera Touring's *Barchetta* style developed for the Ferrari Tipo 166 and 195. This car, designed by John Tojeiro, had originally been conceived as a competition sports-racing car, and several examples had been built, the most successful being the Bristol-engined car raced by Cliff Davis during 1953 and 1954. When A.C. refined the Tojeiro design as a production car, they used their own traditional 6-cylinder in-line 1991 cc single overhead camshaft engine, the origins of which dated back to 1919. One of the most enthusiastic racers and supporters of the Ace was their South Coast dealer Ken Rudd, and it was at his instigation that A.C. adopted the much more powerful Bristol 1971 cc engine in 1956. Later, when supplies of the Bristol engine dried up, it was Rudd who developed a version of the Ace with a Ford 6-cylinder Zephyr 2.6-litre engine.

Before talking to A.C. Cars, Shelby had considered a number of possibilities, including cars based on the Austin-Healey and the Aston Martin DB3S, but he finally turned to A.C. and in 1961 a deal was struck. Shelby managed to interest the American Ford Company in his project and during the winter of 1961–62, A.C. built the first prototype, with 221 cu. in. Ford V-8 and Borg-Warner gearbox. The car was then shipped to the United States for further testing and development. Before long, with strengthened chassis, the Cobra, with financial assistance from Ford, was in production. The first seventy-five cars were powered by the 260 cu. in. 4.2-litre engine, but subsequent cars were powered by the 4.7-litre unit. From 1964, A.C. marketed the car in Britain as the A.C. Cobra, but in fact Shelby claimed the right to the Cobra name, which he in due course sold to Ford, and there was an arrangement made just before the London Motor Show in 1965 whereby the cars marketed by A.C. were known as the A.C. '289', whereas the American cars, now marketed only in 7-litre '428' form, were known as the Shelby American Cobra.

From an early date Shelby recognised the competition potential of the new car, it enjoyed immense success in the United States, and in European racing came to defeat Ferrari in the Grand Touring category, a feat achieved by a combination of sheer brute power, the superb aerodynamics of the later Daytona coupé and, to a certain extent, the sheer number of cars raced. The Cobra was first raced at Riverside Raceway in October 1962, but retired with hub failure; at the end of the year it raced again at Nassau in the Bahamas, but retired once more. By 1963 the teething troubles had been resolved and many successes were gained. In this book of course we are looking only at endurance racing, but it must be remembered that the success in other categories far exceeded those gained in the Classic events.

## 1963

The racing Cobras were extensively modified, especially so far as the engine was concerned, and these modifications included larger valves, general engine tuning and, on Shelby-entered cars, four downdraught Weber 48IDM carburettors. In the Daytona 2000 km race in February there were three entries and MacDonald took fourth place overall, behind two Ferrari 250GTOs. By Sebring the cars were showing greater reliability and impressive speed, but of the three works cars to start the race, there was only one finisher, that of Phil Hill/Ken Miles, which took eleventh place overall and third in the over 3000 cc GT category.

*The seventh-place Cobra of Peter Bolton/Ninian Sanderson at Le Mans in 1963.* (Nigel Snowdon)

The next Championship outing was at Le Mans, where two cars were entered, both managed by Stirling Moss, one entered by A.C. Cars, sponsored by *The Sunday Times* and driven by Peter Bolton and Ninian Sanderson, the other a works entry driven by Hugus/Jopp. The Shelby entry retired with a broken con-rod, but the Bolton/Sanderson car finished seventh overall, behind the Ferraris in the first six places. The Le Mans performance could not be regarded as successful, but it sowed the seeds for a full attack on the Grand Touring Championship in 1964.

## 1964

The biggest problem faced by Shelby, if the team were to tackle the Championship series in 1964, was not that of the poor handling qualities of the car, or its intractability, neither of which were too great problems on fast circuits on which most of the year's events were run, but the sheer lack of aerodynamics of the blunt old-fashioned bodywork of the original car. As a result Peter Brock set about the design of a new aluminium coupé body, and the superb shape of this car, with well-shaped nose with good penetration and Kamm cut-off tail, was sufficient to endow the Cobra with a true maximum speed of 180 mph on the then available power output of 350 bhp. The sheer delicacy of its lines contrasted with the primitive chassis and brute power beneath the bonnet. The one real problem suffered by the coupé in its early days was overheating of the cockpit, and the drivers had a thoroughly miserable time.

Three cars were entered in the Daytona 2000 km race, but two were eliminated, one by a fire in the pits and the other by engine failure, but the surviving car driven by Johnson/Gurney finished fourth overall, beaten in its class by the Ferrari 250GTOs, which took the first three places. However, it was the result of this encouraging debut that gave the coupé its name of 'Daytona'. For the Sebring 12 Hours race Shelby entered a total of five cars, the coupé driven by MacDonald/Holbert, which finished fourth overall, winning the Grand Touring category, together with three open 4.7-litre cars, of which two were fifth and sixth (second and third in their class), together with a 7-litre open prototype which retired with a blown engine. The Ferraris had been trounced and Ford were delighted.

As a result of this success the American Ford Company was persuaded to underwrite the European tour, but there was also sponsorship from Shell Oil. Initially three works cars were entered in the Targa Florio road race in Sicily, an event for which they were totally unsuitable. In addition to the works entries, there were two private cars in the race and the sole finisher was the Shelby-entered car of Gurney/Grant in eighth place, despite broken rear suspension. Of the Cobras in this race, Denis Jenkinson wrote in *Motor Sport*, 'Coming out of a corner there is no rising crescendo to peak rpm before the driver changes gear, there is just a shattering explosive noise and the engine is doing 7000 rpm and the driver is wildly grabbing for the gear-lever and the next moment he is standing on the brakes and trying to scrabble round the next corner.' Next came the Spa 500 km race, where three of the open cars, together with Phil Hill at the wheel of the coupé were entered. On this high-speed circuit the roadsters were outclassed, but whilst Hill set fastest lap of the race, at 129.01 mph, the car was so badly delayed by dirt in the fuel lines and carburettors that he dropped too far behind to feature in the results. At the Nürburgring 1000 km race three open cars were entered. One non-started after a practice crash and of the other two, one retired with an engine blow-up and the other finished at the tail of the field after throttle-linkage problems.

*Sole surviving Cobra in the 1964 Targa Florio was this car driven into eighth place by Dan Gurney and Jerry Grant. (LAT)*

Then came the highlight of the Cobra year, the Le Mans 24 Hours race. At this race there appeared three Daytona coupés. There was a new car which had been built in Italy by Carrozzeria Grand Sport of Modena in accordance with the American specifications, but because of a mistake the car was two inches higher than originally planned, an error corrected on all later cars built at Modena. The new car was driven at Le Mans by Gurney/Bondurant, while the original coupé was handled by Amon/Neerpasch. A third coupé had been built by A.C. Cars on the basis of photographs and drawings supplied by Shelby, backed up by additional telephone instructions. This looked quite different from the works cars, as it featured a flatter roof line, longer nose and pronounced flairs over front and rear wheel arches; in addition the shape of the doors was different and so was the positioning of the side vents. Despite the fact that there were three different Daytona coupés, the scrutineers at Le Mans raised no objections!

Already, however, the A.C.-built car was in trouble. It had made the press in a big way after testing during the night on the M1 motorway, when it was alleged that it had touched 183 mph. This resulted in an assurance from the Society of Motor Manufacturers and Traders that manufacturers would not do high-speed testing on public roads again. Equally interesting, however, was the increase in speed that had been found in the last twelve months, for the maximum speed of the British car in the 1963 race had only been 165 mph. Although Gurney/Bondurant finished fourth overall and their coupé was the first GT car to finish, Amon/Neerpasch were disqualified because of a jump-start from another battery when the car's own battery went flat. The A.C. car driven by Sears/Bolton was involved in a horrific crash on the Saturday night, when it was struck by Baghetti's Ferrari, ended up in a ditch and, sadly, three spectators who had wandered from behind the barriers were killed.

Later in the year both coupés retired at Reims in the 12 Hours race. In the

*This Cobra 'Daytona' coupé driven by Dan Gurney and Bob Bondurant finished fourth overall at Le Mans in 1964 and won the GT class.* (Nigel Snowdon)

Tourist Trophy at Goodwood Gurney with his original coupé finished third overall and won the GT class. Also counting towards the Championship were the Freiburg and Sierra Montana Hill Climbs. At Freiburg, Bondurant and Neerpasch finished first and third in the GT category, while Siffert was fifth with a roadster. The results at Sierra Montana in Switzerland were even better, with Bondurant, Neerpasch and Siffert taking the first three places in the GT category. Oddly enough the Tour de France also counted towards the Championship. In this, in effect, road race, although nominally a rally, there were to be three coupés entered, including a new car. The new car was crashed on the way to the event on its transporter and both the older coupés were eliminated.

In theory at least there remained two rounds in the Championship, the Coppa Europa at Monza and the 500 km race at Bridgehampton near New York. To win the Championship, the Cobras had to win both races, otherwise victory would go to Ferrari. The Monza race was cancelled and Shelby argued that it had been cancelled for political reasons. At Bridgehampton the roadsters took the first four places.

## 1965

For this year Shelby was also responsible for the Ford GT40 programme, in addition to racing the Cobras during their last serious competitive year. The team now had four coupés at its disposal and was destined to dominate the year's GT racing. Because of Ferrari's inability to get the 250LM homologated, the only serious opposition came from the previous year's 250GTO Ferraris, and these were no match for the Cobras in their latest form. At Daytona the car of Keck/Schlesser was second overall (first in the class), with Muther/Timanus fourth overall and second in the class. The Sebring 12 Hours race, run partially on a flooded track, was won by the Chaparral and the Daytona coupés all finished, with Schlesser/Bondurant fourth overall and first in the GT class. The three other coupés also finished well up in the class.

Now the team moved to Europe and appeared in Ferrari's back yard at Monza,

*Bob Olthoff drove this Cobra with hardtop entered by Willment into fifth place in the 1964 Tourist Trophy at Goodwood.* (The Author's Collection)

where a brace of coupés were entered for Shelby by Alan Mann Racing. The race was run on the combined road circuit and bank track, and on the bumpy banking the Cobras took a dreadful pounding. Nevertheless Bondurant/Grant finished eighth overall (first in class), with, immediately behind them, in ninth place, the coupé of Sears/Whitmore. A Daytona was sent for Gurney to drive in the Tourist Trophy at Oulton Park a week later, but in this non-Championship race it proved a complete handful. Next came the Spa 500 km race, where Daytonas were entered for Bondurant and Whitmore. The Alan Mann team had expected something of a walkover, but Whitmore retired because of a transmission vibration and Bondurant, delayed by a broken push-rod, was relegated to fifth overall in this race, which now admitted Prototypes, and second in the GT class to the private Ferrari 250GTO driven by Sutcliffe.

Learning from experience, the Shelby team had given the Targa Florio a miss, but still ran at the Nürburgring, where on paper at least they were likely to be outclassed. Partially because of a switch of tyres for this race from Goodyear to Firestone, the Daytonas showed a remarkable turn of speed on this difficult circuit. Bondurant/Neerpasch finished seventh overall and first in the GT class, with Sears/Gardner tenth overall and second in class. The third car, driven by Schlesser/Simon, and finished in the white and blue colours of Ford France, was 12th overall and fourth in the class.

Next came the Le Mans 24 Hours race, where four Daytonas were entered, but three failed with mechanical problems and the sole finisher driven by Thompson/Sears was a poor eighth overall and second in the GT class behind the Ferrari 275GTB of Mairesse/'Beurlys', which took third place overall. This surviving car had been delayed in a minor accident, which damaged the cooling ducts, and for much of the race it had to be driven at reduced speed. Cobra were now virtually unbeatable in the GT Championship, but the team entered the three remaining rounds. At the Reims 12 Hours race, Bondurant/Schlesser were fifth overall and first in class, with Sears/Whitmore ninth overall and second in class. The team even decided to have a go in the Enna Cup race in Sicily. It was a rough, tough race and the cars finished badly battered, with stone-scarred noses and cracked headlight covers and windscreens. Bondurant finished third overall, first in class, with Sears

63

*Frank Gardner with the Willment 'Daytona' coupé (which was a replica and not in fact built by the works) leads the Alan Mann-entered open car of Sir John Whitmore at Esso Bend in the 1965 Tourist Trophy at Oulton Park. Whitmore finished fourth on aggregate in this two-part race.* (T. C. March)

*Roger Mac in the same race with the Cobra entered by The Chequered Flag. The car has just shed its left hand rear wheel.* (T. C. March)

fifth and second in class. This was the last racing appearance of the Daytona. The final round of the Championship was at Bridgehampton, and here a roadster driven by Johnson finished seventh overall, winning the GT category. Shelby were the undisputed winners of the GT Championship, but it must be remembered that there had been very little in the way of opposition, Ferrari or otherwise.

## Postscript

For 1966 the Ford GT40 in 4.7-litre form was homologated as a Competition Sports Car and so the serious racing days of the Cobra were over. Many private owners continued to race the cars with success, and in 1965 there appeared the Ford Mustang-based Shelby GT350, the car that was in fact to represent the Shelby image in future years. Now the Cobra is one of the most sought-after classic cars, with a reputation that vastly exceeds its merit. While the original A.C. Ace with a Bristol engine was a beautifully balanced, well-performing, sweet-mannered sports car that jostles for a place in anybody's choice of the top ten, the Cobra represented an over-developed beast, of thunderous performance, vulgar manners and behaviour, and totally inadequate road holding. The present glamour surrounding the make and the immense number of replicas that can be bought are in inverse proportion to the original car's true merits.

# De Cadenet (United Kingdom)

Alain de Cadenet has been a long-time motor racing enthusiast, and although the mainstream of his activities has been in the Historic field, during the 1970s he had an amateur but well-organised crack at Le Mans.

The first car, announced only shortly before the 1972 Le Mans race, was designed by Gordon Murray of Motor Racing Developments (Brabham) and largely built by Mike Barney. It was based on a monocoque with a steel spider assembly across the front bulkhead, side-mounted radiators, some Brabham parts, a glass-fibre body built by ProToCo and with a detuned Ford-Cosworth DFV engine prepared by John Nicholson and developing around 400 bhp. The transmission was by a Hewland DG300 5-speed gearbox/final drive unit. The car was entered as the 'Duckhams Special' and driven by Chris Craft and de Cadenet. Prior to Le Mans, it had only been briefly tested at Thruxton and Silverstone. During the race the car ran incredibly well, and not long before the finish it had risen to fourth place. Unfortunately Craft went off in the wet, damaging the bodywork and arriving back at the pits without the front part. After a long time spent in the pits repairing the steering and front suspension, there was a furious argument in the pits because the scrutineers did not consider the car safe enough to rejoin the race. It was eventually agreed that the Duckhams Special would be allowed to complete one more lap at the end of the race to qualify as a finisher and it eventually was classified 12th.

The Duckhams Special reappeared at Le Mans in 1973, by when it had been fitted with new bodywork, featuring a longer tail section and new nose section, designed by de Cadenet, together with modified suspension and an ex-Ligier Cosworth DFV engine rebuilt by John Nicholson. The drivers were again Craft and de Cadenet. Unfortunately the car did not run at all well, plagued by many minor problems, including broken throttle cables, a damaged wheel bearing and electrical failure, and it finally retired with transmission trouble at about half race distance.

*In 1972 Alain de Cadenet/Chris Craft finished 12th at Le Mans with their Ford-Cosworth-powered 'Duckhams Special'.* (Nigel Snowdon)

De Cadenet returned to Le Mans in 1974, but the car was now known as the de Cadenet-Ford, as it had lost its Duckhams' sponsorship and the bright yellow of Duckhams had been replaced by British racing green. In fact this car was also registered for road use and had a tax disc on it. De Cadenet had broken his collar bone in a motor-cycle accident, so the car was driven by Chris Craft and John Nicholson. Mainly because of a comparatively week entry and very high level of retirements, the de Cadenet rose to third place, but shortly after 1.30 a.m. on the Sunday morning, as Craft accelerated up the pit lane, a bolt broke on the left rear radius arm, but Craft managed to jack the car up on his own, change the radius arm single-handed in 25 minutes and complete a lap to get the car back to the pits. The team struggled to sort out their suspension problems, and despite several stops they were still in sixth place by 5.00 a.m. Less than half an hour later, Nicholson had the rear suspension break in front of the pits as he was travelling at high speed, the car slammed into the barrier, bounced off and spun down the track. The team believed that the cause of their problems, something completely new on this car, was the fitting of large Can-Am type constant-velocity joints.

For the 1975 race, de Cadenet decided not to use his old Brabham-based car, but acquired a new Lola T380, a development of the cars raced a couple of years previously by the Bonnier team. Again this was fitted with a Cosworth-Ford DFV engine and Hewland transmission. At Le Mans the de Cadenet team was completely on its own, without support from Lola, and they were shaken to find that the car was nearly 15 mph slower in a straight line than the old de Cadenet. The car was again driven by de Cadenet/Craft, with Guy Edwards as reserve driver and the team was managed by Keith Greene. Again the race was poorly supported, and although at the end of the first hour Craft held fourth place with the de Cadenet Lola, problems followed when the car lost its rear bodywork and a long time was spent in the pits while new bodywork was fitted. The car rejoined the race in 30th position. There were more delays for attention to the bodywork, there were problems with the rear suspension collapsing and time was lost after de Cadenet hit a barrier because of gear-change problems. The car eventually finished in 15th and last place, 45 laps behind the winning Gulf-Ford.

*Three years later at Le Mans de Cadenet entered this Lola T380-Cosworth with striking Union Jack-painted rear aerofoil for himself and Chris Craft, but eventually finished last after a host of problems.* (Nigel Snowdon)

De Cadenet was still preserving with the T380 in 1976, but a new car with revised bodywork that gained 20 mph in top speed. Rumour had it that much of the development work on the bodywork had been carried out on the M4! All de Cadenet's efforts over the years were rewarded by third place behind the winning Porsche Turbo and the second-place Mirage.

De Cadenet returned again to Le Mans in 1977 with a Lola T380, again with Chris Craft as co-driver, and they took fifth place overall. For the 1978 race de Cadenet had another new car, again based on a Lola T380 chassis, developed by designer Len Bailey and built by John Thompson. The power unit was a Cosworth DFV, rebuilt by Nicholson and now developing 460 bhp. Once again Chris Craft was co-driver, and despite gearbox and clutch problems, they struggled on to finish 15th. De Cadenet's 1977 car had been entered by Peter Lovett/John Cooper/Bob Evans, and although it was 19th fastest overall in practice, under the rather peculiar Le Mans qualifying system it was prevented from starting. The 1976 de Cadenet-Lola was entered by owner Simon Phillips, with Nick Faure as co-driver, but was another victim of gearbox problems and eventually they ran out of time to repair the car and were disqualified. Another British entry in this race was the Ibec-Hesketh, with Cosworth DFV engine and Hewland gearbox, entered by Ian Bracey. After Bracey had broken his ankle, the drivers were Guy Edwards and Ian Grob. This car was delayed by a persistent engine misfire during the first half of the race, but after a complete change of electrics, lasting some $2\frac{1}{2}$ hours, it ran well until the engine blew on the Sunday morning.

# De Tomaso Pantera (Italy)

Alejandro De Tomaso, half-Spanish, half-Italian and born in the Argentine, was a fiery amateur racing driver before he embarked on what was to prove an immensely successful industrial career. In the 1950s, together with his wife-to-be, Isobel Haskell, he enjoyed a whole run of successes at the wheel of O.S.C.A. cars. In 1959 De Tomaso, having retired from racing, started his own racing car works in Modena. In addition to the long and not always successful line of cars bearing his own name, De Tomaso in due course acquired both the Maserati factory and Innocenti (manufacturers of the Mini and variants of it under licence in Italy), in addition to successfully building up again, aided by Italian Government sanctions against Japanese motor-cycles, the famous factories of Motor Guzzi and Benelli. He also became President and Chairman of Ghia, the Italian coachbuilders, owned by an American company, Rowan, and subsequently sold to Ford.

In his early days De Tomaso concentrated on single-seaters, building Formula 2, Formula 1 and Formula Junior cars, in the main with O.S.C.A. and Conrero engines. He also built an almost bewildering number of sports and touring cars in prototype form, together with his own flat-8 Formula 1 engine. Very few De Tomaso cars entered production, but the Vallelunga of 1965 onwards with Ford 4-cylinder 1500 cc engine was built in small quantities.

At the Turin Show in 1966, De Tomaso exhibited the Mangusta prototype, closely developed from a 5-litre De Tomaso prototype of 1965. The basis of the Mangusta was a backbone chassis, with sleek coupé body, mid-mounted Ford V-8 engine, independent front suspension by coil springs and unequal-length wishbones with anti-roll bar and, at the rear, coil springs, wishbones, trailing links and anti-roll bar. The production Mangusta had a maximum speed of around 150 mph, with acceleration to match, but it was a typically ill-developed car of poor reliability and construction. Nevertheless it was produced in considerable numbers and Kjell

*The Team Franco Britannic Pantera of Müller/Chasseuil in the paddock at the 1972 Spa 1000 Km race.* (Nigel Snowdon)

*The Team Claude Dubois Pantera of Jacquemin/Deprez which finished 16th at Le Mans in 1972.* (Nigel Snowdon)

Qvale of British Motor Car Distributors in San Francisco ordered more than 250 to sell at an average price of $11,150.

From the Mangusta was developed the Pantera, which was built in collaboration with the American Ford Company and it was at this time that Ford acquired Ghia. The design of the Pantera was the work of Tom Tjaarda, an American citizen who moved to Italy. It was based on a steel monocoque structure, with front suspension by unequal-length wishbones and coil spring/damper units with anti-roll bar and rear suspension by double wishbones, coil spring/damper units and anti-roll bar. The engine was the much improved Ford 'Cleveland' V-8 351 cu. in. (5750 cc), with a power output of 310 bhp at 5400 rpm. As on the Mangusta, there was a German ZF transmission with the 5-speed gearbox in unit with the final drive. It was a singularly handsome car, with coupé body designed by Ghia, but despite its

Ford backing, it proved a production disaster. Ford marketed the car through their Lincoln-Mercury Division, but the assembly line only lasted until 1973, with the last cars for the American market being finished in 1974. De Tomaso bought something over 200 unfinished Panteras from Ford which he finished at his leisure and marketed himself in Europe.

In 1972 there was an effort made to race the Pantera in Europe, with former Autodelta Manager Roberto Bussinello taking control of team management, development work by Bertocchi, and with Mike Parkes as development driver. The cars were extensively modified and raced by three private teams, with works support, Team Claude Dubois, Team Franco Britannic, and Scuderia Brescia Corse. The cars were usually finished in distinctive red and black colours. At Monza in the 1000 km race Locatelli/'Pal Joe' finished fifth and won their class. For the Le Mans race, special 470 bhp engines were flown in from America, but they blew up in practice and were replaced by 440 bhp engines for the race. Throughout the year, Monza apart, no success was achieved.

Panteras were raced throughout the 70s, but their performances were normally abysmal. Rare exceptions were the Imola and Hockenheim races in 1973, where Panteras won their class, but in the main it was a case of retirement after retirement.

Although his own background was very much that of a racing driver, De Tomaso's main concern was the development of his industrial interests and very little attention was paid by the factory to the development of the competition versions of the Pantera.

# Ferrari (Italy)

Apart from Porsche, Ferrari faced little in the way of opposition during the early years of Prototype racing, and even then the German cars only offered stiff opposition on the more difficult circuits. It was much the same in the Grand Touring category, for which Ferrari developed the fabulous 250GTO, and in this category Maranello reigned supreme until toppled, eventually, by the Cobras. When the Prototype rules changed at the end of 1967, Ferrari withdrew from racing for a year, but then returned with the first of a line of 3-litre Prototypes, quickly abandoned in favour of the 5-litre 512S Competition Sports Car. Sadly this proved no real match, in terms of either preparation or performance, for the rival Porsche 917. As a result Ferrari quickly changed track again and built for the 1970 season the new 312P flat-12 Prototype, which was progressively developed and improved during that year, so that a well-organised Ferrari team completely dominated the category in 1972. By 1973 the 312Ps were no real match for the rival Matras. At the end of 1973 Ferrari withdraw from Endurance racing and since then has concentrated exclusively upon Formula 1.

## PROTOTYPES

### The 1962 Cars

During the 1962 season, the Ferrari team fielded a mixed bag of Prototypes, some of which were quite simply modified versions of the sports cars that had been raced the previous year. There were, however, two new models. The first of these was the Tipo 248SP, with a single overhead camshaft V-8 engine of 2458 cc (77 × 66 mm), developing 250 bhp at 7400 rpm. This was also raced as the 268SP with 2645 cc engine developing 265 bhp at 7000 rpm. The 4-speed gearbox was in unit with the final drive and Dunlop disc brakes were fitted. The multi-tubular chassis, with independent suspension front and rear by double wishbones and coil spring/damper units, was very similar to that of the 246SP and the body was virtually identical. The second new car which appeared in 1962 was known variously as the 330LMB and 330GT, front-engined with V-12 power unit of 3967 cc (77 × 71 mm) developing 390 bhp at 7500 rpm, once again with independent suspension front and rear by double wishbones and coil spring/damper units and coupé body.

Ferrari's first race of the year was the Sebring 12 Hours, and this was won by a 1961 front-engined 3-litre V-12 *Testa Rossa* car privately entered by the Scuderia Serenissima. The new V-8 appeared in this race driven by Fulp/Ryan, but retired. In the Targa Florio the winning car was a 1961 246SP, with rear-mounted V-6 Dino, 2417 cc (85 × 71 mm) engine developing 270 bhp at 8000 rpm, driven by Rodriguez/Mairesse. A Tipo 206SP V-6 car driven by Baghetti/Bandini finished second ahead of a works Porsche. The winning car in the Targa Florio was also the winning car at the Nürburgring, here driven by Phil Hill/Gendebien with the 4-litre Tipo 330LMB of Mairesse/Parkes second. Yet another Ferrari victory followed at Le Mans, where the winner was an experimental car with a 4-litre engine and open body similar to the *Testa Rossa* driven by Hill/Gendebien, but the

*Rear view of the winning 250P Ferrari of Scarfiotti/Bandini at Le Mans in 1963. The 250P had superbly balanced lines.* (Daved Phipps)

rest of the works Prototypes retired. The various entries fielded by Ferrari in 1962 were sufficient to confuse journalists and reporters, but preparing so many diverse cars must have proved a sheer nightmare for the works team.

## The 250P and 330LMB, 1963

During 1963, Ferrari raced two main models, which made life much easier for everyone concerned! The first of these, on which the team relied for most of the season, was the 250P, rear-engined with V-12 2953 cc (73 × 58.8 mm) engine with six Weber twin-choke carburettors and a power output of 310 bhp at 7500 rpm. The chassis was basically a slightly lengthened version of that used for the 248SP and 268SP, of multi-tubular construction, with suspension by double wishbones and coil spring/dampers front and rear. There was a 5-speed gearbox in unit with the final drive and Dunlop disc brakes were fitted front and rear, inboard at the rear. It was a car of distinctly attractive appearance with aerofoil section immediately behind the cockpit and it was a major link in the development of the Ferrari Prototypes of this era and from it all the later designs evolved.

The other main model raced by Ferrari in 1963 was the Tipo 330LMB, a coupé derived from the 1962 Le Mans winner and in reality a Prototype for a Grand Touring car that was never proceeded with. Since 1962 the power output of the 4-litre car had been increased to 400 bhp at 7500 rpm.

At Sebring, the first race of the season, the 250P of Surtees/Scarfiotti came through to win, after an early delay caused by spark plug problems, and the similar car of Mairesse/Vaccarella finished second, despite similar problems. The Targa Florio proved a rare disappointment for Ferrari. Maranello entered two of the Tipo 250P cars, which now had modified windscreens and cockpit ventilation. For this

*Ferrari completely dominated the 1963 Le Mans race and took the first six places. This 250P V-12 mid-engined car driven by Parkes/Maglioli finished third.* (Nigel Snowdon)

*Out of luck at Le Mans in 1963 was John Surtees, seen with the 250P he co-drove with Willy Mairesse; the car was eliminated by a fire.* (Daved Phipps)

race Ferrari also produced two 2-litre rear-engined V-6 cars, the Tipo 196S, but one of these was in fact provided for a private entrant. Both the 250Ps were eliminated, but the works 2-litre car shared by Bandini/Scarfiotti/Mairesse led until the last lap, when the Belgian driver spun and wrecked the rear of the car; he was able to carry on slowly to the finish, but he dropped back to second place behind Bonnier's works Porsche. A trio of 250Ps was entered at Nürburgring and Surtees/Mairesse scored a comfortable victory. Three of the 250Ps, together with three of the 4-litre Prototype coupés, were entered at Le Mans, but whilst all were prepared by the works, not all were entered in the name of the works team. The race was won by Scarfiotti/Bandini with a 250P and despite a long list of retirements Ferraris occupied the first six places in the race. Inevitably Ferrari again won the Championship.

## The 275P, the 330P and the 250LM, 1964

For 1964 Ferrari planned what was virtually a production version of the 250P and this was revealed in October 1963 at the Paris Salon. Known as the 250LM, this car originally retained the 2953 cc V-12 engine with six twin-choke Weber carburettors and a power output claimed to be 300 bhp at 7500 rpm. Compared with the 250P, the chassis was much strengthened, the suspension was very similar to that of the 250P and there was a very handsome coupé body with the fuel tanks placed between the fire wall behind the cockpit and the rear wheels. By May 1964, the engine capacity of the 250LM had been increased to 3286 cc (with an increased bore of 77 mm). Although this should strictly speaking, on the basis of Ferrari's own system of designation, have led to the car being known as the 275LM, and it

*Fifth place at Le Mans in 1963 went to this 330LMB car, with 3967 cc engine, driven by Sears/Salmon. It was to all intents and purposes a GTO with larger engine.* (Nigel Snowdon)

*Lorenzo Bandini at the pits at the 1965 Le Mans Test weekend with the 330P2 4-litre Ferrari Prototype.* (Ford of Britain)

*In the 1965 Le Mans 24 Hours race the winner was the Ferrari 250LM entered by the North American Racing Team and driven by Masten Gregory (at the wheel here) and Jochen Rindt. The other car in this photograph is an Alfa Romeo TZ2. (Nigel Snowdon)*

was in fact referred to as such in the press on many occasions, Ferrari always insisted upon it being known as the 250LM. This model was never raced by the works, but was intended for sale to private owners and for homologation as a Grand Touring car. For homologation as a Grand Touring car, it was necessary for a hundred cars to be built. Nothing like this number, only around forty, of the 250GTO were built, and this had been acceptable to the Commission Sportive Internationale, but when Ferrari tried to homologate the 250LM the CSI decided that enough was enough and refused homologation. Accordingly for several years the 250LM ran as a Prototype, something that greatly angered Enzo Ferrari and resulted in him surrendering his entrant's licence for a while, as a result of which the Formula 1 entries in the United States and Mexico in late 1964 were in American colours and entered by the North American Racing Team. Despite the fact that the 250LM was never intended as an outright Prototype race winner, the successes it gained were sensationally good.

Ferrari's own works cars for 1964 were direct developments of the 250P, the 275P with 3286 cc (77 × 58.8 mm) engine developing 320 bhp at 7700 rpm and the 330P with 3967 cc (77 × 71 mm) developing 390 bhp at 7500 rpm. It was to prove another exceptionally successful year for Ferrari, but there was no real opposition in the Prototype class. In addition to the works cars, several of the new Prototypes were from time to time entered in the names of Ferrari agents, in particular the North American Racing Team and Maranello Concessionaires.

At Sebring, once again the first round in the Championship, the Ferrari 330Ps of Parkes/Maglioli, Scarfiotti/Vaccarella and Surtees/Bandini took the first three places. Ferrari decided not to enter the Targa Florio and Porsche were the winners. Another win for Ferrari followed at the Nürburgring, where Scarfiotti/Vaccarella won with a Tipo 275P, although the Maranello Concessionaires-entered 275P of Innes Ireland/Graham Hill had led the race until the fuel tank split. Le Mans proved another Ferrari-dominated event and the Prototypes took the first three

*Frontal view of the Ferrari 250LM driven in British events by Ron Fry.* (The Author)

places in the order Guichet/Vaccarella (275P), Bonnier/Graham Hill (330P) and Bandini/Surtees (330P).

For far too long Ferrari had enjoyed unrivalled success and whilst that was going to last for another season plus, the new Ford GT40, which was eventually to overshadow the Ferraris, had made its somewhat inauspicious debut at the Nüburgring in 1964.

## 275P2 and 330P2, 1965

By now the threat from Ford was a very real menace and as a result Ferrari put a great deal of development work into the new cars for the 1965 season, and most of the work was undertaken by Mauro Forghieri. Although the basic layout of the chassis was unchanged, it was a completely new mutli-tubular structure, with certain of the aluminium panels of the bodywork riveted to chassis tubes for increased ridigity. This was in accordance with the team's Formula 1 practice, as was the new rear suspension, which featured forward-facing radius arms. Up until this point, Ferrari had relied upon wire wheels, but he now adopted cast magnesium wheels; this meant it was possible to use the latest tubeless racing tyres (tubeless tyres could not be used with wire wheels). The most significant changes were, however, to the engines. Although the engine capacities were the same as in 1964, there were now twin overhead camshafts per bank of cylinders and twin-plug ignition systems. Power output for the 3.3-litre car was 350 bhp at 8500 rpm, whilst the 4-litre car had a power output of around 400 bhp at 8000 rpm.

These cars were retained strictly for use by the factory, but Ferrari, recognising the needs of private owners, also produced a model known as the 365P2. The chassis was similar to that of the 1964 cars, but the engine was a single cam per bank 4390 cc unit developing around 390 bhp at 7200 rpm. Although these cars did not figure in Championship races, they did finish first (Rodriguez/Guichet) and second (Surtees/Parkes) in the Reims 12 Hours race in 1965, and David Piper raced one with some success in 1966–67.

Another significant Ferrari development was the introduction of a new smaller-capacity car, still known as the Dino, but completely new in every respect. The V-6 engine had a capacity of 1592 cc (77 × 57 mm) with twin overhead camshafts, twin-plug ignition and an estimated power output of 185 bhp at 9000 rpm. In both chassis design and appearance the new 166P was like a much smaller version of the P2, except that it was built only as a coupé, whereas its bigger brothers were raced in both open and closed forms. By way of comparison, the 166P had a wheelbase of 7 ft 5.76 in. compared with the 7 ft 10.5 in. of the 275P2 and 330P2. Although these cars did not always achieve the success that might be expected in their class, they were delightful and highly desirable mechanical gems, beautifully conceived and superbly styled and constructed.

The first round in the Championship was now the Daytona 2000 km race. Although Ferrari made no official entry in this race, the 275P2 of Surtees/Rodriguez, running in the name of the North American Racing Team was nothing other than a thinly disguised works entry. It retired with transmission problems and the Ford GT40 scored its first and unexpected victory. Because the organisers of the Sebring 12 Hours race had obtained consent to permit unlimited-capacity Sports Cars to run against the Prototypes, Ferrari decided not to enter the race at all. The only serious Maranello contenders were 275Ps and 330Ps in the hands of private owners. The winner was the Chaparral Sports Car, with a Ford in second place and most of the Ferraris retired.

For Ferrari the season started seriously with the Monza 1000 km race, where two of the 330P2s were entered for Surtees/Scarfiotti and Bandini/Vaccarella, with a 275P2 driven by Parkes/Guichet. There was not much in the way of opposition to the Ferraris and Parkes/Guichet and Surtees/Scarfiotti took the first two places. Next came the arduous Targa Florio on the little Madonie circuit in Sicily. Three 275P2s were entered and Vaccarella/Bandini were the winners with a 275P2.

At Monza the Dino had retired on the first lap with engine trouble, but it proved the sensation of the Nürburgring 1000 km race, where it was driven by Bandini/Vaccarella. It ran superbly, trouncing the works Porsche entries on their home territory and leading the 2-litre class until the engine began to misfire; it lost it class victory, but finished the race. Once again outright victory went to Ferrari and the 330P2 of Surtees/Scarfiotti and 275P2 of Parkes/Guichet took the first two places.

At Le Mans eleven Ferraris faced eleven Fords (but five of the Fords were Cobras, where there was only one Grand Touring Ferrari). Of the Ferrari entries, three were works 330P2 cars, but there were five private 250LM cars entered. All the works Ferraris fell by the wayside, but so did the Fords and the day was saved for Maranello by the private 250LMs. The NART-entered car of Masten Gregory/Jochen Rindt went ahead to score an historic victory, after the Belgian-entered 250LM suffered a burst tyre on the Mulsanne Straight, damaging the bodywork and causing delays while repairs were carried out; this car finished second, five laps in arrears.

What was becoming increasingly apparent was that whilst Ferrari still remained dominant in Prototype racing, the Ford GT40s, after an uphill struggle of development and modification, were at long last becoming a serious threat and there was a very real risk that Ferrari would be toppled from supremacy during the coming season.

## 330P3 and 206S, 1966

Despite the threat from Ford, Ferrari had to concentrate on the new 3-litre Formula 1 in 1966 and so entries were restricted throughout the year. The team now raced the new Tipo 330P3, retaining the 3967 cc engine but running on Lucas fuel injection and with output boosted to 420 bhp at 8000 rpm. There was a completely new transmission with multi-disc clutch between the engine and the 5-speed ZF gearbox. The chassis layout was substantially unaltered, but wider wheels were used front and rear, with suitably modified suspension geometry. However, although a multi-tubular frame was retained, the chassis featured a bonded glass-fibre underbody moulded round the tubing. The body was built by Piero Drogo and was substantially different at the front, with four headlamps in vertical pairs, and the cars were raced in both open and closed forms.

The latest version of the Dino was the 206S, in many respects a scaled-down version of the P3 with a capacity of 1987 cc (86 × 57 mm) with single-plug ignition and the same power output of 218 bhp at 9000 rpm.

For private owners there was an updated version of the 365P2, substantially to P3 specification so far as chassis design was concerned. These cars did not, however, prove competitive.

In the face of the Ford onslaught Ferrari adopted a stance of phoney apathy, missing the Daytona race and sending only a single car to Sebring to be driven by

*At Le Mans in 1966 the 330P3 of Scarfiotti/Parkes leads the Chaparral 2D through the Esses. This Ferrari crashed* (Nigel Snowdon)

*The Ferrari Dino 206 of Casoni/Vaccarella, an early victim of engine trouble, leads two other cars through the Esses at Le Mans in 1966. (Nigel Snowdon)*

Mike Parkes/Bob Bondurant. The Ferrari held second place for much of the race, but eventually retired with a seized gearbox. Cannily, Ferrari pulled out of the Le Mans Test Weekend at the last moment, claiming that he was not running because the team had adequate facilities for testing at Monza. This meant that the Ford team had nothing against which to judge their lap times on the Sarthe circuit and no means of knowing just how fast the works Ferraris would prove in June. Ferrari won at Monza at the end of April, with a P3 driven by Surtees/Parkes, in the absence of strong Ford opposition and fielded three cars in the Targa Florio. A P3 was driven by Vaccarella/Bandini with 206S Dinos for Parkes/Scarfiotti and Guichet/Baghetti. The P3 was eliminated when Bandini collided with a 250GTO that he was trying to overtake, Parkes went off the road with his Dino and Baghetti/Guichet took second place behind the winning Porsche of Müller and Mairesse.

Once again Ferrari sent only a single P3 to the Spa 1000 km race, and Parkes/Scarfiotti scored an easy win in the absence of strong opposition. Next came the Nürburgring 1000 km race, in which the American Chaparral made its European debut. Ferrari's sole large-capacity entry was a coupé 330P driven by Surtees/Parkes. There were no works Fords in the race, but Porsche were out in force on home territory. Ferrari had also entered a Dino 206S driven by Scarfiotti/Bandini. Although the P3 led the race, it lost time when a shock absorber broke off, causing the collapse of the suspension, and it eventually retired with transmission problems. The Chaparral was the unexpected winner, but the Dino entered by the works took second place.

At Le Mans Ford fielded a grand total of eight 7-litre Prototypes entered by

*At Le Mans in 1967 this P4 coupé driven by Scarfiotti/Parkes took an excellent second place, beaten by one of the two surviving Ford Mk 4s.* (Nigel Snowdon)

Shelby, Holman and Moody and Alan Mann Racing. Facing these were two works P3 cars driven by Parkes/Scarfiotti and Bandini/Guichet, with a third P3 loaned to the North American Racing Team and driven by Rodriguez/Ginther, backed up by four of the rather uncompetitive 365P2 cars entered by other private teams. It was not to prove a Ferrari race, Parkes/Scarfiotti crashed, Bandini/Guichet retired with a blown cylinder head gasket and the Rodriguez/Ginther car retired with gearbox problems. The result was a clean sweep for Ford, with three of their 7-litre cars crossing the line abreast; but they were not allowed a dead-heat, but were classified in the first three places, a total eclipse for Ferrari, and the highest placed Maranello car, the 275GTB of Pike/Courage was in eighth place.

## The 330P4 and 330P3/4, 1967

Almost inevitably as a result of the poor season suffered by Ferrari in 1966, he fought back the following year with the new 330P4 car, still retaining a 3967 cc engine, but now with two inlet and one exhaust valve per cylinder and with the inlet tracts between the camshafts of each bank of cylinders (in accordance with his Formula 1 practice), with twin plugs per cylinder and four separate coils; in this form power output was boosted to 450 bhp at 8000 rpm. Now that the ZF gearbox had been replaced by the Ferrari-designed and built 5-speed gearbox, generally the chassis and body design followed that of the 330P3, but there was a slightly wider track and shorter wheelbase and the lines had been cleaned up. The P4, for most enthusiasts and in this writer's view quite rightly, represents the acme of Prototype development of the period. Ferrari had succeeded in building a car that, with a comparatively modest engine size, combined a very good performance on high-

79

*The battle-damaged Ferrari P4 of Mairesse/'Beurlys' which finished third at Le Mans in 1967. (Nigel Snowdon)*

speed circuits, with the flexibility and torque for slower, more twisting tracks; it handled superbly, it was beautifully balanced, it could fight it out in a comparatively short 1000 km race, but had the reliability to last 24 hours, and it looked and sounded magnificent.

For private owners the 1966 cars were updated as the 330P3/4 (known at the factory as the 412P) and these consisted of the 1966 works cars updated to take wider wheels. In appearance they were virtually indistinguishable from the latest models. One each of the updated 1966 cars was supplied to the North American Racing Team, Maranello Concessionaires, Équipe Nationale Belge and Scuderia Filipinetti.

For most of the season Ferrari was able to hold his own with the might of the Ford teams. In the Daytona 24 Hours race at the beginning of the season, two works P4s, driven by Bandini/Amon and Scarfiotti/Parkes, took the first two places ahead of the P3/4 of Rodriguez/Guichet. For reasons not clearly explained, Ferrari decided to miss the Sebring 12 Hours race and the cars next appeared at Monza. Here the Ferraris were unopposed by Ford, except by John Wyer's Mirages and the latest 2F Chaparral. Bandini/Amon and Scarfiotti/Parkes took the first two places. Ferrari sent only a single P4 to the Spa 1000 km race, but this car, driven by

Parkes/Scarfiotti, did not run well and eventually finished fifth, with race victory going to the Mirage. Again, in the Targa Florio, Ferrari sent only a single P4 car for Vaccarella/Scarfiotti, but there was also a 206S Dino for Klass/Casoni; this 206S was fitted with three valves per cylinder and fuel injection. Vaccarella crashed the works P4, but the works Dino also crashed and victory went to Porsche. Because of preparations for Le Mans, Ferrari sent only a Dino 206S with 2.46-litre engine for Scarfiotti/Klass to the Nürburgring 1000 km race. However, it blew its engine during practice and was withdrawn.

Le Mans represented the climax of the unlimited capacity Prototype formula. Seven Fords were entered, faced by three works P4s, together with a fourth car entered in the name of Équipe Nationale Belge for Mairesse/'Beurlys'. The Ferraris were driven immensely hard in pursuit of the Fords, which had the edge on this high-speed circuit, and although a Ford won, the Mk. 4, the P4s of Parkes/Scarfiotti and Mairesse/'Beurlys' took second and third places. Ferrari may have been beaten, but it was a very honourable defeat. There remained one other race before the then current Prototype formula came to an end, the first BOAC 500 race at Brands Hatch. The works Fords did not appear, but the Ferraris faced a strong Porsche team, well to the fore on this medium-speed circuit, a solitary Mirage and the Chaparral. The Chaparral scored its only victory of the year, but the P4s of Stewart (having a guest drive with the team)/Amon took second place on the same lap with the other P4s of Scarfiotti/Sutcliffe and Hawkins/Williams in fifth and sixth places. On the strength of this second place, Ferrari ensured that they had won the Prototype Championship.

## The Tipo 312P, 1969

There were no works Ferrari entries in Prototype racing in 1968, but the team returned for 1969 with a car that was something of a hurriedly built compromise, combining an engine similar to that of the then current Maranello Formula 1 car, with a chassis evolved from that of the Tipo 612 car that had run in the last race of the 1968 Can-Am series. The engine was a 60-degree V-12 of 2989 cc (77 × 53.5 mm). In its 1969 form the Lucas fuel injection was in the vee of the engine, with the exhausts on the outside, there were four valves per cylinder and single plug ignition. Twin overhead camshafts per bank of cylinders were chain-driven from the nose of the crankshaft. The power output was 420 bhp at 9800 rpm. Transmission was by a twin-plate clutch and 5-speed gearbox in unit with the final drive.

The chassis was a multi-tubular space-frame, with light alloy panels riveted to give greater strength and rigidity. The suspension was similar to that of the Formula 1 car, with double wishbones and coil spring/dampers at the front, but mounted outboard, and at the rear single top links, reverse lower wishbones, twin radius arms and coil spring/damper units. Girling disc brakes were fitted, initially inboard at the rear, but later moved to the hubs, and there were superbly styled and cast Campagnolo 15 in. wheels. On the prototype, the sleek open body with wedge-shaped nose was panelled in aluminium, but glass-fibre panels were fitted by the time the car was first raced.

Although the 312P was without doubt the most attractive car to be raced in 1969, it was no match for the Porsche 908, lacking the reliability and team management enjoyed by its rival.

The 312P made its debut in the hands of Amon/Andretti at Sebring, and although it led the race twice, it was plagued by overheating and finished second to the Ford GT40 of Ickx/Oliver. The car next ran at the BOAC '500' race at Brands

*Ferrari clinched the Prototype Championship in the BOAC 500 Miles race at Brands Hatch where this open P4 driven by Jackie Stewart/Chris Amon took second place.* (Nigel Snowdon)

*The exceptionally handsome Ferrari 312P seen at the BOAC 500 race at Brands Hatch in 1969 with Pedro Rodriguez at the wheel.* (Nigel Snowdon)

Hatch, in April, and here Amon partnered by Pedro Rodriguez led until a tyre punctured, and after throttle problems finished fourth behind three Porsche 908s. By the Monza race later in the month Ferrari had two 312Ps ready, but both retired. Ferrari missed the Targa Florio, but fielded a single car at Spa for Rodriguez/Piper (the latter deputising for Amon, who was ill). Despite the strength of the Porsche opposition, and despite Rodriguez' collision with a slower car, Ferrari took second place. Only a single car for Amon/Rodriguez was entered at the Nürburgring, and although Amon set a new sports car record, the car was eliminated by electrical problems.

For Le Mans Ferrari entered two superbly elegant and handsome coupé 312Ps, with such good aerodynamics that no trim tabs were used and there was only a very small spoiler at the rear. The cars were driven by Rodriguez/Piper and Amon/Schetty. Amon was eliminated on the first lap of the race when his Ferrari hit the burning fuel tank from a crashed private Porsche; this became wedged under the Ferrari and it caught fire. Rodriguez/Piper retired because of a broken gearbox.

It had only been a token effort in 1969, and Ferrari decided to miss both Watkins Glen and the Austrian Grand Prix. The two cars were disposed of to the North American Racing Team, who ran one in a couple of Can-Am races that year, and they were run in several Championship races by NART in 1970.

*At Le Mans in 1969 Ferrari entered two 312P coupés. One was involved in a first-lap accident and this car driven by Rodriguez/Piper was eliminated by a broken gearbox.* (Nigel Snowdon)

## The Tipo 512S, 1970

It had become common knowledge during the latter part of 1969 that Ferrari, like Porsche, was going to build a full 5-litre Competition Sports car. Originally Ferrari planned to have the car ready for the 1969 Kyalami 9 Hours race, but it was first shown to the press in November and did not race until Daytona in 1970.

Although this Ferrari followed traditional Maranello design practice in many respects, it also incorporated technical lessons learned from the 312P and the 612 car fielded in the 1969 Can-Am series. There was a multi-tubular space-frame constructed from mild steel tubing extending back to the rear of the engine to provide mounting points for this and to locate the rear suspension. The front of the engine was attached to tubes immediately behind the fire wall. The centre-section of the body, forming the cockpit and the fuel tanks, was constructed of stressed alloy, while the nose and the enormous tail were in glass-fibre. Front suspension was by unequal-length wishbones and coil spring/damper units and an anti-roll bar was fitted. At the rear there were single upper arms, lower reversed wishbones, coil spring/damper units and an anti-roll bar.

The 60-degree V-12 engine, mounted ahead of the rear axle, was typical Ferrari in concept and evolved from that used in the Can-Am cars. The capacity was 4993.5 cc (87 × 70 mm). There were twin overhead camshafts for bank of cylinders chain-driven from the nose of the crankshaft, four valves per cylinder, Lucas fuel injection and single-plug ignition with a single distributor unit driven

*The surviving 312P coupe was still being raced in 1970 by the North American Racing Team. At Le Mans it was driven by Posey/de Adamowicz, but failed to finish. Note the bulge in the roof to give extra headroom.* (Nigel Snowdon)

*This open 512S Ferrari driven by Andretti/Merzario, seen here lapping a Chevron, led the 1970 Sebring race for nine hours, but retired with gearbox trouble. The race was won by another works 512S.* (Pete Lyons)

from the rear of the inlet camshaft of the left-hand cylinder block. The inlet ports were in the vee of the engine, and the exhaust on the outsides. In this form power output was 550 bhp at 8500 rpm. Transmission was by a ZF 5-speed gearbox in unit with the final drive. Girling cast iron ventilated disc brakes were hub-mounted and there were Campagnolo 5-spoke cast magnesium wheels.

The 512S looked superb, but with much heavier lines than those of the earlier 312P. It was a very potent and effective piece of machinery, technically much more sophisticated then the rival Porsche 917, but sadly it never proved a match for its German rival. In addition to the works cars, quite a number of 512S models were supplied to private entrants. At Daytona, in January 1970, the cars were all fitted with coupé bodywork. Porsche 917s took the first two places, but a 512S shared by Andretti/Ickx/Merzario finished third. By the Sebring 12 Hours race in March, Ferrari had a new open *Spyder* version of the 512S with a squarer nose, that was lighter and with better front-end adhesion. Sebring proved a race of attrition, with both the 917s and the Ferraris suffering major problems, but the 512S of Andretti/Giunti/Vaccarella came through to score what was to prove the model's only Championship win.

*This 512S 5-litre V-12 car with open top, entered by Scuderia Filipinetti and driven by Müller/Parkes, finished 13th in the 1970 BOAC 500 Miles race at Brands Hatch.* (Nigel Snowdon)

*Practice at the Nürburgring in 1970. This works 512S non-started after it was crashed by Peter Schetty.* (Nigel Snowdon)

Two works cars ran in the BOAC 1000 km race at Brands Hatch, but they were plagued by minor problems and were completely outclassed by the 917 Porsche opposition. Amon/Merzario were a poor fifth and Ickx/Oliver (the latter deputizing for Andretti) were a hopeless eighth. Ony Ickx had been able to match the wet-weather driving of the Gulf team members, Ferrari pit work was much inferior to that of Wyer's team and both cars had wasted time in the pits for bodywork repairs after minor collisions.

The Ferrari team put all their efforts into the Monza 1000 km race and entered three very well-prepared cars. Ickx was out of the team because of burns suffered after a collision in the Spanish Grand Prix and John Surtees was brought into the team. Although the Ferraris were defeated, with Giunti/Vaccarella/Amon in second place, Surtees/Schetty third and Amon/Merzario fourth, there was only the winning 917 in the first six and the second-place Ferrari was less than two minutes in arrears after 175 laps.

Unlike Porsche, who had prepared special 908/03 cars for the races on the two most tortuous circuits, the Targa Florio and the Nürburgring, Ferrari had nothing to race but the 512S. Over the badly maintained, narrow and winding roads of the 44.7-mile Little Madonie circuit of the Targa Florio, the 512S was likely to prove a complete handful and no match for the German opposition. Ferrari entered only a single open car for local hero Nino Vaccarella/Ignazio Giunti. They drove magnificently to finish third behind the two 908/03s. At Spa Ferrari entered three 512S coupés, but again Porsche were the winners, and Ickx/Surtees drove a fine race to finish second, with Giunti/Vaccarella fourth. Although prospects of success were small, Ferrari entered three 512S *Spyders* in the Nürburgring 1000 km race, but the entry was reduced to two after Schetty crashed heavily in practice – it was almost just as well, for Ickx had arrived at the circuit with a sprained wrist and was

*As darkness falls and against the fairground lights, Ickx with his works Ferrari 512S roars through the Esses at Le Mans in 1970. Sadly Ickx crashed during the night hours and a marshall was killed in the accident.* (Nigel Snowdon)

unable to drive. The 908/03s dominated the race, but Surtees/Vaccarella did well to finish third.

The Le Mans 24 hours race in 1970 was one of the most exciting since the race was first run. It witnessed a tremendous three-sided battle between the Porsche 917s of John Wyer's team, those entered by Porsche Konstruktionen and the 512S Ferraris, four of which were works cars. All were fitted with coupé bodies, featuring the original, rounded noses, but with long tails surmounted by small fins. By now power output had risen to 585 bhp.

It proved a disastrous race for the Gulf team, and even more disastrous for Ferrari. During the first hour Vaccarella retired the car he was to share with Giunti with a rod through the side. In one incident alone, four 512S cars were eliminated. After 2½ hours' racing Wisell at the wheel of a 512S entered by the Filipinetti team was driving back to the pits slowly because of an oil-covered windscreen when he was caught by the battling trio of Derek Bell (works 512S), Regazzoni (works 512S) and Parkes (Filipinetti 512S). Bell swerved round the Filipinetti car, missing a gear and breaking his engine, while Regazonni rammed Wisell's car, which was pushed into the crash barrier and rebounded into the centre of the track and it and Regazzoni's car were rammed by Parkes. This left only the 512S of Ickx/Schetty which the young Belgian worked up to second place, only to lose control early in the morning, spinning over a sandbank and killing a marshal. The 917s took the first two places, and the highest placed 512S entries were privately owned cars in fourth and fifth places.

At Watkins Glen the highest placed Ferrari was the Andretti/Giunti car in third place. By the Austrian 1000 km race in October Ferrari contented himself with entering only the prototype, 512M car (see the next section) driven by Ickx/Giunti, and this set an ever-increasing lead in the early laps of the race, only to run into battery trouble, fall out of contention and be withdrawn.

Beyond doubt the 512S was a superbly engineered and well-developed car, but Ferrari team management was no match for that of the Porsche opposition, the 512S was heavier than its 917 rival and it lacked sufficient reliability. It had been a vastly expensive effort by Ferrari, for very little return. Instead of concentrating on

*This 512M driven by Posey/Adamowicz and entered by the North American Racing Team finished third at Le Mans in 1971.* (Nigel Snowdon)

developing the car for 1971, the last year in which 5-litre Competition Sports cars were allowed, Ferrari decided to concentrate on a new 3-litre Prototype in anticipation of 1972.

## The Tipo 512M, 1971

For private owners Ferrari produced this much-improved car, with lighter nose and shorter, cutaway tail. There was a lighter chassis with fewer tubes and a front sub-frame of much reduced proportions. The engine now featured chromed alloy cylinder liners and fuel injection changes which, together with improved inlet and exhaust manifolding, boosted the power output to over 600 bhp. The principal entrants of 512M cars in 1971 were the North American Racing Team, Scuderia Filipinetti, Herbert Müller Racing and Escuderia Montjuich. The best performances achieved by these cars in Championship races in 1971 were a fourth by Müller/Herzog in the BOAC 1000 km race at Brands Hatch, a third place by Posey/Adamowicz at Le Mans, a fourth place by Pasotti/Casoni in the Austrian race and fourth by de Cadenet/Motschenbacher at Watkins Glen.

## The Sunoco-Ferrari, 1971

This, undoubtedly the most potent of all the 512 series Farraris, had started life as a 512S run in a few 1970 Can-Am races. It was bought by Kirk White of Philadelphia, who had it prepared for sports car racing by Roger Penske. The car was completely rebuilt, from the chassis up, with many of the suspension components replaced and major changes made to the steering geometry. The riveted aluminium panelling was replaced and the car was fitted with a new 512M-type body, complete with a full-width rear aerofoil. Other features were a special pressurised fuel refilling system, provision for filling the oil and water reservoirs by compressed air to save time during pit stops and a vacuum device on the brake master cylinders to draw the fluid back from the brakes and to pull the pistons back into the calipers so as to speed up brake pad changes. Another feature, to speed driver changes, was that the drivers wore seat buckles strapped to their waists. Penske sent two of the 5-litre Ferrari engines to Traco, the Chevrolet development specialists, who rebuilt them completely and introduced a number of minor modifications so that the power output comfortably exceeded 600 bhp. The turn-out of this car was magnificent, in blue, with yellow wheels with polished rims.

Unfortunately it had started as something of a short-term project, and one year was not sufficient for a small team to turn this car into a race-winner. Donohue/Hobbs finished third in the Daytona 24 Hours race, despite being rammed by a Porsche 911 which severely damaged the bodywork and resulted in a long time spent in the pits carrying out emergency repairs. At Sebring, with the same drivers, it was in collision with the Rodriguez/Oliver Porsche 917, but 19 laps were lost while the car was repaired and because of damage to the fuel tank on the left-hand side, more frequent fuel stops were required. The drivers did well to bring it across the line in sixth place.

At one stage Penske had considered developing the car for Can-Am racing, but instead it was decided to enter the car at Le Mans. It lacked the sheer speed of the Porsche 917s, although holding second place at one time, and retired with engine

*At Brands Hatch in the 1971 BOAC 1000 Km race Jacky Ickx with the new Ferrari 312P
leads the Porsche 917 of Kauhsen/Jöst. (Nigel Snowdon)*

trouble on the Sunday evening. At Watkins Glen it was fastest in practice and faster
on the straight than the Gulf 917s and it led the race initially, but retired with
suspension problems.

## The Tipo 312P, 1971

In abandoning the 512 cars, Ferrari was looking ahead to 1972 when these would
be banned and racing would be limited to 3-litre Sports Cars. Throughout 1971 the
team ran what might best be described as a 'prototype' Prototype. This was a new,
low, open car with a very compact wedge-shaped body, as first seen on small sports
cars such as the Chevron B19.

The basis of the new car was a tubular space-frame, with aluminium sheet
riveted to give a semi-monocoque, a common feature of Ferrari design practice. A
tubular structure running rearwards from the cockpit formed the mounting for the
engine, which became the 'backbone' of the car. At the front there were double
wishbones and coil spring/damper units, whilst at the rear there were single
transverse links, twin radius arms and lower wishbones. Rack-and-pinion steering
was fitted, the disc brakes were outboard front and rear and there were twin
radiators mounted on either side of the cockpit, with ducting in the bodywork to
feed air to them.

Powering the new car was the Ferrari flat-12 Formula 1 engine of 2993 cc (78.5
× 51.5 mm) with power output 440 bhp at 10,800 rpm, considerably detuned
compared to the Formula 1 configuration of 480 bhp at 11,500 rpm. There was a

5-speed gearbox in unit with the final drive. During 1971 a revised gearbox was fitted, which made it much easier to change ratios. The two-piece glass-fibre body could be raced with three different tails, a very short tail for tight circuits, an intermediate style used for most of the season, and a long tail that was used only during Le Mans testing in 1971.

1971 was very much a season of testing and development for the team and although the car performed very strongly, outstanding results were neither expected nor achieved. The car was driven on its debut at Buenos Aires by Giunti/Merzario, but during the race Giunti crashed into the Matra of Beltoise that was being pushed along the track. The Ferrari caught fire and Giunti suffered burns and injuries that were fatal. Two months later Ferrari had a new 312P ready for Sebring and it was driven by Ickx/Andretti. Although it led the race, it retired with transmission problems. In most European races the drivers were Ickx and Regazzoni. At Brands Hatch they finished second, three laps behind the winning Alfa Romeo, after the Porsche 917s had run into trouble and despite delays caused by a collision and throttle problems. It was a very encouraging performance. At Monza the 312P was eliminated by an accident and again it was forced out at Spa by an accident, this time a collision with the Dulon-Porsche. Ferrari missed the Targa Florio and, after leading at the Nürburgring, the Ferrari retired with loss of water and engine problems. Le Mans was another race that the team missed. In Austria

*Tim Schenken with his 312P Ferrari at La Source hairpin in the 1972 Spa 1000 Km race.*
*He was co-driving with Ronnie Peterson, but they did not finish in this race.*

the Ferrari again built up an enormous speed, only to crash near the finish, possibly because the front suspension broke. At Watkins Glen Ickx was partnered by Andretti, and was again leading when the engine refused to start after a pit stop.

At the end of the year Ferrari completed a second car, with modified cockpit to comply with the 1972 Sports Cars regulations and modified suspension. The two cars were entered in the Kyalami 9 Hours race and Regazzoni/Redman won from Ickx/Andretti in second place.

## The Tipo 312P, 1972

In Prototype racing 1972 was the most successful year in Ferrari's racing history and the team scored ten wins, without a single failure. A batch of six new cars had been built so that three-car teams could be fielded at each race without having to run the cars in successive races. Ferrari had an immensely strong team of drivers consisting of Ickx, Regazzoni and Andretti (all members of the Ferrari Formula 1 team), together with Brian Redman, Ronnie Peterson and Tim Schenken.

Apart from the fact that the cars were superbly engineered, the full year's testing in 1971 proved of immense benefit, the team was well managed by Peter Schetty and standards of preparation, the responsibility of Ermanno Cuoghi, formerly with the Gulf team, but now joint chief Ferrari mechanic, were better than at any time in Ferrari history. Admittedly there was not much in the way of opposition, for the Alfas, despite a very successful year in 1971, were totally uncompetitive, Matra ran only at Le Mans and the Lolas were purely an amateur effort. The one race during the year which Ferrari missed was the Le Mans 24 Hours, and it was stated quite unequivocally that the team did not consider the flat-12 Formula 1 engine suitable for an event of this length. For the record the wins were as follows:

| | | | |
|---|---|---|---|
| Buenos Aires 1000 km race | 1st | Peterson/Schenken | 108.05 mph |
| Daytona Continental 6 Hours race | | Ickx/Andretti | 124.72 mph |
| Sebring 12 Hours race | | Ickx/Andretti | 111.51 mph |
| BOAC 1000 km race | | IckxAndretti | 105.12 mph |
| Monza 1000 km race | | Ickx/Regazzoni | 105.94 mph |
| Spa 1000 km race | | Redman/Merzario | 145.05 mph |
| Targa Florio | | Merzario/Munari | 76.14 mph |

(in this race only the one Ferrari was entered, defeating a team of four Alfa Romeos),

| | | |
|---|---|---|
| Nürburgring 1000 km race | Peterson/Schenken | 103.59 mph |
| Austrian 1000 km race | Ickx/Redman | 125.46 mph |
| Watkins Glen 6 Hours race | Peterson/Schenken | 103.59 mph |

## The Tipo 312P, 1973

For the 1973 season Ferrari made a number of modifications to the 312P cars, including the adoption of a slightly longer wheelbase, modified nose and power increased to 460 bhp at 11,000 rpm. Most onlookers had anticipated that Ferrari's run of success would continue, but it had been overlooked just how much work Matra had put into their cars, now that they had the resources available after withdrawing from Formula 1. The first shock came at Vallelunga, Ferrari's first race of the season, and Matra won this 6-hour event, with the Ferraris trailing

*The winning 312P at Spa in 1972 was driven by Brian Redman (seen here) and Merzario.* (Nigel Snowdon)

behind in second, third and fourth places. Another defeat followed at Dijon, where Matra again won and the Ferraris were pushed back into second and fourth places. At Monza, there was a furious battle between the Matra and Ferrari teams, but this came to an end when the gearbox of the leading French car seized and Ickx/Redman were the winners from team-mates Schenken/Reutemann.

After the leading Matra punctured a tyre at Spa, a Ferrari victory seemed certain, but the 312P of Ickx/Redman lost the oil in its gearbox and was eliminated. The unexpected winner was the Mirage of Bell/Hailwood. Both Ferraris were eliminated by crashes in the Targo Florio, and Ferrari regained some prestige at the Nürburgring, where Ickx/Redman and Merzario/Pace took first and second places after the failure of the leading Matra. At this race the Ferraris were fitted for the first time with a new engine air box above the roll bar. Despite what Ferrari had said in 1972, a team of three cars was entered at Le Mans. The race proved another Matra benefit, with the French cars finishing first and third, but Merzario/Pace brought their Ferrari home in second place, having lost the lead and spent a great deal of time in the pits while the exhaust system was replaced. More defeats followed in Austria, where the highest placed Ferrari, that of Ickx/Redman, was third, and at Watkins Glen where Ickx/ Redman finished second.

Ferrari withdrew from Sports Car racing at the end of 1973, a year of Matra domination followed and then the category simply died through lack of support and interest.


# GRAND TOURING CARS

Throughout the 1950s Ferrari GT cars had enjoyed a substantial measure of success and this design theme reached its acme in the SWB (short-wheelbase) 250 GT Berlinetta, which had appeared in late 1959. This car, developed by engineer Giotto Bizzarini, was powered by the Colombo-designed 2953 cc (73 × 58.8 mm) V-12 engine with single overhead camshaft per bank of cylinders and a power output, in later form, of 280 bhp at 7000 rpm; it was broadly similar to the engine that powered the *Testa Rossa* Sports-Racing car. The chassis had a short, 7 ft 10.5 in. wheelbase, rigid rear axle, and a very elegant body styled by Pininfarina, but built by Scaglietti. It has been estimated that around 250 of these cars in all were built, of which around 20 per cent were lightweight competition cars. SWB Berlinettas enjoyed a good run of success in 1960, with wins in the Tourist Trophy at Goodwood (by Stirling Moss at the wheel of a car entered by Rob Walker), the Tour de France (Mairesse/Berger), with similar cars in second and third places and a win in the Paris 1000 km Race at Montlhéry (Gendebien/Bianchi). This run of successes continued in 1961, with many class wins, and the outstanding successes included fourth place at the Nürburgring 1000 km race (Abate/Davis with a 1960 car), third place overall at Le Mans (Noblet/Guichet), and wins by Stirling Moss with Rob Walker's car in the GT race at Silverstone in July, at Brands Hatch in August, and again in the Tourist Trophy at Goodwood. Other wins included the Auvergne 6 Hours race (Mairesse with a 1960 car), a class win in the Pescara Grand Prix and a win in the Coppa Inter-Europa race at Monza in September. In the Tour de France Berlinettas took the first four places. Yet another victory followed in the Paris 1000 km race, where Pedro and Ricardo Rodriguez were the winners. Despite the brilliant successes of the 250 GT Berlinetta, Ferrari was planning a new and even more successful car for the coming year.

*Even before the appearance of the 250GTO Ferrari enjoyed immense success in GT events. Above is Luigi Tarramazzo with his winning 250GT in the 1958 Coppa da Roma and below Mike Parkes with his Maranello Concessionaires-entered 250GT on his way to a win at Brands Hatch in 1961. (John Ross and British Petroleum)*

## 250GTO, 1962

The Prototype of the 250GTO is regarded as having been a special car that ran at Le Mans in 1961. This featured a prototype Pininfarina body, inspired by the 'Superfast II' aerodynamic coupé exhibited in 1960, powered by a 2953 cc engine brought up to Testa Rossa specification, with sports-racing camshafts and pistons, converted to dry sump lubrication and developing 300 bhp at 7500 rpm. At Le Mans this car was driven by Fernando Tavano and Giancarlo Baghetti, but retired with engine problems. A second car was also built to this design. One of these cars was driven by Stirling Moss in the Daytona 3 Hours race in February 1962 and he finished fourth overall. From these were developed the definitive GTO, with much smoother and more aerodynamic bodywork evolved by Pininfarina, but built by Scaglietti, and with dry sump engine, 6 twin-choke Weber 38 DCN carburettors, with a power output of 300 bhp at 7500 rpm and a 5-speed all-synchromesh gearbox. For homologation as a Grand Turismo car, strictly speaking Ferrari should have built 100, but it seems that total production amounted to only around 40, but no objection was received over the question of homologation. This was to cause Ferrari great anger when he was later unable to homologate the 250LM (referred to above).

During 1962 the new cars enjoyed an immense run of success. The model made its competition debut in the Sebring 12 Hours race, and was driven into second place overall and first in class by Gendebien/Phil Hill. In May Scarlatti and Ferraro drove their 250GTO into fourth place overall and first in class in the Targa Florio. At the International Silverstone Meeting in May Parkes and Gregory took the first two places in the GT race. Another success followed at the Nürburgring, where Nöcker/Seidel finished fifth overall and first in the GT class with a 1960 SWB

*Mike Parkes with this 250GTO entered by Maranello Concessionaires won the GT race at Silverstone in May 1962.* (British Petroleum)

*The start of the 1962 Le Mans race with, nearest the camera, the Ferrari 250GTO of 'Beurlys'/Langlois which finished second overall.* (David Phipps)

Berlinetta. The class had been led by a GTO, but this was forced to retire when the starter motor failed at a pit stop. At Le Mans the 250GTOs of Noblet/Guichet and 'Elde' 'Beurlys' finished second and third, ahead of two lightweight E-type Jaguars. In the Tourist Trophy at Goodwood the 250GTOs of Innes Ireland, Graham Hill and Parkes took the first three places. Yet another victory followed in the Paris 1000 km race for Grand Touring Cars in October, when brothers Ricardo and Pedro Rodriguez repeated their 1961 victory, but this time at the wheel of a 250GTO, leading home five other Ferraris.

Mention should also be made of a variation of the GTO theme; Giotto Bizzarini, who had left Ferrari early in 1962, worked with bodybuilder Piero Drogo to build a number of Berlinettas based, in the main, on Ferrari SWB Berlinetta components. None of these cars achieved much in the way of success, but the so-called 'Bread-van' with square-back raced by the Scuderia Serenissima Republica di Venezia in 1961 acquired quite a degree of fame, partly because of the fascinating complexity of its entrant's name and partly because of its rather outré lines.

## The 250GTO, 1963

The GTO continued into 1963 without modification and its run of success was unabated. In February Pedro Rodriguez won the Daytona 3 Hours race, at Sebring Penske/Pabst finished fourth overall with a 250GTO, Bulgari/Grana finished fourth overall in the Targa Florio and Noblet/Guichet turned in a brilliant drive at the Nürburgring to finish second overall with their 250GTO. It was much the same story at Le Mans where the GTO of 'Beurlys'/Langlois finished second overall behind the winning 250P Prototype. Ferrari's fourth successive win in the Tourist Trophy followed, with Graham Hill in a GTO leading home Mike Parkes in a similar car. Parkes also finished second overall and first in the 3-litre GT Class, behind Salvadori's Aston Martin, in the Coppa Inter-Europa race at Monza in September, and this was an exceptionally closely fought event. Again the Tour de France was won by a Ferrari, for the eighth year in succession, with Guichet/José Behra winning in their GTO from a similar car driven by Mauro Bianchi/Abate.

## The 250GTO64, 1964

Originally Ferrari had hoped to homologate the 250LM in 1964, but after homologation was refused, Maranello entrants were forced to rely in the GT category on an improved version of the 250GTO. With this car Ferrari produced one of the most handsome of all his competition models, a design with basically similar lines to the mid-engined 250 Le Mans, with sleeker nose, sweeping and very raked windscreen and very abbreviated coupé featuring an angular aerofoil roof and high rear wings. Throughout the year Ferrari faced a strong challenge from Cobra, but the GTO64s achieved a substantial measure of success. With the new car Phil Hill and Pedro Rodriguez won the Daytona 2000 km race, ahead of two earlier GTOs, and with the Cobras soundly trounced. However, in March at Sebring the Cobras finished ahead of a 250GTO64, which was pushed back into seventh place overall. Felaino/Taramazzo finished fourth overall with 'Beurlys'/Lucien Bianchi fifth in the Targa Florio, a race in which the Cobras failed, and Parkes/Guichet finished second overall and first in the GT category at the Nürburgring. At Le Mans the surviving Cobra coupé finished fourth overall and won the class, but the GTO of 'Beurlys'/Bianchi finished fifth overall and second in the class. The model took third and fourth places in the Reims 12 Hours race, but the Cobras beat the GTO64 in the Tourist Trophy. An older-style GTO won the Tour de France and this clinched Ferrari's victory in the GT Championship. At the end of the year the GTO64 of Rodriguez/Schlesser finished second in the Paris 1000 km race. Although GTO64s, and indeed the earlier cars, continued to be raced through into 1965, Ferrari indicated that he would not be contesting the GT Championship in 1965. This, however, proved not be quite the case.

## The 275GTB, 1965

In 1964 Ferrari introduced at the Paris Salon the new 275GTB Berlinetta with 3258 cc (77 × 58.8 mm) engine, a new 5-speed all-synchromesh gearbox in unit with the final drive, completely revised rear suspension and a very elegant body designed by Pininfarina, but built by Scaglietti. In its standard form the GTB had a power output of 280 bhp, but Ferrari was unable to resist producing a special version of this car for GT racing in 1965 and it is believed that it was powered by a full 250LM engine developing 310 bhp at 7500 rpm. The car featured a light alloy body with longer nose and swept-up rear bodywork. This car, painted in Belgian yellow racing colours and entered by Scuderia Francorchamps, was driven at Le Mans by Mairesse and 'Beurlys'. Despite overheating problems, which meant that the nose was cut open during the race to improve the cooling, it finished third overall and won the GT class. Later in the year it was driven to victory in the Nassau Tourist Trophy in the Bahamas by Charlie Kolb.

In 1966 a 275GTB driven by Noblet/Dubois finished tenth and won its class.

For many collectors, the SWB Berlinetta and 250GTO represent the ultimate in front-engined Ferrari design and development. They have become so sought after and desirable that samples have changed hands at close to $1,000,000.

*With this 250GTO64 Graham Hill, entered by Maranello Concessionaires, won the Sussex Trophy race at the Easter Goodwood meeting in 1964.* (David Phipps)

*At Le Mans in 1966 this Ferrari 275GTB driven by Noblet/Dubois finished tenth overall and won its class.* (Nigel Snowdon)

*This Ferrari 365 GTB4 Daytona entered in the 1972 Spa 1000 Km race by Charles Pozzi and driven by Ballot-Lena/Rouveyran retired because of a burst tyre.* (Nigel Snowdon)

### The Daytona

From 1972 onwards private owners raced a modified version of the production Daytona car. This, developed from the 275GTB4, featured a front-engined V-12 4390 cc engine, developing in production form 352 bhp at 7500 rpm. Transmission was by a 5-speed gearbox in unit with the final drive. The body was a dramatic Berlinetta designed by Pininfarina. At Le Mans in 1972 one of these cars driven by Andruet/Ballot-Lena finished fifth overall, winning the GT class, and leading home four other Daytonas. The model also won its class at Watkins Glen, where it was driven into sixth place by Jarier/Young. The model won its class at Le Mans in 1973 and 1974. As late as 1977 Daytonas finished fifth and sixth overall at Daytona. Although the mid-engined Berlinetta Boxers, with flat-12 engines, have been raced, the front-engined Daytona represented the last successful foray by Ferrari in the GT class.

# Ford GT40 (United States)

Ford's break into international motor racing was a remarkable phenomenon. It arose from a decision made in 1962 by Henry Ford II to break with the traditional U.S. Manufacturers' agreement not to enter racing. Initially the American Ford company turned its efforts towards Indianapolis and the local scene, but early in

1963 the decision was made to enter the new international class of Grand Touring Prototype Cars. In 1962 this category had been subject to a capacity limit of 4 litres, but for 1963 this restriction was abandoned and it made it much easier for the Ford Company to enter the fray. To attain success proved an immense, uphill struggle, but after the expenditure of vast sums of money and an intensive development programme, Ford came to dominate both prototype racing and the class for homologated Competition GT Cars. In all, including the later victories by the John Wyer-entered cars, Ford won Le Mans four times.

## Development of the GT40

In the autumn of 1962 Roy Lunn, a Yorkshireman who had at one time worked for the Jowett Company, was given the task of starting his design studies on a Prototype, to be powered by the existing Ford 4.2-litre Indianapolis engine. Already Eric Broadley's small Lola concern at Bromley was working on a similar project and the Lola GT with Shelby-modified Ford V-8 engine mounted ahead of the rear axle line, Colotti 4-speed gearbox and glass-fibre coupé body appeared at the Racing Car Show in London in January 1963. The racing history of the Lola GT is described under that heading in this book and it suffices to say here that Ford immediately recognised that what Broadley had achieved was very comparable with the project that they were aiming to create. It was in 1963 that Ford conducted abortive negotiations with Ferrari with a view to taking over the Maranello concern, but these came to nothing, and in June 1963 Ford came to an arrangement with Broadley whereby they took over Lola for what was to be originally a year; Broadley was to work with Roy Lunn to develop the new Ford GT. Three months later, at the end of September, they were joined, as Technical Director and General Manager, by John Wyer, formerly of Aston Martin. The new company, Ford Advanced Vehicles, was set up at Slough as a subsidiary of the British Ford company.

Ford's first step was a complete appraisal of the Lola GT, in theory at Dearborn and in practice at Monza, where it was driven by Richie Ginther, Bruce McLaren and Roy Salvadori. By the tests at Monza, Ford had fitted their own 4.2-litre Indianapolis engine and there were a number of other Ford modifications. Of these tests, Salvadori has written, 'When I first tested the Lola-based car at Monza in October 1963, I found that there was virtually nothing about it I liked. The car was unstable on the approach to the Curva Grande and the faster parts of the circuit. . . . My initial reaction was not to blame the car and I was wondering whether I was at fault – perhaps my driving was getting rusty and I ought to give up competition driving.' It was only too obvious that a great deal of work was needed before the team could race a really competitive car.

Work went ahead on the definitive GT40, which was an amalgam of the design features of the original Lola coupled with the input of Lunn and his design team. The basis of the car was a sheet-steel semi-monocoque with square-tube stiffening and glass-fibre body panels. The front suspension was by double wishbones, coil springs/dampers and an anti-roll bar, while at the rear there were twin trailing arms, transverse top links, lower wishbones, coil spring/damper units and an anti-roll bar. In its original form the engine was the Ford V-8 of 4195cc (95.5 × 72.9 mm) with aluminium cylinder block and heads, dry sump lubrication, four twin-choke Weber carburettors, 12.5:1 compression ratio and a power output of 350 bhp at 7200 rpm. This engine was used in conjunction with a Borg and Beck dry 3-plate clutch and combined Colotti 4-speed gearbox and final drive unit without synchromesh. There was rack-and-pinion steering, Girling disc brakes front and rear and a new body, with the doors cut extensively into the roof to provide easy entry and exit and very pugnacious but not unattractive styling. All the cars were painted in American white and blue colours at this stage.

## The GT40, 1964

The car was tested again in March 1964 at the Motor Industry Research Association track near Rugby, at Silverstone and at Goodwood. Salvadori felt that the car was only a marginal improvement over the Lola-based car driven at Monza the previous autumn. The GT40s had their first public outing at the Le Mans test weekend in April and the cars were found to be suffering very badly from aerodynamic stability. The weekend was wet and windy and on the Saturday Schlesser lost one of the cars at around 170 mph on the Mulsanne straight, crashing heavily. The following day Salvadon over-braked and smacked into a concrete barrier, damaging the car too badly for it to be repaired that day. Salvadori was so disenchanted with the car he decided to pull out of the Ford team, but took part in a

*The Ford GT40 of Attwood/Schlesser at Le Mans in 1964. It is leading the class-winning Cobra and the Simon/Trintignant Maserati. This Ford rose to sixth place, but a fuel line split and it caught fire. (Nigel Snowdon)*

final test section at MIRA, and the addition of a spoiler, at the suggestion of John Wyer, did much to improve the car's stability. Interestingly enough, the idea of using a spoiler had been rejected after wind-tunnel tests, but when applied practically the result was very different. Although the team's efforts were firmly fixed on a successful outing at Le Mans, it was felt that further development under racing conditions was needed and so a single car for Phil Hill and Bruce McLaren were entered in the Nürburgring 1000 km race. Ford was second fastest in practice and at one stage Phil Hill held second place behind Surtees' Ferrari, but the car had to be withdrawn because of the failure of a rear suspension mounting bracket caused by an incorrect welding process. Back at Slough, when the car was more thoroughly examined, it became obvious that a number of other welding points were near failure. At least the team had the opportunity of incorporating these hastily learned lessons in the three cars being built for Le Mans.

At Le Mans the three cars were driven by Hill/McLaren, Ginther/Gregory and Attwood/Schlesser. Although the GT40s ran well in practice, second, fourth and ninth fastest, they were plagued by a tendency for the nose to lift at high speeds. At the end of the first hour the Ginther/Gregory car led, it held second place for another three and a half hours, but then retired with gearbox selector failure. Attwood/Schlesser rose to sixth place before a fuel pipe split and the car caught fire. As the race progressed, Hill/McLaren, having made five pit stops in the first hour, drove faster and faster, working the car up to fourth place with Hill setting a new circuit record of 131.29 mph before the car was retired on the Sunday morning with gearbox trouble.

Two other racing appearances were made in 1964, in the Reims 12 Hours race, where all three cars retired, and in the Tourist Trophy at Nassau in the Bahamas, where Hill drove a single car but again retired.

## The GT40 and Mk 2, 1965

Whilst Ford were bitterly disappointed by the poor performances during 1964, and this had led to an erosion of confidence in the existing set-up, they realised that the basic design was right, subject to development, and for 1965 split up the operations between a number of different organisations. Roy Lunn and his staff were moved out to a Ford acquisition, Kar Kraft, a small and very specialist unit, around four miles from the main plant at Dearborn. Their aim was to work on the new Mk 2 version of the car, to which reference will be made later.

Development of the existing GT40 was passed to Shelby-American, who were very highly rated because of their efforts with the Cobra and indeed were significantly overrated. Shelby made a substantial number of changes to the existing car, including the substitution of the 4.7-litre Cobra version of the Ford 289 Fairlane engine in place of the Indianapolis unit. This engine, with a capacity of 4736 cc (101.6 × 72.9 mm) featured a cast-iron cylinder block, it weighed somewhat more than the previous light-alloy engine, it had a wet sump in place of the dry sump of the 1964 cars and after the first two races of the 1965 season (Daytona and Sebring) a ZF gearbox was substituted for the previous Colotti unit. Pending the availability of the ZF gearboxes, quite substantial changes were made to the Colotti gearboxes. Cast alloy wheels replaced the original wire wheels and there were now Goodyear tyres instead of Dunlop. Some of the additional weight of the cast-iron block engine was compensated for by the elimination of the front-mounted oil tank and the piping.

At Slough John Wyer had been pushed into something of a backwater, being forced to rely on the development of a production version of the GT40 and building

*The open Ford-France-entered Ford GT40 of Trintignant/Ligier at Le Mans in 1965. It retired because of gearbox problems.* (Ford of Britain)

an open roadster version, which retained the wire wheels of the original but suffered from lack of stiffness of the basic structure and resulted in very little weight reduction, and that at the price of increased drag and cockpit noise.

At Daytona, in the 2000 km Continental race, two of the now improved original GT40 cars were entered; the opposition was weak, the Ferraris entered by North American Racing Team were plagued by transmission trouble and, thanks to new-found reliability, Ken Miles/Lloyd Ruby scored the GT40's first and unexpected but fairly easy victory, followed home by a Cobra Daytona coupé and the other GT40 driven by Ginther/Bondurant, 28 laps behind because of mechanical problems. Two cars were again entered in the Sebring 12 Hours race, an event that was also open to sports cars not complying with Prototype rules, and in a race run in the most appalling conditions, including a flooded track, the Chaparral of Hall and Sharp scored a good victory. The surviving GT40 of McLaren/Miles took second place, although the other car of Hill/Ginther retired because of a fractured spring mounting.

Now the European season started and at the Le Mans Test Weekend Shelby appeared with two cars, rather tatty-looking, and John Wyer brought along his open GT40 as well as two coupés. The Ferraris put on a show of force, with the five fastest cars. Fastest of the Fords, sixth fastest, was Dickie Attwood with a John Wyer-entered car. Ford was contesting the whole of the European season and, for the first race, the Monza 1000 km event, two cars were driven by McLaren/Miles and Amon/Maglioli and the preparation and race organization were delegated to Alan Mann Racing. The Ferraris took the first two places, but the Ford of McLaren/Miles finished third, never having been able to challenge for the lead. The other Ford GT40, driven by Amon/Maglioli, had run with a 5.3-litre engine, but it had drive-shaft trouble both in practice and during the race. Wyer entered the open 4.7-litre car for Whitmore/Bondurant in the Targo Florio road race in Sicily, but after suffering from a misfiring engine in the early laps of the race, it lost a wheel (which was replaced by the spare) and later, with Bondurant at the wheel, bounced off a wall, tearing off its front suspension and a wheel. It was not really a suitable car for this event. Ford tried again at the Nürburgring 1000 km race, with a total of four entries: Attwood/Whitmore drove the open car entered by FAV (engine bearer problems caused its retirement); Phil Hill/McLaren with 5.3-litre engine entered by Shelby (still suffering from drive-shaft problems and retiring on the seventh lap when one broke); Amon/Maglioli (surviving a slow race to finish eighth) and a car for Trintignant/Ligier entered by Ford-France and retaining wire wheels (suffered a failed engine mounting). So far the season had been an appalling disappointment.

Next came the Le Mans 24 Hours race, where Ford entered two of the new 7-litre Mk 2 cars, a title which was given to the model retrospectively. The Mk 2 used the 6977 cc (107.5 × 96.1 mm) V-8 Ford Galaxie engine in the form developed for stock-car racing, weighing all of 600 lbs but with a single Holley 4-choke carburettor, dry sump lubrication and 10.5:1 compression ratio, developing a massive 485 bhp at 6200 rpm. This engine was used with a Ford T-44 4-speed gearbox in unit with the final drive and with synchromesh on all four gears. To accommodate this engine, the rear bulkhead of the GT40 chassis had to be moved, the nose was altered to accommodate an engine oil tank as well as a larger radiator and the transmission was much stronger than that used previously. The first car had been completed in April and tested at the Romeo proving ground at Riverside, which belonged to Ford, but, by the Le Mans Race, the second car had not even been tested. In addition there were four of the 4.7-litre cars, two of which were prepared by Shelby-American for Scuderia Filipinetti and Rob Walker, while Ford Advanced Vehicles and Ford-France each entered a car. Two of these cars should have run with 5.3-litre engines, but after problems in practice 4.7-litre engines were substituted. The handling of the Mk 2 cars was horrific and after the first practice session both cars were fitted with spoilers and stabilising fins and the rear anti-roll bar was dispensed with. At the start of the race the Mk 2 Fords ran away from the rest of the entry, progressively reducing the lap record, but by midnight, a mere eight hours after the start, the Ford challenge had failed. Both 7-litre cars retired with a transmission problem and all the 4.7-litre cars were eliminated either by gearbox trouble or cylinder head failure. It was a bloody defeat and the blood-red Ferraris which imposed it also fell by the wayside, so that privately entered Ferrari 250LM cars took the first two places, ahead of a 275GTB Grand Touring Ferrari.

As a result of this débâcle Ford withdrew from the Reims 12 Hours race and the cars appeared in only a limited number of races during the remainder of the year. An interesting development was the X-1 7-litre open car which was entered in

*This Ford GT40 was entered at Le Mans in 1965 by Ford Advanced Vehicles and was driven by Sir John Whitmore/Innes Ireland. It retired with cylinder head trouble. (Ford of Britain)*

Cam-Am races for Ford by the McLaren team with Chris Amon at the wheel. It retired in the Canadian Grand Prix, but finished fifth at the Times Grand Prix at Riverside Raceway. At the end of the year Amon drove it in two races in Nassau, but retired in both. A private car acquired by Peter Sutcliffe finished second in the Kyalami 9 Hours race, with Innes Ireland as co-driver, and Sutcliffe also won the Pietermaritzburg 3 Hours race in South Africa.

## The GT40 Mk 1 and Mk 2, 1966

Development work continued in the United States and Kar Kraft concentrated on making the Mk 2 cars competitive. Both Shelby and Holman and Moody built up cars from rolling chassis supplied from Slough and in addition to Ford Advanced Vehicles, both Shelby-American and Alan Mann Racing were permitted to build cars. The Alan Mann team built five cars at Byfleet which were much lighter than the original, with modified suspension and light alloy bodies. Production of the cars was now sufficient for the GT40 to qualify as a Competition GT Car (minimum production of 50) and during 1966 a very competitive team of these cars was entered by the American Essex Wire Corporation, prepared by John Wyer and with David Yorke as Racing Manager.

The 1966 version of the Mk 2, known as the Mk 2A, featured a shorter nose, rear brake scoops, improved ducting and radiators, strengthened chassis, reduced engine weight and ventilated disc brakes. At the same time Kar Kraft had developed the new J-Car, which used the same suspension and engine as the Mk 2, albeit with new exhaust system, but featured a completely new chassis built from epoxy-bonded aluminium honeycomb sandwich, bonded and riveted to the stress-bearing chassis unit, very much in accordance with aircraft practice, and weighing some 400 lb less than the Mk 2 and with a smaller frontal area. Transmission was by a Ford 2-speed automatic transmission. After testing at the Ford proving ground, this car appeared at the Le Mans Test Weekend, but whilst it was almost as fast as the new Mk 2As there was power loss in the torque converter.

*Peter Sutcliffe drove his private GT40 to third place overall in the 1966 Tourist Trophy at Oulton Park.* (Nigel Snowdon)

*Ford completely dominated the results at Le Mans in 1966 and this Mk 2 7-litre car driven by McLaren/Amon was the winner.* (Nigel Snowdon)

Ford's task in 1966 was made easier by the fact that Ferrari's effort was not of the most intense, and his efforts were split between Prototype racing and Formula 1. In the Daytona Race, now extended to 24 hours, in the face of very limited opposition, the Fords took first, second, third and fifth places in the order Miles/Ruby and Gurney/Grant (both Shelby entries), with the Holman and Moody car of Hansgen/Donohue third and the other Shelby car of McLaren/Amon fifth. The only retirement was a Holman and Moody-entered Mk 2 with automatic transmission. It was much the same story at Sebring, where Ford took the first two places; the winning car was the open X-1, now fitted with a completely new body more closely resembling that of the closed cars and looking like a coupé with the top removed rather than a true open car. After this race the X-1 was broken up. Second place went to the Holman and Moody entered Mk 2 of Hansgen/Donohue. In third place came the Essex Wire-entered standard GT40 of Revson/Scott and this of course won its class. Two Alan Mann Racing cars appeared in this event, but both retired.

Although Ferrari withdrew from the Le Mans Test Weekend, the Fords were out in force. The team brought along the J-Car, together with two Mk 2 7-litre cars, and Alan Mann entered two cars with 4.7-litre engines. Sadly on the Saturday morning Walter Hansgen lost his Mk 2 in the wet at the Dunlop Bridge bend and aquaplaned up the escape road and into a sand barrier. The car was completely destroyed and Hansgen, who suffered terrible injuries, died shortly afterwards. The Shelby-American and Holmann and Moody teams did not run in the races prior to Le Mans, but the GT40s were out in considerable strength. Ferrari won the Monza 1000 km race, but Whitmore/Gregory finished second with their Essex Wire Corporation car, and Müller/Mairesse finished third with the Filipinetti car. A GT40 entered by Ford-France, managed by John Wyer, ran in the Targa Florio driven by Ligier/Greder. Despite its unsuitability for the circuit it ran well, but retired with a broken stub axle about eight miles from the finishing line. The car was excluded from the results, but reinstated after a protest by John Wyer on the grounds that it had covered more than nine-tenths of the winners' distance. As a result it was given 12th place overall and gained a victory in the over 2000 cc Sports

Class that would otherwise have gone to a 250LM Ferrari. At Spa, now extended to 1000 km, the winner was the works P3 Ferrari of Parkes/Scarfiotti, but Fords took the second, third, fourth and fifth places. In second place came a 7-litre Mk 2 entered by Alan Mann Racing and driven by Whitmore/Gardner. The third-place GT40 of Scott/Revson entered by Essex Wire won the Sports Car class and the cars in fourth and fifth places were Sutcliffe's GT40 shared with Redman and the F. English, Ford Dealers, car painted pale blue and driven by Ireland/Amon. Only Sports Ford GT40s were entered in the Nürbugring 1000 km race; the race was won by Chaparral, with Ferrari Dinos second and third and the highest placed Ford, which won its class, was the Ford-France GT40 of Ligier/Schlesser. This was of course not a circuit on which the GT40s shone and in the circumstances the results were more than satisfactory.

At Le Mans Ford made a massive onslaught with eight of the 7-litre Mk 2 cars, three entered by Shelby-American, three by Holman and Moody and two by Alan Mann Racing. Backing these up were five Sports GT40s, two from the Essex Wire Corporation and one each from F. English Ltd, Scuderia Filipinetti and Ford-France. Ford even faced some driver problems with such a formidable team, for three of the drivers originally entered were not available because of accidents, and Dick Thompson, entered at the wheel of an Alan Mann car, was disbarred from driving after a collision with another GT40.

In sheer numbers the opposition was substantially weaker, for Ferrari could field only three P3 cars, one entered in the name of the North American Racing Team, with another four of the 365/P2 cars appearing in the names of Ferrari 'supporters'. The Ferrari effort was weakened by dissension in the team resulting from Surtees' withdrawal as a result of internal Ferrari politics. There was one other serious contender, the Chaparral 2D, which had just won at the Nürburgring. Although the Ferraris were down in terms of sheer power compared with the Fords they had other advantages on their side, economy in fuel, tyres and brakes, and in reality the two teams were well matched. At 10.30 pm, after six and a half hours' racing, Ferraris were in the first two places, with the third-place leading Ford two laps behind. By midnight Fords were in the first two places and the Ferrari attack was broken, and soon all three P3s were out of the race. Of the eight Ford Mk 2 entries, only three made it to the chequered flag, to line up for a formation finish, and the order was first Amon/McLaren (Shelby-American), second Miles/Hulme (Shelby-

*Second place at Le Mans in 1966 went to another Ford GT40 Mk 2, this car driven by Ken Miles/Denis Hulme. (British Petroleum)*

American), and third Bucknum/Hutcherson (Holman and Moody). None of the five Sports GT40s finished.

During the remainder of the season there were only minor events, but GT40s scored successes in the Surfers' Paradise 12 Hours race in Australia (Sutcliffe/Matich second), in the Austrian Grand Prix (Salmon fourth), in the Coupe de Paris at Montlhéry (Ireland was the winner) and the Pietermaritzburg 3 Hours race (Hobbs/Hailwood first). Kar Kraft continued development work on the J-car and produced an open version intended for American events. Sadly veteran driver Ken Miles was killed while testing this at Riverside Raceway.

## The GT40 Mk 2 and Mk 4, 1967

In late 1966 John Wyer, together with John Willment, took over both the Slough Works from Ford Advanced Vehicles and responsibility for the manufacture of road-going and Group 4 versions of the GT40, and set up a new company known as J. W. Automotive Engineering. At the New York International Motor Show in April 1967 J. W. revealed the new Mk 3, road-going version of the GT40, for which two prototypes and a production run of 20 cars were planned. In fact only the two prototypes and five production cars were completed. As a result of the success of the Essex Wire Corporation cars in 1966, Wyer had been able to enter into a deal with Gulf Oil for the entry of GT40 cars in their name and in their distinctive light blue and orange colours. From the standard GT40s were developed the first Mirages (qv).

Kar Kraft had concentrated their efforts on the production of the new Mk 4, derived from the J-car, but the honeycomb panels incorporated greater use of rivets, there were crash-resistant 'fuel cell' tanks, an immensely strong roll-over cage, much improved aerodynamics and it was in every way a more functional and more potent piece of machinery than its immediate predecessors. The Mk 2s, which continued to be raced, now featured new glass-fibre noses and tail sections, with repositioned frontal air ducts, and new-type magnesium wheels designed to pump air across the brakes.

Ford's first outing of the year was in the Daytona 24 Hours race, where six cars were entered in the names of Shelby-American and Holman and Moody, but in each team one of the cars was entered as a 'Mercury' to reflect one of Ford's other brand names in the United States. The race proved a complete disaster for the Ford team and the new works P4 Ferraris took the first two places ahead of a P3 entered by the North American Racing Team. The highest placed Ford was the J.W-entered Sports GT40 of Ickx/Thompson, which finished sixth and won its class. The mainstream entry of Fords were all cars to the latest specification, three brand new and three updated, which had never been tested in this form. Improperly machined gears were Ford's downfall and the only remedy was a gearbox change. As the race progressed gearbox after gearbox was changed until eventually the team ran out of spare gearboxes, all of which in any case suffered from the same trouble. The only survivor from the Mk 2 cars was the seventh place Shelby-American entry of McLaren/Bianchi. Ferrari did not enter the Sebring race, and Ford entered only two cars, both by Shelby-American, and one was the new Mk 4. This won the race, driven by McLaren/Andretti, and the Mk 2A driven by Foyt/Ruby finished second, despite the fact that it had spent the last half-hour of the race in the pits because of a broken camshaft.

Ford sent just two cars to the Le Mans Test Weekend, a Mk 4 and a Mk 2A; although it was apparent from lap times that the drivers were instructed not to try too hard and give too much away, the Fords were the only cars to exceed 200 mph

*Ford line-up before the start of the 1967 Le Mans race, with nearest the camera, the Mk 4 cars of Gurney/Foyt and McLaren/Donohue.* (Nigel Snowdon)

on the Mulsanne straight and McLaren with the Mk 4 was timed at 205.05 mph. In the absence of serious Ford opposition Ferrari took the first two places in the Monza 1000 km race, but Schlesser/Ligier with a Ford-France GT40 finished sixth and won the Sports class. It was much the same story at Spa, save that the winner was the Mirage and the highest-placed Ferrari was third, but the victory in the Sports class went to the GT40 owned by Lord Downe and driven by Mike Salmon/Oliver. A remarkable performance followed in the Targa Florio, in which the GT40 of Henri Grédé/Jean-Michele Giorgi entered by Ford-France finished fifth overall and won the Sports class. A minor success followed in the Martini 150-Mile Race at Silverstone in May, when Paul Hawkins with his ex-Alan Mann car won from Mike Salmon with Lord Downe's car.

At Le Mans the battle was renewed between Ford and Ferrari, with outsiders in the shape of Chaparral, Mirage and Lola. In all there were seven of the 7-litre Fords, all superbly prepared and each painted a different colour. From Shelby-American came Mk 4s for Gurney/Foyt and McLaren/Donohue, while Hawkins/Bucknam drove a Mk 2A entered by this team. Holman and Moody entered Mk 4s for Bianchi/Andretti and Hulme/Ruby, while they had a Mk 2 for Gardner/McClusky. In addition there was a Holman and Moody-prepared Mk 2A entered by Ford-France for Schlesser/Ligier. Ferrari entered three works P4 cars with a fourth on loan to Équipe Nationale Belge, and there were three private P3/4s. In practice the Ford Mk 4s were plagued by cracking windscreens and indeed one car's windscreen actually cracked while it was stationary in the pits. The problem was solved by flying replacement screens from the United States. Ford suffered mechanical attrition. Ruby crashed the Ford which earlier in the race had set a new lap record, and during the early hours of the Sunday morning the Ford team suffered a shattering blow, Jo Schlesser, driver of the Ford-France car, walked into the pits to report that there had been Fords all over the road, and he had been forced to hit the bank to miss them. What had happened was that Andretti had a brake lock-up as he went into the Esses, smashing into the bank, and McClusky in trying to avoid him had hit the bank on the other side of the road. Schlesser avoided both cars, but rammed the bank himself. At the end of the 24 hours Foyt/Gurney with their Shelby-American Mk 4 were the winners at 132.49 mph, leading home

*The winning Mk 4 in 1967 driven by Gurney/Foyt and seen here at Mulsanne corner. Note the bulge in the roof to clear the lanky Gurney's head.* (Nigel Snowdon)

two P4 Ferraris, and with the other Shelby-American Mk 4 of McLaren/Donohue in fourth place.

The season was a long way from over and the Fords were prominent in many more races during the year. Paul Hawkins with his private car won the Auvergne Trophy at Clermont-Ferrand from Sutcliffe and Schlesser. Another good victory followed at Reims, where Schlesser/Ligier with the Ford-France Mk 2 won the 12 Hours race from the private Ferrari P2/3 of Piper/Siffert. There was one more round in the Championship, the BOAC 500 Miles race at Brands Hatch, but Ford had now pulled out of Endurance racing and so the event was a battle between the works Ferraris, the Chaparral and the Mirage. Chaparral won with Ferrari second, and because Mirage was counted as a separate make for the purposes of the FIA Championship, Ford lost out in the Championship to Ferrari. Private owners continued to enjoy success, with Paul Hawkins scoring a fine victory in the Sports Car Championship in the Austrian Grand Prix at Zeltweg. Later Hawkins finished second at Brands Hatch and first at Oulton Park, which gave him victory in the *Autosport* Championship. After Le Mans the Mirages scored quite a number of successes, but they are dealt with under that section of this book.

## The GT40, 1968

After Le Mans and before the FIA had decided to restrict Prototypes to 3 litres in 1968 and Competition Sports Cars to 5 litres, Ford had already made the decision to withdraw from European racing. The career of the 7-litre Prototype was over, but the racing days of the original GT40 were by no means finished. While John Wyer developed a new 3-litre Mirage, he continued to race the GT40s, one of which was a rebuilt Mirage, and two were newly built-up cars in Gulf's blue and orange colours. Initially these cars were in the usual 4727 cc form, but they were developed as the year progressed, with Gurney-Weslake cylinder heads; later the engines were stroked to 4942 cc and the Gulf cars featured improved brakes, modified engine and gearbox lubrication systems and the glass-fibre panels

*Pedro Rodriguez corrects a slide with the winning Gulf GT40 at Le Mans in 1968. He was partnered by Lucien Bianchi.* (Nigel Snowdon)

strengthened by reinforcing carbon filament. In Le Mans trim the maximum speed was 205 mph. In theory the Ford GT40s were no match for the strength of Porsche, but thanks to exceptionally careful and detailed preparation, superb team control by David Yorke and a fine team of drivers, the Gulf team was a constant thorn in Porsche's side and scored several significant victories.

Both John Wyer entries retired at Daytona and Sebring, but in the BOAC 500 Miles race at Brands Hatch the sole Gulf car entered by Ickx/Redman won from a brace of Porsche 907s, with the private bright red Castrol-sponsored GT40 of Hawkins/Hobbs in fourth place. By Monza the Gulf team was up to strength again with two cars for Ickx/Redman and Hawkins/Hobbs; Redman retired after spinning at Lesmo and battering the rear of the car, but the other entry had both the speed and stamina to beat the Porsche 907s and Hawkins/Hobbs finished over two minutes ahead of the Porsche 907 of Stommelen/Neerpasch. Wisely Wyer missed the Targa Florio, but entered two cars at the Nürburgring. Here the Porsche team was dominant, with the new 908 of Siffert/Elford finishing first ahead of the 907 of team-mates Herrmann/Stommelen. Ickx/Hawkins did well to finish third and the other Gulf car driven by Hobbs/Redman took sixth place, a lap in arrears. Again, in the rain-soaked Spa 1000 km race the reliability of the GT40s proved more than a match for the speed of the 908s, and Ickx, the Belgian maestro on his home circuit, partnered by Redman won the race from the 907 Porsche of Mitter/Schlesser and the 908 of Herrmann/Stommelen with Gulf team-mates Hawkins/Hobbs in fourth place. Yet another victory for Gulf followed at Watkins Glen, where the two GT40s were fitted with 4942 cc engines with Gurney/Weslake cylinder heads; wheel-bearing problems plagued the 908s and Ickx, partnered by fellow-countryman Lucien Bianchi won from Hobbs/Hawkins. John Wyer withdrew his entry from the Austrian Grand Prix run over 500 kilometres at Zeltweg so that he could concentrate on preparation for the postponed Le Mans 24 Hours race. Although Porsche took the first two places in Austria, Paul Hawkins drove a fine race with his private GT40 to finish third overall.

At Le Mans Wyer entered three GT40s, all with Gurney-Weslake heads, 4942 cc engines and with two cars fitted with Sullivan profile flat-tappet camshafts. The Rodriguez/Bianchi car was fitted with a special dry-deck GT40 engine, with block water passages welded up, and this engine had been specially flown from Dearborn. All the engines had run for 24 hours on the test-bed with simulated gear changes and braking and the power output was claimed to be around 415 bhp. The cars were restricted to 6000 rpm in the lower ratios, but 6500 rpm was frequently achieved in top. Wider front rims were fitted and the wet-sump engines had additional baffles to prevent surge under hard braking. Because of driver shortages, Redman having crashed in Belgium and Ickx having broken a leg in practice for the Canadian Grand Prix, the pairings were Rodriguez/Bianchi, Hawkins/Hobbs and Muir/Oliver. As the race progressed, so the Porsche onslaught crumbled and Rodriguez/Bianchi were able to ease their pace to win by a margin of 45 miles at an average of 115.29 mph from two Porsche entries and achieve a Ford 'hat-trick' at the Sarthe circuit. The Oliver/Muir car was embedded by Muir in the sand at Mulsanne corner early in the race, and although he eventually dug it out and drove it back to the pits, the clutch was so badly weakened by constant reversing that there was no alternative but retirement. The Hawkins/Hobbs GT40 retired with engine failure at Mulsanne shortly before midnight. The race was run in cold and wet conditions during the night, and in any case at a lower temperature than a race would have been run earlier in the year, and the winning GT40 was under no pressure during the hours of Sunday. Accordingly the 'dry-deck' engine was not stressed, but later events proved that it was only reliable at low temperatures.

## The GT40, 1969

For 1969 Wyer was developing his 3-litre B.R.M-engined Mirage, but in the meantime he had no alternative but to soldier on with the now, apparently obsolescent, GT40s. Two cars with 'dry-deck' engines ran at Daytona, but on one, driven by Hobbs/Hailwood, the block cracked down one bore, and although Ickx pranged the other car, in fact the engine was about to go. From this time Wyer abandoned the 'dry-deck' engines and relied on the older units. At Sebring Ickx/Oliver scored a totally unexpected victory, despite delays to repair a damaged nose after the throttles had jammed open and the car had run into the marker cones, but

At Le Mans in 1969 the winning GT40 of Ickx/Oliver leads the third-place car of Hobbs/Hailwood and two Porsche 908s. (Nigel Snowdon)

the Ford was the beneficiary of Porsche unreliability. The Mirage 3-litre made its debut in the BOAC race at Brands Hatch, but Wyer also entered a GT40 for Hobbs/Hailwood.

The results were Porsche-dominated, but the GT40 finished fifth. Wyer decided to miss the Monza race because he considered the GT40s no longer fast enough for this course, and Porsche took the first three places; however, the GT40 of Kelleners/Jöst finished fourth, ahead of a Lola and an Alpine. Wyer had no alternative but to give the Targa Florio a miss, Mirages were entered at Spa and the Nürburgring, but the GT40s reappeared at Le Mans. The engines of both cars had been extensively tested at the Maidenhead factory of Vandervell Products and power output was now 412 bhp. An interesting entry in this race was the GT40 of Malcolm Guthrie, with Frank Gardner as co-driver. This car had been built up from a bare hull by Alan Mann Racing, and its 5-litre engine was fitted with Tecalemit fuel injection, Weslake-Gurney cylinder heads and had a power output of around 465 bhp. Despite the apparently overwhelmingly strong Porsche opposition, the cars from Zuffenhusen failed badly and after a bitter struggle in the closing laps of the race between Ickx with the 5-litre GT40 and Herrmann with the Porsche 908 3-litre, Ickx won by just over 100 yards. The other JW car of Hobbs/Hailwood finished third. In addition Kelleners/Jöst took sixth place. The special Gardner/Guthrie GT40 was plagued by drive-shaft doughnut trouble. Subsequently there was litigation between Guthrie and Alan Mann Racing. Although JW did not race their GT40s again in 1969, the Kelleners/Jöst car had one more successful outing, in the Watkins Glen 6 Hours race, in which it took fifth place.

The serious racing career of the GT40 was now at an end, extended for two seasons beyond what Ford had anticipated when they withdrew from racing at the end of 1967 and the cars had won at Le Mans four times in succession. By any standards, to build such a competitive car from scratch and achieve such a high level of success in such a comparatively short time was unusual. It was not just a simple question of the millions of dollars pumped into the project by Ford, but sound technical development and learning lessons the hard way from experience gained. The GT40 was a magnificently successful car and, quite rightly, is now regarded as one of the most sought-after classics.

For John Wyer it was also a particularly successful era. During his long days with Aston Martin, and subsequently with Ford, he had never been left alone, free from interference, to conduct a racing programme in accordance with his own judge-

*The third-place GT40 of Hobbs/Hailwood seen during the Saturday afternoon (the patches over the headlamps have not yet been removed).* (Nigel Snowdon)

ment and discretion. With Aston Martin he always had to tolerate the interference and quirks of David Brown and at Ford policy had been decided by committee. At long last, unfettered by outside influences, he had achieved substantial international success consistently, not with the most advanced or fast cars, but as a result of careful preparation, careful planning and superb team management.

# Ford (Alan Mann) (United Kingdom)

After the American Ford company withdrew from racing at the end of 1967, the British Ford Motor Company commissioned a completely new car, the design and construction of which was entrusted to Alan Mann Racing, who had worked successfully with Ford on the racing programme of the GT40 and the Cobra. The new car, designated the P68 F3L, was designed by Len Baillie, who had worked on the Ford GT40 project, and it was constructed in Alan Mann's workshops at Byfleet. The basis of the new car was a very elaborate monocoque constructed from riveted and bonded light alloy panels. Apart from the nose, all panels were stressed and the tail and the outside skin of the car were made from a malleable aircraft alloy with a thickness of only $\frac{1}{30}$ in. The body was low and exceedingly shapely, with a long tail that was vortex-creating, ie, the aerodynamic effect was as if the tail had been even longer still. It also featured the shortest wheelbase of any car using the Ford-Cosworth DFV 3-litre engine, shorter even than that of the Formula 1 cars using this engine, and the result was an exceptionally cramped cockpit. The Ford-Cosworth V-8 engine needs little description, as at one time it was used in every Formula 1 car with the exception of the B.R.M.s and Ferraris and in its 1968 form developed 420 bhp at 9000 rpm. Transmission was by either a 5-speed ZF or Hewland gearbox. The suspension design also followed Formula 1 practice with double wishbones and coil spring/damper units at the front and with lower reversed wishbones, upper straight tubular links, twin radius arms and coil spring/damper units at the rear. Girling 11.5 in. disc brakes were fitted front and rear, 3 in. inboard of the suspension uprights, a mounting intended to achieve good heat dissipation, and these brakes were driven from the hubs by short shafts.

Whilst there was obviously a question mark over the reliability of the Cosworth-Ford engine in endurance racing, Alan Mann had great confidence in the car's

*This photograph shows to good advantage the clean uncluttered lines of the Ford P68 driven in the 1968 BOAC race at Brands Hatch by McLaren/Spence* (Nigel Snowdon)

*The Ford P69 in practice for the 1969 BOAC race. It non-started after the engine blew and was never again entered.* (Nigel Snowdon)

prospects and it was believed that its aerodynamics were so good that it would be capable of attaining 200 mph on a long straight. Initially two cars were built, the second featuring a slightly longer wheelbase so as to give better cockpit accommodation. Both cars were finished in the Alan Mann Racing colours of red with central gold stripe.

Although no substantial success was expected in 1968, which was to be a year of testing and development, in fact the season proved so disastrous that the cars were withdrawn from racing after only a few events.

The cars were to make their debut in the BOAC 500 race at Brands Hatch in April. Originally one car, that with the longer wheelbase and Hewland gearbox, was to have been driven by Graham Hill and Jim Clark, but because of a problem over tyre contracts, they were unable to appear and instead drove Lotus Formula 2 cars at Hockenheim. It was at this Hockenheim race that Jim Clark was so tragically killed. Accordingly Alan Mann arranged for Bruce McLaren and Denis Hulme to take their place alongside the car to be driven by Mike Spence and Jochen Rindt. The earlier car broke its engine in practice and so the sole starter was driven by McLaren and Spence. Although McLaren took the lead early in the race, not long after he had been relieved by Spence, the Ford was eliminated by a broken inner drive-shaft coupling which had damaged the exhaust pipe and rear chassis bulkhead.

Both cars were entered in the Nürburgring 1000 km race, to be driven by Pedro Rodriguez/Chris Irwin (this was a brand new car) and the car that had run at Brands Hatch was to be driven by Frank Gardner and Richard Attwood. In practice Irwin lost control at the Flugplatz. The car rolled and Irwin suffered appalling head injuries, from which he eventually recovered. The second car started the race with Attwood at the wheel, but after delays in the pits, retired out on the circuit with engine failure. The surviving P68 next appeared at Spa driven by Gardner/Hahne and was fastest in practice. The race started in heavy rain and at the end of the first lap the Ford was back in the pits with the electrics waterlogged, and after an unsuccessful attempt to dry out the engine it was pushed away into retirement.

At this stage it was decided to curtail the season's racing and the P68 was not seen again until 1969. By then there had been a relaxation in the Prototype regulations, so Len Bailey produced another version, known as the P69, with an open body, 15 in. shorter than that of the coupé, and both lower and wider. It was a most odd-looking car, completely encased in light alloy panels, apart from a small hole at the cockpit for the driver's head. As a result of studies which Bailey had made of the Chaparral, the P69 incorporated a system of interconnected spoilers, mounted in the nose between the front wings of the car and across the tail, and these were activated mechanically and hydraulically with the pitch angle adjusted by wind pressure. Unfortunately, however, the P69 proved so unstable both on the straight

*Denis Hulme at the wheel of the P68 at Brands Hatch in 1969. After only 25 minutes of racing he brought the car into the pits to retire because of a loose aerofoil and low oil pressure.* (Nigel Snowdon)

and on cornering during testing that it was decided that it should run on its debut at the BOAC race at Brands Hatch with large front and rear suspension-mounted aerofoils, with the supports passing through the bodywork. In addition the team entered the P68, now fitted with larger brakes and an enormous suspension-mounted rear aerofoil. After the P69 broke its engine in practice only the P68 driven by Frank Gardner and Denis Hulme started the race, but this car was retired with a loose aerofoil and low oil pressure after less than half an hour's racing.

At this point Ford said enough was enough and the team withdrew altogether. The reason given officially was the ban on aerodynamic aids imposed at the Monaco Grand Prix in May, which in effect banned movable spoilers. It was clear, however, that both cars were inherently unstable designs and there was very little future for them even with a major redesign.

# Ginetta (United Kingdom)

Never serious international contenders, Ginettas were primarily built for the home market and were widely raced in British events. Although the company did build a number of competition cars, throughout its history it has primarily been a manufacturer of production sports cars on a limited scale. The company, based in Suffolk, has always been run by the Walklett Brothers, with Bob as managing director, Ivor as designer, Trevor responsible for chassis work and Douglas as works manager. The marque originated with a Special based on a pre-war Wolseley Hornet built by Ivor Walklett and this was followed by a production sports 2-seater, the G2, that appeared in 1958. Two years later Ginetta introduced the G3 with glass-fibre aerodynamic body and this was followed by the widely raced G4 in 1961, another 2-seater sports car with glass-fibre body and Ford Anglia engine. A number of other production and prototype sports cars followed until the G12 appeared in 1966. The claim has been made for this that it was the first British mid-engined GT car, but this is unlikely.

The basis of the G12 was a multi-tubular space-frame with the glass-fibre cockpit and centre parts of the body bonded to the chassis. Front suspension was by coil spring/damper units, incorporating Triumph suspension uprights, with an anti-roll bar. At the rear there were lower reversed wishbones, single upper transverse links, twin radius arms, coil spring/damper units and an adjustable anti-roll bar. Minilite 13 in. cast magnesium wheels were used and Girling 9.5 in. disc brakes were mounted outboard front and rear. The usual power unit was the Cosworth-Ford SCA 997 cc used in conjunction with a Hewland gearbox/final drive unit. The body was a neat and stylish glass-fibre coupé of striking appearance. Because of the low price – a mere £1200 in component form – the demand was considerable and in all over a period of three years something over 50 were sold.

The most successful driver of the G12 was Willie Green, now racing tester for *Classic and Sportscar* magazine, who won 11 races in 1966, and broke his class lap record five times. The following year Green raced a second G12 car powered by a 1594 cc Ford twin-cam engine. Other G12s were raced for *Motoring News* by Editor Mike Twite (who had close associations with the Walklett family) and Ian Tee, and the Worcestershire Racing Association, who fielded two cars during the year. Another car was fitted with the Martin V-8 2-litre engine, but this proved hopelessly unreliable, and driver John Burton reverted to a Cosworth SCA engine before the end of the season. Much less success was gained in 1967, primarily because the G12s were no match for the latest Chevrons, and by 1968 it had been superseded by the G16 open Group 6 Prototype.

In all essentials the G16 followed the design of the earlier model, but with open bodywork. The main problem with the car was that the factory, committed to other projects, handed over development work to the first purchasers, the Worcestershire Racing Association, whose cars were driven by John Bamford and John Burton. Little success was gained during the year. Cars were also raced with a Coventry Climax 2-litre engine by Jeremy Richardson, and on occasions Bamford's car was fitted with a 2-litre B.M.W. engine. For 1969 Ginetta marketed an improved version of the G16 with a smaller windscreen (said to lower frontal area by 30 per cent), changed spring rates, stronger drive-shafts, a glass-fibre tonneau and wider wheels. The company also produced the G16A with 2-litre B.R.M. V-8 engine. One of the G16As was retained by the works, whilst the other was acquired by Ian Tee. Not much in the way of success was gained. One of the rare international appearances was the BOAC 500 Miles race at Brands Hatch, but the Tee entry retired early in the race because of an oil leak.

The Ginetta Company continued to build competition cars, mainly single-

*The Ginetta G16A with B.R.M. 2-litre V-8 engine driven by Ian Tee and Willie Green in the 1969 BOAC 500 Miles race. It retired very early because of an oil leak.*

seater, without success and actually started work on a Formula 1 car, but it was never finished. Ginetta suffered badly in the economic recession of the 1970s, but still exists as a very small-scale manufacturer.

# Healey (United Kingdom)

During a long career in the motor industry, Donald Healey worked with Invicta, Triumph and, during the war years, with Humber on armoured fighting vehicle development. After the war he set up his own company, building initially Riley-powered sporting cars of great performance and distinction, as well as the later Alvis and Nash-powered cars, before the first Austin-Healey appeared at the 1952 Motor Show. From that point onwards Healey enjoyed a close relationship with the Austin Company and with its successor the British Motor Corporation. Competition versions of Healey's designs were raced and built from 1953 onwards, but it was not until 1968 that the Healey Company considered building a completely new Prototype, a car aimed at providing Healey with publicity and an enhanced image at around the time they were involved in the development of the car that was to be announced in 1972 as the Jensen-Healey.

## The SR, 1968 and 1969

For Le Mans in 1968, the Healey organisation built the mid-engine SR (the initials stood for *sub rosa*, but apart from the normal meaning of this tag, the reason for the choice of name is not known). The car was based on a sheet-steel centre-section platform of somewhat elaborate construction, with sponsons to house flexible fuel bags and with built-in roll-bars. The front suspension consisted of unequal-length wishbones and coil spring/damper units, whilst at the back there

119

*Throughout the 1960s the Donald Healey Motor Company raced Austin-Healeys under contract from the British Motor Corporation. This is the Sprite of Enever/Poole which finished 15th and last at Le Mans in 1968.* (Nigel Snowdon)

were links, radius arms and coil spring/damper units, and the rear suspension was rose-jointed throughout and fully adjustable in accordance with contemporary practice. The rack-and-pinion steering, supplied by Cam Gears, was a modified MGB steering rack, Girling cast iron discs were mounted at the hubs and there were Dunlop Elektron alloy wheels, with centre-lock, five-peg-drive system. Powering this car was a Coventry Climax FWMV engine in 2-litre form, developing 240 bhp at 9000 rpm and loaned to Healey by the manufacturers. Transmission was by a Hewland DG300 5-speed gearbox/final drive unit with a twin-plate competition clutch. The alloy coupé body incorporated a deep, sloping windscreen, curved cockpit roof, cut-off tail and large intakes either side ahead of the rear wheels to draw air to the twin rear-mounted radiators. The oil cooler and a 2-gallon oil tank were mounted immediately behind the nose cowling and the fuel capacity was 21 gallons. Maximum speed was estimated at 180 mph. The design of the car was the responsibility of Barry Bilbie, but the concept was in accordance with Donald Healey's wish that it should be of a type with which the Company was familiar and which conceivably might form the basis of a production car. As events were to prove, the real problems were that the car was vastly overweight for its engine capacity and it was to prove sadly unsuccessful.

At Le Mans in 1968 it was driven by Clive Baker and Andrew Hedges, and ran steadily if not spectacularly until the clutch jammed in the 'out' position, because of bearing failure. The same car, again with a V-8 Coventry Climax engine, ran at Le Mans in 1969. In the meantime some modifications had been carried out to eliminate the slight oversteer suffered in 1968 and to improve high-speed stability. Already the car was outdated when it appeared at Le Mans because of the relaxation in Prototype regulations, but nevertheless Healey persevered. The drivers were, again, Clive Baker, but now partnered by John Harris. It proved another unlucky outing for the team, for when John Woolfe crashed his 917 with fatal results at White House on the first lap, completely blocking the road, all the cars had to wait until the track was cleared and they could proceed. As a result of this hold-up the

Healey overheated, a water leak developed at the cylinder head joint and the car had to be withdrawn.

## XR37, 1970

Because of the favourable change in the regulations, the car was substantially modified for 1970 and in this form became known as the XR37. Gone was the closed fixed-head bodywork and it was replaced by a new open body, with small Perspex screen and roll-over bar. It was decided to seek an engine of greater capacity and eventually Healey arranged with Jack Brabham to borrow a 3-litre single cam per bank Repco Formula 1 engine developing 322 bhp at 8500 rpm. The engine was rebuilt for Healey by the now famous developer John Judd. The car was driven by Andrew Hedges and Roger Enever at Le Mans, but it was once again out of luck, because it was involved in a collision early in the race that severely damaged the front bodywork. After lengthy delays for body repairs, the car began to climb its way up through the field, but it was again delayed with problems with one of the dog clutches in the gearbox which necessitated a gearbox rebuild, but shortly before the end of the race the car broke down because of ignition problems.

Despite its failures the Healey at least added a little more variety to the Prototype scene.

*The Healey XR37 with Repco 3-litre engine at Le Mans in 1970. The front bodywork was damaged early in the race and the car retired shortly before the finish because of ignition problems.* (Nigel Snowdon)

# Howmet (United States)

In 1963 and 1965 Rover had run gas-turbine cars successfully at Le Mans, but when the Howmet Turbine appeared in 1968, the concept was still very much of an innovation. In fact it remains something of a novelty, because the only gas-turbine competition cars built since have been the Lotus Indianapolis and Grand Prix cars. Designed by Ray Heppenstall, the Howmet used a Continental TS325-1 shaft turbine engine designed for use in helicopters, and under the Equivalency rules

*Two views of the gas-turbine Howmet in the pits at the 1968 BOAC 500 Miles race at Brands Hatch. Note the Ford Cortina rear lights.* (Nigel Snowdon)

laid down by the Federation Internationale de l'Automobile it was treated as having a capacity of 3 litres. This engine, which weighed only 170 lb, had one centrifugal stage and one axial stage compressor, followed by an annular-type combuster, a two-stage gas generator turbine and a single-stage free-power turbine. There was a wastegate valve between the gas generator turbine and the power turbine which improved throttle response by varying the hot gas flow to the power turbine. The gas generator ran at 57,500 rpm and the power turbine at 44,000 rpm. With reduction gearing the power output of 330 hp was developed at 6789 rpm.

The chassis of the Howmet was built by McKee Engineering Corporation and was a multi-tubular frame, based on a Cam-Am design. There were double wishbones and coil spring/damper units at the front with, at the rear, lower wishbones, single upper links and radius arms with coil springs. The coupé body was panelled in aluminium panelling supplied by the Howmet Corporation, which was a specialist alloy supplier, and the company also supplied the turbine blades used in the engine.

A very distinctive feature of the car was the roof-mounted intake for the gas turbine. Superficially, at least, from the front the car had a passing resemblance to the 1966 Chaparral 2D.

Howmet tested the TX (standing for Turbine Experimental) at Daytona and it lapped the banked circuit at 176.58 mph. The company regarded the test session as successful and accordingly it was decided to take on a full season's racing in 1968. In fact the Howmet appeared in only five Championship races.

The Howmet's competition debut was in the Daytona Continental 24 Hours race at the beginning of February and here it was driven by Dick Thompson and Ed Lowther. Ray Heppenstall also shared the driving. In practice the car was seventh fastest, but during the race the wastegate valve caused the throttle to jam open and the Howmet hit the concrete retaining wall of the banking, damaging the suspension and bending the chassis slightly so that the car had to be withdrawn. With the same drivers the Howmet reappeared at Sebring and was third fastest in practice. The car was never in contention in the race and was retired after a couple of off-course excursions broke two engine mountings. For the BOAC 500 race at Brands Hatch the driving was shared by Dick Thompson and Hugh Dibley. Again it suffered throttle problems and was retired after the throttle jammed open and Thompson hit the bank.

The team did not race again until the Watkins Glen 6 Hours event in July and now fielded two cars driven by Heppenstall/Thompson and Dibley/Tullius. In a race that was not only poorly supported, but in which the Porsche team ran into severe mechanical problems, towards the end of the race the Howmets held third and fourth places. Eventually Thompson/Heppenstall finished third, despite a long pit stop to change the starter motor and voltage regulator, whilst Dibley/Tullius dropped to twelfth place after a long pit stop because of differential problems. The team returned to Europe to compete in the Le Mans race, which had been postponed until the end of September, and again the cars were driven by Thompson/Heppenstall and Dibley/Tullius. The Howmets were geared for the Mulsanne

*The Howmet of Thompson/Tullius at Le Mans in 1968. It was rolled later in the race.*
(Nigel Snowdon)

straight, because they had only the single gear, and they proved very difficult to handle on the slower corners. The Dibley/Tullius car was disqualified under the minimum distance regulations in the race after a three-hour pit stop to change a rear hub bearing. The Thompson/Heppenstall car had a faulty fuel control which reduced power by some 30 per cent, it was not exceeding 100 mph on the Mulsanne straight and was eventually eliminated on the Saturday evening, when Thompson lost control at Indianapolis and the car rolled.

From Howmet's point of view, the season had been one of interesting and worthwhile experiment and although the cars had failed in Championship races, with the exception of Watkins Glen, they had won a 25-lap race at Huntsville in Alabama and the 300-mile Marlboro race in Maryland. There were no real prospects of ever making the cars competitive because they were hampered by heavy fuel consumption, which necessitated refuelling stops every forty to fifty minutes, and other problems arose from the lack of engine braking and the very slow throttle response.

# Iso Grifo (Italy)

Not frequently seen in competitions, there is no real good excuse for including the Iso Grifo in this book, other than the fact that it had such strikingly handsome styling and was one of the very best cars built with an American power unit. Giotto Bizzarini was one of the engineers who left Ferrari in the big walkout in 1962. He joined the Iso company and played a role in the development of the Iso Rivolta GT

*Entered as an Iso Rivolta this car, running as a Prototype, was driven into 14th place at Le Mans in 1964 by Berney/Noblet.* (Nigel Snowdon)

production car. From this was developed the Iso Grifo, the touring version of which was made in the Iso factory, and the Bizzarini, which was made in his own small works after he left Iso's.

The Iso Grifo was based on the Iso Rivolta chassis, which featured large-diameter steel main tubular members, with sheet steel stiffening members. At the front suspension was by double unequal-length wishbones and coil spring/damper units. On the early cars there was a de Dion rear axle located by radius arms and a Watts linkage, but later cars featured fully independent rear suspension. Disc brakes were fitted front and rear, mounted inboard at the rear, there were Campagnolo alloy wheels and a Powr-Lok limited slip differential. The power unit was the Chevrolet Corvette and transmission was by a close-ratio all-synchromesh 4-speed gearbox. The degree of engine tune varied enormously, but the most powerful versions developed around 425 bhp with four Weber carburettors. The early cars featured a lightweight aluminium body, but on later cars this was replaced by glass-fibre. Maximum speed was anything up to 180 mph, depending on the state of engine tune and the axle ratio fitted. One of the rare Iso Grifo appearances was at Le Mans in 1965, where one of these cars finished ninth.

*Rare competition appearance of the Iso Grifo was at Le Mans in 1965. De Mortemart and Fraissinet drove this car into ninth place.* (British Petroleum)

# Jaguar E-Type (United Kingdom)

The great sports car sensation of the 1960s was the E-type Jaguar, direct descendant of the sports-racing D-type which had won at Le Mans in 1955–57 and the E2A car that ran at the Sarthe circuit in 1960, and offered to the public at a remarkably low price for a car of such high performance. In its original production form, the E-type, introduced at the 1961 Geneva Motor Show, used the classic Jaguar XK engine in 3781 cc (87 × 106 mm) form, developing 265 bhp at 5500 rpm. The chassis of the E-type was formed by a complex monocoque built up of welded steel panels, forming the passenger compartment and rear of the car; from the monocoque there projected a framework constructed in square-section Reynolds 541 steel tubing, carrying the engine and front suspension. A smaller framework of tubular-section members on the front of this carried the cross-flow radiator and the pivot for the bonnet. At the front, suspension was independent by double wishbones, with longitudinal torsion bars, and at the rear there were lower wishbones, upper drive-shaft links, radius arms, coil springs and an anti-roll bar. Dunlop disc brakes were fitted front and rear, inboard at the rear. Transmission was by a 4-speed gearbox based on the original far from satisfactory Moss gearbox, with a single-plate Borg and Beck clutch. It was a dramatically styled car with long nose and available either in open form or as a coupé. When the open car was tested by *The Motor* in 1961, the testers obtained a maximum speed of 149.1 mph, and although this car was rather specially tuned as a road test car, it still was a remarkable package for the then UK price of £2,098 in open form. Jaguar's attitude to motor racing was ambivalent, in theory eschewing it, but in practice offering a great deal of support to private entrants. Throughout 1961 E-types were raced by the Coombs and Équipe Endeavour teams, which had the strongest track record in saloon car racing with Jaguars. Jaguar did put in hand the development of a competition version of the E-type, but development was slow and never kept pace with the Ferrari opposition.

The origins of the 'lightweight' E-type lay in the Coombs car which Salvadori crashed at Goodwood on Easter Monday in 1962, which was rebuilt with many non-standard parts and constantly modified and improved throughout 1962 by the works. In fact the Coombs car achieved very little during 1962, although Salvadori finished fourth in the GT Tourist Trophy at Goodwood behind three Ferraris. The E-type's best performance was at Le Mans, where three cars were entered. Briggs Cunningham had a coupé, prepared at the works with extensively modified dry-sump cast-iron block engine, which Briggs himself with Salvadori drove into fourth place overall, one place ahead of the E-type of Peters Lumsden and Sargent,

*Graham Hill with Coombs' Lightweight E-type on his way to win in the GT race at the May Silverstone meeting in 1963.* (T. C. March)

*In the Silverstone race Roy Salvadori took second place with the 'Tommy' Atkins Lightweight E-type.* (T. C. March)

which had run very strongly, with its sights on third place, when it stuck in top gear and was forced to lap at reduced speed. The third car was entered for John Coundley/Maurice Charles, with an engine loaned by the works, but this retired during the third hour with engine trouble.

Work which had started at the factory in 1961 on a special coupé (further reference to which will be made later) led directly to the 1963 competition 'lightweight' E-type. In all there were 15 special-build E-types created by the works, including the prototype and the Coombs car, and not all were to precisely the same specification. What is said here is broadly true, but not necessarily true of every example. The centre monocoque, together with inner and outer body panels including the bonnet, were made from aluminium sheet. Many suspension parts were completely new, the engine featured an aluminium block, together with Lucas fuel injection, dry-sump lubrication, 'wide angle' cylinder head (as used on the D-type at Le Mans) and a power output varying from between 290 and 320 bhp (although this was eventually increased to 344 bhp on certain cars). The transmission was now by a ZF 5-speed gearbox. The bodywork was of the open type, but with a hard top. Among exceptions to this was one car supplied to Briggs Cunningham for Le Mans in 1963.

Both Graham Hill with the Coombs car and Roy Salvadori, now driving a 'lightweight' for 'Tommy' Atkins, achieved an immense run of successes in British events. However, successes in the broader area of international racing were few and far between. In the Sebring 12 Hours race, Leslie/Morrill, with a car entered by Kjell Qvale, finished seventh at Sebring, with the Cunningham-entered car of Hansgen/McLaren eighth, but delayed by brake trouble. At the Nürburgring two cars were entered by Peter Lindner/Peter Nöcker and Peter Lumsden/Peter Sargent. Lindner, despite a lack of familiarity with right-hand drive, was initially the sensation of the race, making a superb start and leading the entire field for more than a lap. He was still leading the GT class when the car was eliminated by engine failure. The second car, which had gradually been moving up through the field, was crashed by Lumsden.

At Le Mans the Cunningham team entered three 'lightweight' E-types, two of which were brand new. Two of the cars were plagued by gearbox problems (the

127

*At Le Mans in 1963 this Lightweight E-type entered by Briggs Cunningham and driven by Richards/Grossman finished ninth.* (Nigel Snowdon)

gearboxes were all-synchromesh, prototypes of the design adopted on later E-types) and this caused the retirement of Hansgen/Pabst. The second car was driven by Salvadori/Richards, lapping using fourth and fifth gears only, but Salvadori was involved in an horrendous accident, caused by oil dropped from McLaren's Aston Martin which blew its engine at the kink at the end of the Mulsanne straight. The E-type went completely out of control and hit the bank, and Salvadori, who had been unable to do up his seat belt at his last pit stop, was thrown out through the back window. Four cars altogether were involved in this accident and one driver was killed and another critically injured. Salvadori escaped with the most terrible bruising, but the E-type was virtually destroyed. The remaining Cunningham-entered E-type lost its brakes at Mulsanne and carried on through the straw-bales. Bob Grossman crawled back to the pits, where the front of the car was rebuilt, and this E-type eventually finished ninth, Jaguar's last finish at Le Mans for 22 years.

In June Dick Protheroe had taken delivery of the original 'lightweight' E-type prototype coupé, and in July ran the car at an all-comers 25-lap race at Reims. The fastest cars, Parkes' 4-litre Ferrari Prototype and Schlesser's Aston Martin, retired, and the race was won by a front-engined Ferrari *Testa Rossa* driven by Carlo Abate, but Protheroe finished second overall and won the GT category from Ferrari 250GTOs driven by Bianchi and Noblet. It was one of the very best performances achieved by the 'lightweight' E-type. In the Tourist Trophy at Goodwood the GTOs were dominant, but Salvadori finished third with the 'Tommy' Atkins' E-type and Jack Sears brought the Coombs-entered E-type across the line in fourth place.

By 1964 the 'lightweight' E-type could no longer be regarded as a serious competitor in international GT racing. Frustrated by his inability to homologate the 250LM, Ferrari was racing a new and slightly more potent 250GTO and the dominant force in the class was to be the Cobra Daytona coupé. Private owners, however, persisted with their E-types and the works continued to give both support and continued development. Over the winter the Lindner/Nöcker car was modified with a low-drag roof, similar to that of the original works prototype that passed to Protheroe, and Lumsden had his car fitted with a new Frank Costin-developed low-drag body. Both Lumsden/Sargent and Lindner/Nöcker ran their cars again at Le Mans in 1964 and the German entry was prepared at the works. At Le Mans the cars were substantially slower than the rival Cobras and Aston Martins and both retired. At the end of the year, in torrential rain, Lindner crashed in the Paris 1000 km race at Montlhéry, suffering injuries from which he died, and the car was a write-off, but resurrected in the 1980s.

Although the cars continued to be raced in British events, their serious competition days were over. No Jaguar was ever an instant winner in the hands of private owners at an international level. But what Jaguar have always done, and continued to do with the E-type, was to offer a car to private owners that was properly supported by the works, was competitive and with the right driver could achieve a reasonable measure of success. Nowadays the 'lightweight' E-type is one of the most coveted cars of the 1960s.

# Ligier (France)

Before setting up his own manufacturing company, Guy Ligier had played international rugby football for France, he had raced in Formula 1 as a private entrant and, as the head of a very substantial construction company in France, he was adequately financed to set up his own racing organisation. All Ligier cars had been typed in the JS series in memory of Ligier's very close friend Jo Schlesser, who died in an accident with a Honda in the 1968 French Grand Prix. The first prototype raced during 1970 featured a Y-shaped backbone chassis, a Cosworth FVC 1.8-litre engine, Hewland gearbox/final drive unit and a very neat coupé body. This car, typed the JS1, was a true prototype for the intended line of production Ligiers. It appeared at Le Mans in 1970 driven by Ligier and Andruet, but after running well down the field, as might be expected, it was eliminated by a broken distributor.

In 1971 Ligier introduced his production car, the JS2, built at his base at Vichy and of which it was intended to produce about 100 annually. This car designed by Michel Tetu, of Renault Formula 1 fame, was powered by the German Ford Taunus V-6 2.6-litre engine, running on fuel injection and modified to develop 165 bhp, and in unit with a 5-speed Citroën SM transmission. The claimed top speed was 150 mph.

*The JS1 Ligier seen in front of the pits before the start of the 1970 Le Mans race. It was driven by Ligier/Andruet, but retired shortly before the finish because of ignition problems.*
(Nigel Snowdon)

*At Le Mans in 1971 Ligier entered the JS3 Prototype with Ford-Cosworth V-8 engine. It was unclassified.* (Nigel Snowdon)

The same year Ligier introduced his JS3 Prototype, powered by a mid-mounted Cosworth-Ford DFV V-8 3-litre and with very shapely open glass-fibre bodywork. Driven at Le Mans by Ligier/Depailler, the car was plagued by transmission troubles, the gearbox was virtually rebuilt and although the JS3 rejoined the race after three and a half hours and was still running at the finish, it was not classified.

Ligier returned to Le Mans in 1972 with two of the JS2 coupés, yellow-painted, and looking very much like Grand Touring cars. Undoubtedly they would have run in that category if production had been sufficient. The car shared by Maublanc/Laffite survived until almost the end of the race, when it retired with engine trouble. The other Ligiers driven by Laurent/Marche/Delaland and Ligier/Piot also both retired with engine problems.

Ligier was still struggling with the JS2 in 1973 and again three cars were entered, but only one finished, right down the field in 19th place, shared by Laurent/Marche/Delaland. In 1974, in the face of much weaker opposition, the JS2s, now powered by Maserati SM6 engines, scored a little more success, taking

*Ligier's greatest success came in 1975 when this Cosworth-powered JS2 driven by Chasseuil/Lafosse finished second to the winning Gulf.* (Nigel Snowdon)

an eighth place at Monza (Lafitte/Serpaggi) and eighth again at Le Mans by the same drivers. By 1975 the JS2s were back on Cosworth-Ford DFV V-8 engines. In the early part of the season nothing much was gained, although Beltoise/Jarier finished seventh at Mugello, Migault/Jarier were sixth at Dijon and then came Le Mans, not a round in the World Championship of Makes because of fuel consumption impositions, and here the heavy Ligier coupé running with 410 bhp engine (retaining a higher output than that of other Cosworth V-8 users) achieved its best performance of the season and Chasseuil/Lafosse finished second, a mere lap behind the winning Gulf GR8. Of the other two Ligiers in this race, one car, that driven by Beltoise/Jarier, retained a Maserati engine, mainly because the drivers thought it would prove more reliable in a 24 Hours race; both these cars, however, retired.

After this encouraging performance, Ligier turned his attention towards Formula 1 and since 1976 has been racing in the premier single-seater category, with cars variously powered by Matra, Cosworth, Renault and Megatron engines.

# Lister-Jaguar (United Kingdom)

From 1954 onwards Brian Lister of Cambridge had been building successful cars based on twin steel tubular members, with unequal-length wishbones and coil spring/damper units at the front and at the rear a de Dion rear axle with the tube located by a vertical centre-slide, twin parallel radius arms and coil spring/damper units. The first car was powered by an M.G. engine, and the first Bristol-powered example appeared later in 1954 and enjoyed a fantastic run of success in the hands of Archie Scott-Brown, and a small number were made for sale to private owners. From this car was developed the unsuccessful Lister-Maserati with 2-litre 6-cylinder twin overhead camshaft A6CGS engine. In 1957 came the first of the Jaguar-powered cars which with Scott-Brown at the wheel proved immensely successful in British events. By 1958 these cars were in limited production with Jaguar or Chevrolet engines and it was at the wheel of the works car that the brilliant Scott-Brown lost his life at the Spa-Francorchamps in May 1958. Lister continued racing into 1959 with what was basically the same chassis design, but with a new body designed by Frank Costin, former de Havilland aerodynamicist and designer

131

*The Lister-Jaguar raced at Le Mans by Sargent/Lumsden seen in the paddock at Prescott hill climb in the mid-1960s.* (The Author)

of Lotus and Vanwall bodies. Although aerodynamically efficient, the body was big and bulbous, with flaired front wings, higher bonnet line and high-level tail. Drivers simply did not like the new Lister design. In international long-distance events these Listers were plagued by reliability problems with the 3-litre version of the Jaguar engine, whilst in short-circuit British events they were no longer a match for the Lotus 15s and Cooper Monacos. Lister had already decided to withdraw from racing at the end of 1959, when his Number one driver Ivor Bueb suffered fatal injuries in a Formula 2 race in late July at Clermont-Ferrand and died a few days later. Lister then withdrew from racing on the spot and the team was immediately disbanded.

There was, however, one Lister that was never raced by the works, a new Jaguar sports car with multi-tubular space-frame, the development of which had cost Lister vast sums of money but which remained uncompleted. The car was built up for garage owner Jim Diggory at his premises at Rhostyllen near Wrexham in 1960. Diggory entered the car in a number of events, sometimes with Bruce Halford, a well-established Lister and Lotus driver, at the wheel, but later sold it to John Coundley. It was then acquired by Peter Sargent with the registration WTM 446 and Sargent had carried out by Playfords of South London a magnificent coupé body conversion with double-bubble roof line, rather as pioneered by Zagato. It was powered by a well-developed 3781 cc Jaguar D-type engine, and so there were prospects of good reliability.

It was entered at Le Mans in 1963, first appearing in unpainted form at the Le Mans Test Weekend in April so that its owner could be satisfied that it would be acceptable to the scrutineers. Although it went well in the opening laps of the Le Mans race, it was eliminated when the clutch bolts sheared, the result of a supply from a bad batch. Afterwards the car was sold back to John Coundley, who entered it in the 1964 Nürburgring 1000 km race with Jack Fairman as co-driver. The coupé bodywork overheated appallingly and the drivers suffered very badly, but the car ran well before retiring with rear suspension problems. It was an interesting effort to go Prototype racing at relatively low cost, but obviously prospects of success were minimal.

# Lola (United Kingdom)

Above all else Eric Broadley was an enthusiast, building and racing his own 'Special' to comply with the 750 Motor Club's 1172 formula for Ford side-valve-powered cars, which he raced from 1956 onwards and soon moving on to the design and construction of an 1100 cc Coventry Climax-powered sports-racing car that first appeared in the middle of 1958. The Mk 1 Lola, as it was later designated, soon came to be the dominant force in British 1,100 cc Sports Car racing and remained in production until 1962. From 1960 onwards Broadley also built front-engined Formula Junior single-seater racing cars, a rear-engined Formula Junior followed in 1961 and for 1962 Lola built the team of Mk 4 Formula 1 cars for the Bowmaker/Yeoman team. However, at that point Broadley switched his attention to Prototype racing, and built a dramatic and potentially immensely successful car which first appeared at the 1963 Racing Car Show at Olympia.

## Mk 6 Lola GT, 1963

The basis of the new car was a monocoque central section forming a stiff, light and wide passenger compartment, based on a pair of large box-members which formed the door sills on either side and served as the fuel tanks. Each box-member had an inner face of sheet steel bent to a U-section, and an outer face of duralumin sheet. Inside the box-members were four cast magnesium formers with bosses to take attachment bolts for the door frame and roof structure. The two side-members were linked by a steel floor pan, with small, boxed bracing members for mounting the seats and the central remote control gear change. From the rear of each side-member extended a fabricated extension to which the coil spring/damper units were attached. The rear suspension consisted of wishbones, transverse links and long forward-facing radius arms. Forwards from the scuttle of the new Lola was a mainly square-section tubular structure extending to provide the front suspension mountings, to carry the cross-flow radiators and the spare wheel. The front suspension was by unequal-length wishbones and coil spring/damper units. This chassis was clothed in a shapely and aerodynamic glass-fibre coupé body, marred only by the use of proprietary fittings, such as the Cortina rear lights. The power unit was originally the 4.2-litre Ford V-8 engine, with Shelby modifications, including the fitting of four twin-choke downdraught Weber carburettors, and developing 260 bhp at 6500 rpm. Transmission was by a combined Colotti 4-speed gearbox and final drive unit.

After an initial debut at the May Silverstone Meeting, where the 4.2-litre engine was still fitted with only a single downdraught carburettor, and where Tony Maggs finished fifth in the over 2000 cc class, the car ran at the Nürburgring 1000 km race, but was delayed by a rear wheel working loose and finally retired with engine trouble. Two cars had been entered at Le Mans, but eventually only one, a new car with a 4.7-litre engine started the race. It was driven by Attwood/Hobbs, but

*At Le Mans in 1963 the Lola GT driven by Dickie Attwood/David Hobbs displayed immense promise, but retired because of an accident at Tertre Rouge when Hobbs was unable to engage third gear.*

retired on the Sunday morning when Hobbs, unable to engage third gear on the approach to Tertre Rouge, lost control and crashed. The third car was built in time for the August Bank Holiday Meeting at Brands Hatch and a Lola GT was also supplied to the American John Mecom team. Later, fitted with a 6-litre Chevrolet engine, Augie Pabst drove the Mecom car to a win in the Nassau Tourist Trophy in the Bahamas.

Undoubtedly the Lola GT was a very ambitious project for a small company, and clearly Lola lacked the resources to develop it fully. What at the time seemed the perfect answer came when Broadley was invited to join Ford Advanced Vehicles with the intention that the Lola should form the basis of the new Ford GT40 Prototype. For Broadley this was a desperate interlude, as he was thoroughly unhappy working within the Ford organization. No longer did he have autonomy and freedom, development seemed to be governed by committee rather than by individuals and most of Broadley's sound practical ideas based on experience were ignored. By 1965 he was back in business on his own at Slough and soon there appeared a new sports-racing car from the Lola stable.

## T70 Mk 3 GT, 1967

In 1965, Broadley had introduced his new T70 Group 7 sports-racing car based on a monocoque chassis, fabricated from sheet steel and alloy with the front suspension by double wishbones, coil spring/damper units and anti-roll bar, and rear suspension by reversed lower wishbones, single top links, twin radius rods, coil spring/damper units and anti-roll bar. Rack-and-pinion steering was fitted, there were Girling disc brakes front and rear, 15 in. cast magnesium wheels and an aerodynamically effective glass-fibre body built by Specialised Mouldings. Powered by either a Traco-modified Chevrolet or 4.7-litre Ford V-8 engine, these cars enjoyed immense success during 1965–66. The 1966 version was the improved Mk 2 with all-alloy centre monocoque. John Surtees ran his own red Chevrolet-engined car and other cars were driven with success by David Hobbs (Ford-powered) and Denis Hulme (entered by Sid Taylor). At the end of 1966, Group 7

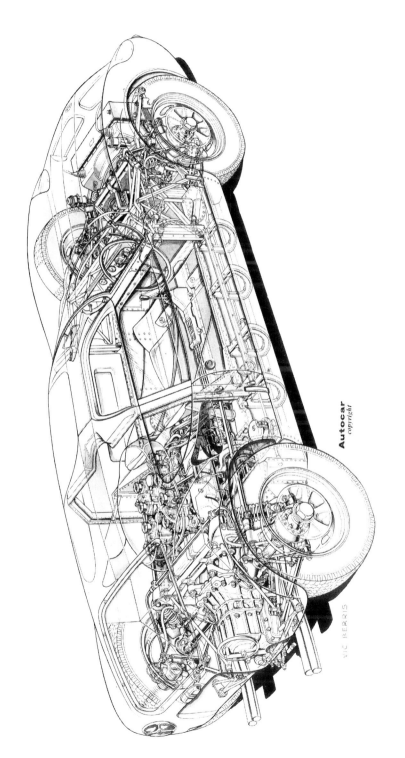

**Autocar**
*copyright*

VIC BERRIS

*This cutaway drawing by Vic Berris, the true master of the art, reveals just how advanced was the concept of the 1963 Lola GT.*
(The Quadrant Library)

135

racing came to an end and so the only market for these very fast sports-racing cars was now in Can-Am racing. Accordingly Broadley developed a GT version of the T70 for Prototype racing. In this form the T70s sported handsome gull-wing door coupé bodywork. It was intended it should eventually be homologated as a Competition Sports Car, but until then was obliged to run in the Prototype class.

In this form it was usually raced with a Chevrolet 5.9-litre engine and Hewland LG500 gearbox/final drive unit. However, there was also a quasi-works team run by Lola and John Surtees known as Lola Racing to race cars with the Aston Martin V-8 engine. Although this 5064 cc (98 × 83 mm) design with light alloy cylinder block and twin overhead camshafts per bank of cylinders was a bulky, heavy unit, both Broadley and Surtees believed that it had considerable potential for competition work. In this form it was modified to dry sump lubrication and was fitted with four twin-choke Weber carburettors.

Early testing was not encouraging, as there were many engine problems, but with certain regrets Lola Racing decided to press on. At the Le Mans Test Weekend, Surtees appeared with the new car, distinguished by its dark green paintwork and white arrowhead, and set third fastest lap. The new car made its race debut at the Nürburgring, where it was driven by Surtees and Hobbs, but running in seventh place it retired with broken rear suspension. By Le Mans Lola Racing had two cars ready, now fitted with Lucas fuel injection, and these were driven by Surtees/Hobbs and Irwin/de Klerk. Early in the race both cars retired with major engine problems. After this race Lola Racing abandoned the use of the Aston Martin engines and switched to Chevrolet units. Neither Lola Racing nor private owners gained much in the way of success apart from minor wins at the Norisring in Germany and the Cape 3 Hours race.

## T70 Mk 3 GT, 1968

For 1968 the rules were changed and henceforth Prototypes were limited to a 3 litres and Competition Sports Cars, of which not fewer than fifty had been built, to 5 litres. The Lola was accepted as a Competition Sports Car, but only on the basis of adding together the total number of Group 7 sports-racing cars and GT versions built in total. Lola Racing had now been disbanded, although a quasi-works Lola was entered by Sid Taylor, but almost exclusively in British events. In international racing, the team's chances rested purely with private owners and very little success was gained. The best performances during the year were a sixth place in the BOAC 500 Race at Brands Hatch by Bonnier/Axellson, the only finish by a Lola in the first six at a Championship race during the year, wins in minor British events by the Sid Taylor-entered car and overseas victories at Anderstorp, Vila Real and Innsbruck.

## The T70 Mk 3B GT, 1969

An improved version, known as the 3B, was introduced for 1969, but the changes were limited to improved handling and minor modifications to the bodywork, which was now lighter and incorporated front-hinged instead of gull-wing doors. This was to be the last year in which the model was built.

At the Daytona 24 Hours race in 1969 a new Mk 3B coupé was entered by Roger Penske Racing, sponsored by Sunoco. Already Penske had an outstanding repu-

*The first Lola T70 Mk 3-Aston Martin, driven by John Surtees at the Le Mans Test Weekend in 1967.* (David Phipps)

tation for preparation and development work, stretching back to 1962, when he had first appeared with his own Cooper-based Zerex Special. Since the T70 had arrived in Penske's workshop, a month before the race, the team reckoned that it spent an average of eighteen working hours a day on preparation. The T70 looked magnificent, in royal blue with gold lining, and was powered by a Traco-built 5-litre Chevrolet engine running on fuel injection. It was driven by Mark Donohue and Ronnie Bucknum. Despite all the preparation work, however, the car was plagued in the race by fuel pick-up problems and dropped back to seventh place and over an hour was lost in the pits whilst the exhaust system was repaired; luckily for Penske, the front runners, the Porsche 908s, suffered from cracked exhausts and other mechanical problems, both of the Wyer-entered Fords were eliminated and Donohue/Parsons came through to win this race from another Lola T70 Mk3, an older car not raced since Sebring in 1968, driven by Motschenbacher/Leslie. By the Sebring race the Penske Lola was running on carburettors, but it retired early in

*The Lola T70 Mk 3-Chevrolet driven into sixth place in the 1968 BOAC 500 Miles race by Bonnier/Axelsson. Note the handle for the gull-wing door.* (Nigel Snowdon)

*With this T70 Mk 3B-Chevrolet entered by Scuderia Filipinetti, Bonnier/Müller finished fifth in the 1969 Spa 1000 Km race. Conventional doors were fitted to the Mk 3B.* (Nigel Snowdon)

the race when a radius rod pulled loose from the monocoque, and it failed to run in any more Championship events during the year. At Sebring, however, the older Mk 3 of Motschenbacher/Leslie did manage to finish in sixth place.

Despite the inherent unreliability of the T70, in fact the model enjoyed a better year than in 1968. At the Monza 1000 km race the Mk 3B of Sid Taylor was driven by Andrea de Adamich and Frank Gardner into fifth place, only just missing fourth spot by 1.2 second. One of the outstanding Lola drives of the year was that of Herbert Müller with the Scuderia Filipinetti car in the Targa Florio. Although the Lola was inherently an impractical car for the Sicilian road race, both in terms of handling and manoeuvrability and reliability, it had been very carefully prepared for the race and had been considerably strengthened, especially the suspension. In practice this car was fifth fastest behind the Porsche 908 opposition, and despite losing two minutes at the start because of ignition trouble, Müller overtook 60 cars on the first lap to hold third place at the end of the lap. Unfortunately he suffered a puncture, which apparently damaged the suspension, and Bonnier retired the car on lap three with deteriorating handling. Filipinetti were in fact the most successful Lola entrants in 1969 and later in the year Bonnier/Müller finished fifth in the Spa race and took second place at the Österreichring, due entirely to the unreliability of the opposition.

In short-distance British events, many minor successes were gained by both the Sid Taylor car and other private owners. Sadly in the Tourist Trophy at Oulton Park in May, Australian driver Paul Hawkins, who had already won races during the year at Snetterton and Dijon, crashed his red Lola with fatal results. He went off the road at Island bend and hit a tree and the car rolled and caught fire. The writer was present at this accident; there was no possibility of saving the driver and Hawkins' death was a particularly sad loss to motor racing. Other successes during the year included Hans Herrmann's win in the Solitudenrennen, by Bonnier at Montlhéry, Redman at Karlskoga, and Gardner at Innsbruck. Lola also won four of the five races in the Springbok series in South Africa at the end of the year. None of these successes counted for much in international terms, but they did at least show that when the cars ran well, they were competitive.

## T70 Mk 3B GT and T210, 1970

Although the T70 could no longer be regarded as a serious racing proposition, teams including the Belgian team VDS, and David Piper, continued to race the cars. Dickie Attwood (with Piper's car) and Pilette (VDS entry) took the first two places in a minor race at Montlhéry in May, Attwood won at Dijon and Pilette won at Montlhéry again in June, whilst Gosselin won a minor race at Vila Real in Portugal. So far as Sports Cars were concerned, most of Lola's efforts were concentrated on the T210 car, with the Cosworth FVC 1798 cc engine developing 230 bhp and a 'tub'-type monocoque with multi-tubular space-frame engine compartment and conventional suspension. These cars appeared in Endurance Championship races, but they were mainly intended for the new European Constructors Championship for Group 5 and 6 cars under 2 litres. The first car was supplied to Joakim Bonnier, and with victories at the Saltzburgring, Anderstorp, Hockenheim and Enna, together with second places at the Paul Ricard and Spa circuits, Lola finished second in the Championship to the Chrevon driven by Brian Redman.

## T212, 1971

This was an improved version of the 1970 1.8-litre car and these were now more frequently seen in Championship races. In the Targa Florio one of these cars driven by Bonnier/Attwood finished third overall behind the winning Alfa Romeos and another driven by Parkes/Westbury finished fifth. Remarkably enough there was another finish in the Championship points during the year, by the T70 Mk 3B of Pilette/Gosselin, who took sixth place in the Spa 1000 km race. In the European 2-litre Constructors Championship there was a total of nine races, and of these five were won by Lolas, and Lola took the Championship from Chevron with 57 points to 46.

*The class-winning Lola T212 of Joakim Bonnier/Richard Attwood which was entered in the 1971 Targa Florio by Scuderia Filipinetti and finished third overall. These cars achieved some remarkable performances in long-distance races.* (Nigel Snowdon)

*At Le Mans in 1972 this Lola T280-Cosworth was entered by Ecurie Bonnier for Bonnier/Larrousse/van Lennep, but sadly crashed with fatal results with veteran driver Joakim Bonnier at the wheel.* (Nigel Snowdon)

## T280 and 290, 1972

For 1972, Lola offered, and built in considerable numbers, an improved T290 car, but in addition there was a T280 variant, powered by the Cosworth-Ford DFV V-8 Grand Prix engine and built for Joakim Bonnier's Écurie Bonnier. Despite a strong team of drivers, the cars proved unreliable and one of the main problems was Bonnier's lack of finance. The team's first finish in the points came at Sebring, where Bonnier/Wisell/Larrousse finished sixth, Larrousse/de Fierlandt were fifth at Spa and Larrousse/Bonnier finished sixth at the Nürburgring. By the Le Mans 24 Hours race the team had sponsorship from the Swiss Cheese Federation and were hopeful of doing well. It was thought that the Ford V-8 engine would last the distance, but there were serious doubts about the Hewland DG300 gearboxes and so the team had been practising gearbox changes to the point where they could change a 'box in twenty minutes. One car was delayed by a host of minor problems and was eventually abandoned out on the circuit with clutch problems, but the second car was eliminated from the race in tragic circumstances on the Sunday morning; Bonnier collided with a Ferrari Daytona, the Lola rebounded over the barrier and into the trees and Bonnier died in the ensuing fire. Although the cars continued to appear on something of a half-hearted basis during the remainder of the season, and towards the end of the year an improved 1973 T282 was delivered, all the impetus was lost with Bonnier's death and the team faded away.

In the European 2-litre Championship there was a total of nine races, but Lola could win only two and the marque finished third in the Championship.


## T282, 1973

During 1973, Jean-Louis la Fosse and Reine Wisell raced a Lola T282, an improved car, with better aerodynamics and still powered by the Ford V-8 engine, with financial support from the Gitanes French cigarette company. Throughout the season Lola design engineer Bob Marston supervised the operation, but the car crashed twice as a result of failure of the suspension. By the middle of the year it had been extensively modified and after further testing it was due to appear at Watkins Glen, but crashed once more because of a jammed throttle during pre-race testing.

In the European 2-litre Sports Car Championship, Lola were dominant once again with their new and improved T292 car and of the year's eight races, four were won by the Lolas, twice with Chris Craft at the wheel and twice with Guy Edwards. Lola won the Championship by a comfortable margin from Chevron.


## Postscript

1973 represented the last year in which Lola showed any interest in Endurance racing, but their T294 cars, the 1974 version of the 2-litre model, continued to run in the European 2-litre Sports Car Championship. This was now dominated by Alpine-Renault and Lola failed to win a single race, finishing fourth overall in the Championship with the best performances fourth places at Hockenheim and Jarama. By 1975 this Championship had lost support and consisted of a mere two rounds, so that it no longer received FIA recognition and it was not again held.

# Lotus (United Kingdom)

## 23 and Elite, 1962

The first year of Prototype racing reflected the gradual eclipse of one long-standing Lotus design and the rise to fame of a new model from Chapman's stable. The Lotus Elite had been the greatest surprise and the very real star of the 1957 London Motor Show. This car, intended to establish Lotus as serious manufacturers of production cars, featured a unique monocoque constructed in glass-fibre, and it featured suspension very similar to that of the early front-engined Lotus 12 Formula 2 cars, with double wishbones at the front and the famous Chapman strut rear suspension. The power unit was a Coventry Climax 1216 cc engine developing in production form 75 bhp at 6100 rpm and transmission was by a B.M.C. gearbox. The body was an exceptionally elegant coupé designed by Peter Kirwan-Taylor. As a production car, the Elite proved unsatisfactory, firstly because Lotus could not produce it at an economic price and make a profit, and secondly because it proved more than a little unreliable and temperamental in the hands of ordinary users. However, its great successes came on the racing circuit in the GT class. By 1962 these included eighth place by Lumsden/Riley at Le Mans in 1959 (together with second place in the Index of Thermal Efficiency), 13th and 14th places at Le Mans in 1960 (together with a win in the Index of Thermal Efficiency) and 12th place overall (together with second place in the Index of Thermal Efficiency) at Le Mans in 1961. In addition Lotus Elites had won their class at the Nürburgring in 1959, 1960 and 1961.

The real sensation of the Lotus line-up for 1962 was the new 23 sports-racing car, an adaptation of the company's 22 Formula Junior design. As with the single-seater, there was a multi-tubular space-frame but wider and with suspension at the front by double wishbones and coil spring/damper units and at the rear on a system similar to that of the team's Formula 1 cars, by lower wishbones, top links, parallel radius arms, and coil spring/damper units. The usual power unit was the 1098 cc Cosworth-Ford (as used in Formula Junior cars) in conjunction with a modified Volkswagen gearbox. The low and very aerodynamic body was made in glass-fibre with detachable panels. In the main this car was intended for racing in British short-circuit events, but it made a couple of appearances, albeit somewhat unfortunate, at Endurance races during the year.

At the Nürburgring a works car was entered in the name of Essex Racing Team under the control of Lotus director Mike Costin. What was so very different about this car was that it was powered by the new Lotus twin overhead camshaft engine developed by Harry Mundy and based on a Ford block. The original development work had been carried out with a 997 cc Ford Anglia engine, but the new engine was based on the as yet unannounced 116E Ford block to be used in the new production Classic. In this form it had a capacity of 1498 cc and, as raced, a power output of around 140 bhp; it was the engine that was destined to power the new production Elan model. At the Nürburgring this Lotus was entered for works Formula 1 Lotus drivers Jim Clark and Trevor Taylor. When the race started the track was wet and treacherous. Clark with the small, light Lotus was beaten into the first corner by the Aston Martin DBR1/300 of Bruce McLaren, but soon the Lotus was in front and as the race progressed so he built up an ever-extending lead, heading the field by 27 seconds at the end of the first lap and extending this to over two minutes by the end of lap eight. As the circuit dried out, so Clark lost ground and on lap 12 he failed to correct a slide at Kesselschen, the result of fumes from a leaking exhaust, and the Lotus finished its race in a ditch. Even if the car had failed in this unfortunate way, it had still performed magnificently and the 1000 cc class was won by a standard Lotus 23 entered by Ian Walker Racing and driven by Peter Ashdown and Bruce Johnstone. In addition the Elite of Wagstaff/Fergusson took second place in the class for GT cars up to 1300 cc.

At Le Mans two 23s were entered, a 997 cc twin-cam car by Lotus Engineering to be driven by Jim Clark/Trevor Taylor and in addition a car with a 745 cc Coventry Climax engine by UDT-Laystall for Les Leston/Tony Shelly. However, when the cars were presented for scrutineering, they were rejected because the front wheels had four-stud fixing and the rear wheels six-stud. The Technical Committee of the organising club argued that the spare wheel could replace only one pair of wheels. Immediately Colin Chapman had the rear wheels modified to a four-stud fixing and the cars were represented for scrutineering. The officials then refused to look at them again, taking the attitude that since the wheels had originally been designed for six-stud fixing, modification to four-stud made the cars unsafe. Despite strenuous arguments and representations on Chapman's behalf made by the Royal Automobile Club, the cars were not permitted to run. Lotus never again entered at Le Mans. However, there was more than a little consolation for Lotus in the results, as the Elites of Hobbs/Gardner and Hunt/Wyllie finished eighth and 11th overall, taking the first two places in the Index of Thermal Efficiency, with the leading car finishing third in the Index Performance and winning the up to 1300 cc class. Other successful Elite performances during the year were class wins by Sir John Whitmore with an Elite owned by band leader Chris Barber in the Spa Grand Prix and by Clive Hunt in the Tourist Trophy at Goodwood.

## Elite, 1963

During 1963, the Elites continued to achieve a measure of success and this included sixth place overall and a win in the 1300 cc class of the Spa Grand Prix by Pat Fergusson, entered by Team Elite, a class win for GT cars up to 1300 cc by Wagstaff/Baird at the Nürburgring and tenth place by Wagstaff/Fergusson at Le Mans, together with third place in the Index of Thermal Efficiency, despite delays

*This Lotus Elite entered by Team Elite at Le Mans in 1963 and driven by Wagstaff/Fergusson finished tenth overall, won its class and finished third in the Index of Thermal Efficiency.* (Nigel Snowdon)

143

caused by an off-course excursion into the sandbanks at Mulsanne corner by Fergusson. This was the Elite's last year of success in international racing. From now on the emphasis would be on the Elan with the Lotus twin-cam engine, first raced by Graham Warner at Silverstone in May and a prototype of which was entered by Stirling Moss at the Nürburgring for Innes Ireland/Sir John Whitmore, but withdrawn because of handling problems. Although the Elan scored an enormous number of successes in minor British events, it in reality lacked the international potential of the Elite and failed to shine at all in international events. In 1964 the Ian Walker team entered a special-bodied Elan, intended for Le Mans, at the Nürburgring. It was, however, written off when Mike Spence crashed in practice as a result of brake failure.

## 47, 1967

At the last race of the year in 1966, the meeting at Brands Hatch on Boxing Day, John Miles appeared at the wheel of a new competition Lotus model. This was the 47, based on the production Lotus Europa, with similar backbone chassis, double wishbone front suspension (but with stronger fabricated upper wishbones which were fully adjustable), and rear suspension by single upper links, reversed lower wishbones and twin radius rods. On the 47 the mid-mounted engine was the Cosworth-Ford Mk 13 twin-cam, fitted with Tecalemit-Jackson fuel injection and developing 165 bhp (instead of the Renault fitted to the production Europa); this engine was mated to a 5-speed Hewland FT200 gearbox/final drive unit. There were two fuel tanks mounted on each side behind the doors, the oil tank and spare

*A rare international appearance for the Elan was in the 1967 BOAC 500 Miles race in which this car was driven by Keith Burnand/Peter Taggart, but was too far behind at the finish to be classified.* (Nigel Snowdon)

*This Lotus 47 driven by John Miles/Jack Oliver finished ninth overall in the 1967 BOAC 500 Miles race and won its class.* (Nigel Snowdon)

wheel were in the nose ahead on the passenger side of the car, knock-on cast magnesium spoked wheels were fitted, and there were outboard Girling disc brakes front and rear. At Brands Hatch John Miles won the British Eagle Trophy race for Grand Touring cars, whilst Jack Oliver with the second car, after receiving a push-start, finished second on the road, but was classified well down the field because of the penalty imposed.

Following the Brands Hatch race, Lotus put a great deal of development work into the cars, and by the time the prototype was tested by John Blunsden for *Motor Racing* magazine (March 1967) it was a much improved car. Blunsden commented 'to the extent that any car of this calibre can be, the Lotus feels relatively easy to handle. Initial reactions are of the comparatively soft ride, and of a certain deadness in the steering, suggesting that maybe only 3 degrees of castor is on the low side. But the steering is quick and light, and so the lack of feel is soon forgotten, until occasionally the tail breaks loose a little quicker than anticipated (because you backed off when you had more lock on than you thought).

'The car understeers (but not excessively) round slow corners, and runs more or less neutrally through the faster curves. A momentary back-off tightens up the line at the hairpin (this is when you have to be prepared to do some smart unwinding), and the car reveals outstanding traction in the way it rockets out of a corner; the power really gets through to the road on this one.

'The production version is being turned out with Cosworth's Mark 13C 1.6-litre Lotus-Ford twin-cam, giving 160 bhp at 7000 rpm with Tecalemit-Jackson fuel injection. The works cars are similar, but have a special development head, and probably produce another 10 bhp at the same revs. The normal rev range is between 5000 and 7000 rpm with an extra 500 rpm on tap when really needed. Most of the time I confined myself to 7000 revs, although I took it up to 7400 in fourth on the top straight before changing to fifth halfway along the pits, and I had to watch the needle carefully at that point because it was still climbing quite quickly!

'. . . One or two recent Lotuses . . . have not exactly flattered their owners. This one is very different . . . and flattery will get you anywhere!'

In the same issue of *Motor Racing* Lotus Cars (Sales) Limited were offering the

47 at 'from £2,600' and in fact a total of 55 of these competition cars in all were built. They scored a whole string of successes in British events but never made their mark in international racing. The best performance of the year was in the BOAC 500 race at Brands Hatch at the end of July in which Jack Oliver and John Miles with the Lotus Components entry took ninth place overall and won the 2-litre Prototype category. John Wagstaff entered his 47 under the name of the re-formed Team Elite in the Nürburgring 500 km race with Trevor Taylor at the wheel, and Taylor came close to winning the race from strong Alpine opposition, but was eliminated by an electrical fault.

In 1968 a brace of these cars were entered in the red, white and gold colours of Gold Leaf Team Lotus and were driven by John Miles and Jack Oliver to many successes in British events. However, nothing was gained on the international front.

## 62, 1968

For 1968 Lotus produced a new Prototype, derived from the Lotus 47, and with the intention that it should be used as a testbed for the new Lotus-Vauxhall LV/220 slant-4 engine. This engine was modified for racing by Lotus, but later units would be of Lotus manufacture and power the range of Lotus production cars. It featured a light alloy cylinder block and cylinder head with twin overhead camshafts, Tecalemit-Jackson fuel injection and a capacity of 1992 cc; power was 220 bhp at 8000 rpm. Transmission was by a ZF 5-speed gearbox. Under the glass-fibre panels, the 62 was very different from its predecessor and featured a multi-tubular space-frame of round, square and rectangular section tubing, in place of the backbone structure of the earlier 47. Front suspension was by double wishbones and coil spring/damper units, while at the rear there were links, radius arms,

*Driven on its racing debut by John Miles/Brian Muir, the Lotus 62 finished 13th in the 1969 BOAC 500 Miles race and won its class.* (Nigel Snowdon)

wishbones and coil spring/damper units. Two of these cars were built, finished in Golf Leaf colours and entered under the name Lotus Europa, and they were amongst the noisiest Prototypes on the racing circuits. In addition Lotus Components were still offering the 47A, a modified version of the original Competition coupé, with the main difference that there was a detachable backbone chassis, whereas on the original the body shell had been bonded to the backbone. Both accessibility and ease of maintenance were vastly improved, but the cars achieved no more success than they had previously.

The first 62 made its debut in the BOAC 500 miles race at Brands Hatch in April 1969 and was driven by John Miles/Brian Muir. Despite a multitude of minor problems, because it was largely untested, it finished 13th overall and won its class. These two drivers drove two of the 62s in many minor events during the year, but when Miles was driving a four-wheel-drive Formula 1 car for the Lotus team, then Roy Pike took his place. The best performances during the year were in the Tourist Trophy at Oulton Park in May in which John Miles took third place, beating Chevron and Porsche 910 opposition, and in the Trophy of the Dunes at Zandvoort, where Miles finished fourth and Muir sixth. Because all the necessary development work on the Vauxhall-based engine had been completed, the cars were not raced by the works after the end of the year, but a 62 was acquired from the works by band leader Chris Barber in 1971 and driven for him by Dave Brodie. During the previous year or so, Barber had been struggling to make raceworthy a new Piper Prototype, without success.

# *Marcos (United Kingdom)*

Not exactly an inspiring design, or one from which much in the way of success could be expected, the Marcos Mantis built by Jem Marsh of Marcos raced once during the 1968 season. Originally Marsh had planned to use the B.R.M. V-12 engine, which had been developed for sale to private customers, but because of the high cost of this, Marsh chose the less expensive Repco V-8 engine with a single camshaft per bank of cylinders and developing around 315 bhp at 7250 rpm. This engine, which had been used by the Brabham Formula 1 team, was now regarded as redundant for their purposes. This was used in conjunction with a Hewland gearbox and featured conventional double wishbone suspension front and rear.

*Photographed before it was raced, the Marcos Mantis with Repco V-8 engine instead of the B.R.M. V-12 that it was originally planned to use.*

There were, however, two remarkable features about the car; firstly, it featured stressed plywood monocoque construction, as used on all Marcos cars, and as evolved by former de Havilland engineer Frank Costin. Secondly, the bodywork designed by Dennis Adams, who was responsible for the styling of production Marcos cars, featured extremely angular lines with a very large cockpit area. The whole concept looked rather flimsy and impracticable.

The car only raced once, in the Spa 1000 km race, and it arrived after only brief testing at Castle Combe and Goodwood. Originally Formula 2 driver Robin Widdows was nominated to drive the Marcos with constructor Jim Marsh, but he thought that it was too untested for such a difficult circuit and his place was taken by Ed Nelson. It arrived only in time for the final practice session, was plagued by alternator trouble, and started from the back of the grid. After only a few laps, it was withdrawn because of loss of engine oil and more alternator troubles. Originally Marsh had planned to run the car at Le Mans and was trying to save the engine for that race (he had only the one engine), but any further plans to race the Mantis were abandoned following a flood at Marcos' Wiltshire works.

*The Mantis on its sole race outing in the 1968 Spa 1000 Km race, on a rain-soaked track, in which it was delayed by wet electrics and eliminated by low oil pressure.* (LAT)

# Maserati (Italy)

From 1926 to 1957, the war years apart, Maserati had enjoyed an unbroken record of entering motor racing, not always with works cars, as very often the company had been content to supply cars to private owners and assist them so far as they were able on their limited resources. In 1938 control of Maserati had passed to the Orsi family. Managing Director Omer Orsi took a much more serious interest in running works cars and in particular during the years 1953 to 1957 entered strong teams of both single-seaters and sports cars. In 1957 Juan Fangio had won his fifth World Championship at the wheel of a Maserati 250F Formula 1 car. That year had been a disaster for Maserati, with substantial trading losses in South America, partly as a result of the collapse of the Peron regime, the vast expense of the team's competition programme and the loss of cars worth more than £20,000 through accidents in the Venezuelan Grand Prix at Caracas in November. Accordingly Maserati announced their retirement from motor racing, but in fact it is very difficult for a team so deeply steeped in motor racing history and with so many close ties to simply pull out. Lightweight versions of the 250F were built in 1958 and these were followed in 1959 by the Tipo 60, the first of the so called 'Bird-cage' cars designed by Giulio Alfieri. The nickname given to the car came from the construction of the chassis, which was formed by a multiplicity of small-diameter tubes welded together to form a frame of remarkable lightness, and with additional strengthening provided by the lower body panels. Double wishbone/coil spring front suspension was used, with a de Dion axle and transverse leaf spring at the rear. The first cars used the 4-cylinder 200S 1990 cc unit, but for 1960 the team built the Tipo 61 car with 2890 cc engine. Cars entered by the Camoradi Team won the Nürburgring 1000 km race in both 1960 and 1961. During 1961 Maserati also introduced the more advanced Tipo 63 car with mid-mounted engine, independent rear suspension by coil springs and wishbones and fitted either with a 4-cylinder 2890 cc engine or with a V-12 of 2989 cc. Mainly because of unreliability and lack of development, these cars scored nothing in the way of success during 1961, which was of course the last year of the World Sports Car Championship.

## Tipo 61 and 63, 1962

During the first year of the Prototype Championship, the old Tipo 61 front-engined car was accepted at some races. The V-12 Tipo 63 was also raced by Briggs Cunningham, but without success, and Maserati produced a new version of the 'Bird-cage', the Tipo 64, which was entered by the Scuderia Serenissima in the Targa Florio for Abate/Davis. The chassis was virtually unchanged, but there was revised bodywork and the V-12 engine was still used. The car retired in the Sicilian race because of steering trouble, without showing any real form. Casner partnered by Masten Gregory entered his old Tipo 61 fitted with a new body in the Nürburgring 1000 km race, but it was plagued by overheating and many other minor problems and although it finished 19th on the road, winning its class, it was completely uncompetitive. Tipo 61 cars did, however, appear in international events as late as 1963.

## Tipo 151, 1962

Maserati built three new cars for Le Mans in 1962. These were the Tipo 151, which featured a front-mounted engine because Alfieri believed that it was easier to resolve the handling problems of a front-engined car than with a mid-engined design. To power this new car Alfieri adopted the 1957 Tipo 450S engine, but with the capacity reduced to 3944 cc (91 × 75.8 mm), as it had to be under four litres to comply with the 1962 regulations. The specification of this engine included twin overhead camshafts per bank of cylinders, twin-plug ignition and four twin-choke

*The Tipo 64 'Bird-cage' entered in the 1962 Targa Florio by the Scuderia Serenissima Republica di Venezia for Abate/Davis. It retired because of steering problems.* (The Author's Collection)

Weber carburettors, and power output was 360 bhp at 7000 rpm. There was a 5-speed all-synchromesh gearbox in unit with the final drive. Gone were the complexities of the earlier 'Bird-cages', and instead Alfieri had designed a simpler chassis constructed from large-diameter tubes. At the front he used unequal-length wishbones and coil spring/damper units, while the rear suspension was formed by a de Dion axle, twin trailing arms and coil springs. This de Dion axle had a sliding trunnion mounted centrally at the rear of the final drive unit to provide lateral location, and at either end of the de Dion tube there were separate arm sections which gave greater roll resistance and a limited degree of independent movement. The coupé bodies of the new cars were dramatically stark, characterised by long, tapering noses, originally perspex covers over the bonnet-top air intakes – by the Le Mans race metal cowls had been adopted in their place – and Kamm cut-off tails.

Without doubt the new Tipo 151 cars were amongst the most potent entered at Le Mans in 1962, but their reliability was with reason more than suspect. Two of the cars were entered by Briggs Cunningham for McLaren/Hansgen and Thompson/Kimberly (originally Roy Salvadori should have driven this car, but he was unable to accommodate himself in the cockpit at all comfortably and so the driver-switch was made). The third car was entered by Maserati-France for Maurice Trintignant/Lucien Bianchi. During the race the cars displayed a magnificent performance, achieving close to 190 mph on the Mulsanne straight, but their handling through the corners was vastly inferior to the Ferraris. The Thompson/Kimberly car held second place early in the race, taking the lead for a short while during refuelling stops, but Thompson crashed at the Esses, the petrol tank burst and the car was eliminated on the spot. By the early hours of Sunday morning the surviving cars were in seventh and ninth places, with Maserati-France leading

*One of two Maserati Tipo 151s entered by Briggs Cunningham in the 1962 Le Mans race, seen lined up in front of the pits before the start. It was driven by Hansgen/McLaren, but retired with transmission problems.* (David Phipps)

*In the same race this Tipo 151 entered by Maserati-France was driven by Maurice Trintignant/Lucien Bianchi, but it too was eliminated by suspension and transmission problems.* (LAT)

Cunningham, but the red French-entered car was eliminated by suspension and transmission problems and shortly after 5 am the Hansgen/McLaren car, which had peculiar noises emanating from its transmission, finally retired.

## The Tipo 151, 1963

Now only Maserati-France, run by Colonel Simon, continued to race a Maserati in major events. For 1963 his Tipo 151 was rebuilt with shorter wheelbase, modified rear suspension and a new engine of 4941 (94 × 89 mm) developing 430 bhp at 7000 rpm. At Le Mans the car was driven by Simon and Lloyd Casner. Simon led the race during the first hour, but fell back, handed over to Casner, who took the lead again, only to retire very early in the race with engine trouble. Simon later drove the car in a race for Prototypes at Reims, but crashed on the first lap. The car again appeared in the Guards Trophy at Brands Hatch in August, but it was uncompetitive on this circuit and finished well down the field.

## The Tipo 151, 1964

Very minor modifications were made to the Maserati-France car for 1964 and it again appeared at Le Mans driven by Trintignant/Simon. Although it was undoubtedly the fastest car in the race, timed on the Mulsanne straight at 191.30 mph, it was an early retirement because of electrical problems. The same car and drivers appeared in the Reims 12 Hours race, but again it retired, this time with ignition trouble.

*The Maserati-France Tipo 151 lined up in front of the pits before the 1963 Le Mans race.* (The Author's Collection)

*The Tipo 151 led during the first hour in 1963 at Le Mans, with André Simon at the wheel, but dropped back and retired with engine trouble.* (Nigel Snowdon)

## The Tipo 65, 1965

The Tipo 151 reappeared at the Le Mans Test Weekend, with the engine bored out to 5046 cc, modified suspension, semi-outboard brakes and fuel capacity increased from 140 to 160 litres. It was driven by Lloyd Casner, but sadly he

*This hastily built Tipo 65 car was entered in the 1965 Le Mans race by Maserati-France for Siffert/Neerpasch, but crashed on the first lap.* (The Author's Collection)

crashed on the Saturday at the end of the Mulsanne straight, possibly as a result of brake failure, and suffered fatal injuries.

This was not quite the end of Maserati racing activities, as a new car designed by Giulio Alfieri was hastily built for the race itself in June. This new car, the Tipo 65, featured a multi-tubular space-frame constructed from even smaller-diameter tubing than that used on the original 'Bird-cage' cars, suspension by double wishbones and coil spring/damper units at the front and double wishbones and longitudinal torsion bars at the rear. The rear-mounted 5046 cc V-8 engine, with Lucas fuel injection, developed 430 bhp at 6500 rpm. Transmission was by a 5-speed all-synchromesh gearbox and the body was now a very smooth open two-seater. At Le Mans the car was driven by Siffert/Neerpasch, but it suffered from the most appalling handling problems and crashed on the first lap of the race. It was subsequently driven at Reims by Trintignant/Simon, but soon retired. This was the last Maserati specifically built for racing.

# Matra (France)

From 1965, the French Matra organization grew to be a significant force in motor racing. Between 1968 and 1972 it competed in Formula 1, in the main with its own V-12 engine, but its greatest years were 1968–69, when Jackie Stewart raced Ford-powered Matras for the Tyrrell Organisation. Matra themselves were mainly successful with their Prototypes, and these were racing through until the end of 1974. Even after the team withdrew from racing itself, it continued to supply Formula 1 engines to the Shadow team in 1975 and to the French Ligier team in 1976 and 1981.

Whilst nothing could be more serious than Matra's efforts to succeed in international racing, the involvement of Engins Matra, a major French aerospace and defence company, came almost by chance. Marcel Chassagny, who had founded Engins Matra (in full, Engins Mecanique Aviation-Traction), had a close friendship with René Bonnet, who, in partnership with Charles Deutsch, built the DB-Panhard 750 cc cars that competed with enormous success at Le Mans and elsewhere. Bonnet and Deutsch split up in 1961, going their separate ways. Deutsch initiated the C.D. Prototypes and Bonnet continued to build competition and road coupés powered by Renault engines. The new René Bonnet company was not commercially successful and when the company got into severe difficulties in 1964, at Chassagny's instigation, it was acquired by Engins Matra. Matra wanted to continue production of the René Bonnet Djet, now known as the Matra Djet, and it was put into production at Romorantin under the control of a young and very enthusiastic director, Jean-Luc Lagardère. Lagardère believed that the best way to promote the new marque was by participation in motor sport and obtained the main board's sanction for the construction of competition cars. First came a Formula 3 single-seater and this was followed by Formula 2 cars and Prototypes. As the motor racing programme developed, so did the extent of the main company's financial backing and enthusiasm. It was rare indeed to see a French car at the forefront of either Formula 1 or sports car racing, and over the years of the company's participation it did much to enhance both the international reputation of Matra and of France generally. The expense was vast, but the returns more than worthwhile.

## The M620, 1966

For 1966, Matra decided to enter a limited number of Prototype races and built three cars for this category. The basis was a multi-tubular space-frame chassis, with semi-monocoque skinning round the centre-section, independent suspension front and rear, similar to that of the team's single-seaters, the V-8 B.R.M. four overhead camshaft Grand Prix engine of 1962–65, enlarged to 1915 cc Tasman form, as used by B.R.M. themselves in Formula 1 in 1966–67 and with transmission by a 5-speed ZF gearbox. Girling disc brakes and magnesium-alloy wheels were fitted. The most striking feature of the M620 was the coupé body, with pronounced angular lines, but nevertheless the result of wind-tunnel tests in the company's aerospace department. It was hoped at least that the cars would prove mechanically reliable, because the B.R.M. engine was well tested and maintenance was left with B.R.M. themselves, in the hands of Wilkie Wilkinson, their chief mechanic. The cars first appeared at the Le Mans Practice Weekend, but no success was gained throughout the year, partly because of mechanical problems, in the main nothing to do with the engines, and partly because of a number of driver errors.

## M620 and M630, 1967

Matra had learned the hard way from their 1966 experiences, and at the 1967 Le Mans Test Weekend produced the new M630 model, with more aerodynamic bodywork, the radiators moved to each side of the car ahead of the rear wheels, a new nose very much closer to the ground, larger wheels and the later, 1998 cc

*The Matra M630-B.R.M. of Beltoise/Servoz-Gavin leads a Ford through the Esses at Le Mans in 1967. This Matra was eliminated by engine problems.* (Nigel Snowdon)

B.R.M. V-8 engine with centre exhausts. In addition the team also brought along an M620 powered by a Ford 4.7-litre V-8 engine, similar to that used in the Ford GT40. At the end of the first day's testing, the popular young French driver Roby Weber lost control of the new M630 on the Mulsanne straight, the car went off the track, rolled and burst into flames. The driver died. So far as the V-8-powered car was concerned, it was never raced in this form.

Matra did not race their latest Prototypes until Le Mans in June and at this race the cars appeared in practice with the choice of short, angular or long, tapering tails, but settled for the short tails for the race. Both cars were eliminated by minor problems. A week later, Jean-Pierre Beltoise drove one of the cars into fourth place in the 300 km Trophée d'Auvergne, despite a lot of time lost in the pits with fuel-injection problems. Another retirement followed in the Reims 12 Hours Race. In September the Matra scored its first victory when Beltoise won a minor race at Magny-Cours. By the Paris 1000 km race at Montlhéry in October, one of the M630 cars had been fitted with the Ford V-8 engine. It retired with a broken gearbox, but the 2-litre coupé driven by Jaussaud and Servoz-Gavin finished ninth overall and third in the 2-litre class.

## M630, 1968

In 1968, the new MS11 Formula 1 car with the four overhead camshaft V-12 engine with the inlets between the camshafts and a capacity of 2985 cc (79.7 × 50 mm) was ready to race. Its power output of 390 bhp at 10,500 rpm was not really sufficient for Formula 1, although the car enjoyed a good first season. It was, however, decided to adopt this engine also for Prototype racing and it was installed in one of the M630 chassis, with the tubular rear bay extensively modified and with

*The M630 with V-12 engine driven by Pescarolo/Servoz-Gavin at Le Mans in 1968. It was in third place when it retired not long before the finish.* (Nigel Snowdon)

a much restyled and more aerodynamic body. Mainly because of the team's Formula 1 commitments, it was raced only three times during the year. It retired at Spa in May, and at Le Mans, postponed until September, it ran strongly for much of the race with Servoz-Gavin and Pescarolo, despite minor problems, holding second place until near the end of the race, when a front tyre punctured on the debris from Bianchi's crashed Alpine. It suffered yet another puncture, went off the road, and an electrical fire damaged the wiring. Its third and final appearance of the year was at Montlhéry, where Beltoise and Servoz-Gavin retired with a broken oil pipe.

## M630, MS640 and MS650, 1969

By the Daytona 24 Hours Race in February 1969, Matra had built a fourth M630 coupé powered by the V-12 engine. It non-started after it was crashed badly by Pescarolo in practice. There was considerable dissension amongst the Matra team as to whether they should concentrate their efforts on open or closed cars, and eventually both were built. Two of the existing M630 cars were rebuilt with open bodywork (in this form known as *Barquettes*, as opposed to the closed *Berlinettes*). These open cars took the designation MS630/650.

The first MS630/650 appeared at the Le Mans Practice Weekend, and here Servoz-Gavin set second fastest time. Encouraged by this performance, the team entered the car in the Monza 1000 km race, but it retired with engine problems.

In the meantime work had been progressing on the new MS640 with coupé bodywork designed by consultant aerodynamicist Robert Choulet. Matra Sports were able to persuade the local police to arrange the closure of the road at Le Mans for a private testing session, but whilst Pescarolo was doing his warming up lap, he lost control on the Mulsanne straight and crashed heavily. The accident was just as inexplicable as had been Weber's, and the car was not rebuilt.

Work was progressing on a new MS650 with improved tubular chassis, and the used suspension similar to that of the MS80 Formula 1 car. This was crashed in testing at Marigny with Servoz-Gavin at the wheel because a front suspension upright broke. There was then a desperate rush to get the cars ready for Le Mans. Four cars were entered, two MS630/650s, distinguishable from the new MS650 by six-stud wheel fixing and short tails (the 650 had a longer streamlined tail and a

*Another view of the M630 seen here at Le Mans in 1969, showing its long, low, sleek lines. Driven by Guichet/Vaccarella, it finished fifth.* (Nigel Snowdon)

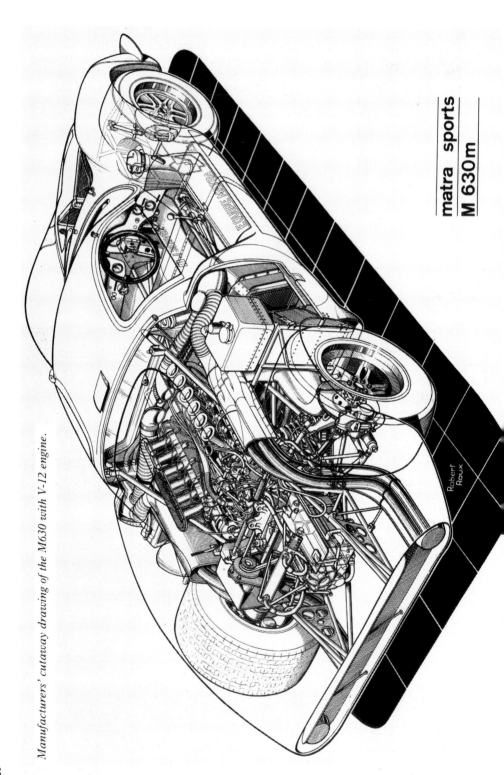

matra sports
M 630m

Robert
Roux

*Manufacturers' cutaway drawing of the M630 with V-12 engine.*

single centre-lock nut-wheel fixing), the new MS650 and an M630. Although the cars were less reliable than hoped and a long time was spent in the pits, Beltoise and Piers Courage finished fourth overall with the repaired MS650, distinguished by its long boom-like rear wings, the M630 driven by Guichet/Vaccarella was fifth and the MS630/650 of Widdows/'Nanni' Galli was seventh. The team ran at Watkins Glen and in Austria without success, but in the 1000 km race at Montlhéry in October Beltoise/Pescarolo (MS650) and Rodriguez/Redman (MS630/650) finished first and second.

### MS630/650, MS650 and MS660, 1970

In December 1969, Chrysler France acquired the Matra car division and henceforth the competition cars bore the legend 'Matra-Simca'. Matra were planning a full season of Prototype racing, but because of slow development of the new models, the season became somewhat abbreviated.

At the beginning of the year the team ran the MS630/650 for the last time in the Argentine and Beltoise/Pescarolo won the Buenos Aires 1000 km race and finished third in the 200-miles race the following weekend.

When the writer visited the Matra works at Vélizy in late 1969, Gérard Duca-

*The new 650 Matra, driven by Beltoise/Courage, finished fourth at Le Mans in 1969.*
(Nigel Snowdon)

rouge made no secret of the team's dislike of the then current racing regulations, which meant that the Matra 3-litre Prototypes were forced to run against the 5-litre Sports Cars of equally advanced concept and far greater performance. This posed a major dilemma for Matra, as their main ambition was to win at Le Mans, but at the same time their prospects of victory were far greater on slower circuits. The result was that Matra efforts in Prototype racing were comparatively restricted during 1970–71 and it was not until 1972, by when 5-litre Sports Cars were banned, that they put their maximum efforts into this class of racing.

Nevertheless Matra attracted a strong team of drivers that included Jack Brabham (and it was far from clear why he should want to drive for them), together with Beltoise, Pescarolo and Cevert. It was, however, sad to see Matra turn up at circuits with a very well-prepared team of cars and first-class drivers only to reduce their chances of success substantially by their sheer inefficiency in the pits. Only Matra (and perhaps Autodelta) could succeed in calling all three cars into the pits simultaneously for routine refuelling and driver changes, to forget to check the oil and have to call all the cars back again a lap or so later.

After running in the Championship races at Daytona, Sebring and Brands Hatch, all without any success, the team did not run again until Le Mans. Here two MS650s, together with the new MS660 with monocoque chassis, were entered, but all three cars retiring with engine failure. The team ran in only two more events during the year. In September two MS650s were modified for use on public roads with long-travel suspension, passenger accommodation of a very basic nature, sump guards and the necessary additional lighting so that they could compete in the Tour de France. The Matras took the first two places. The following month the team competed once more in the Paris 1000 km and the winners were Brabham/Cevert with Beltoise/Pescarolo fourth, both team pairings at the wheel of MS660 cars.

## MS650 and MS660, 1971

The team's Prototype racing activities this year were very restricted and in fact the MS650s made only one appearance late in the year, and then not in a racing event. Matra's short racing season was struck by tragedy right at the start, at the first round of the Championship, the Buenos Aires 1000 km race. The team had entered a single MS660 for Beltoise/Jabouille. Beltoise ran out of fuel on the circuit and whilst pushing his car back to the pits it was struck by Giunti's Ferrari. Giunti had been racing in Parkes' slipstream and was completely unsighted. The Ferrari burst into flames and the charming and able young Italian driver suffered such serious injuries and burns that he was dead on arrival at hospital. Buenos Aires was the most inefficiently organised race of the series and the cause of the accident was not so much Beltoise's obsession with getting the car back to the pits, but the blatant incompetence of the marshals in permitting him to do so. Beltoise's licence was suspended.

The team did not run again until Le Mans, where a single MS660 was entered for Chris Amon/Beltoise, and this retired on the Sunday morning with failure of the fuel injection metering unit. Gérard Larrousse took a third place at Clermont-Ferrand in the Auvergne 300 km race, but this was a very parochial event. The MS650s ran again in the Tour de France and won on the model's final appearance, Larrousse/Rive and Fiorentino/Gelin finishing first and retiring respectively. In October only a single MS660 for Beltoise/Amon was entered in the Paris 1000 km race. It led until just before the second round of refuelling stops, took the lead

*Only this single MS660 was entered at Le Mans in 1971 for Beltoise/Amon, but it retired on the Sunday morning with fuel metering problems when in third place.* (Nigel Snowdon)

again, but was eliminated when Beltoise, troubled by gearbox problems, lost control and crashed.

## MS660 and MS670, 1972

Although Matra had originally planned a full season in 1972, now that there was a 3-litre capacity limit they took a look at the opposition, which was in effect the flat-12 Ferraris, and decided to restrict their entry to one event only, Le Mans, which was the obvious goal for any French constructor.

The team entered four cars, a modified MS660, known as the MS660C, which had reprofiled bodywork and revised suspension and was driven by Jabouille/David Hobbs, while three of the brand new MS670 cars were driven by Amon/Beltoise, Cevert/Howden Ganley and Pescarolo/Graham Hill. The main changes to the MS670 were 13 in. front wheels (permitting the use of a lower nose section), 8 ft 4 in. wheel base (two inches longer than that of the MS660), four Marchal headlamps (instead of two) and Girling disc brakes (instead of ATE). Two of the cars, those driven by Cevert/Ganley and Beltoise/Amon, had the latest MS72

*In 1972 Matra ran only at Le Mans and took the first two places. This is the winning MS670 driven by Henri Pescarolo/Graham Hill.* (Nigel Snowdon)

*Second place in 1972 went to this long-tail MS670 driven by François Cevert (seen here at the wheel) and Howden Ganley.* (Nigel Snowdon)

engine with narrower angle valves and steel instead of titanium conrods. The new engine developed 450 bhp at 8400 rpm, was more economical and in theory more reliable. Ferrari had the Prototype championship in the bag and decided to miss the race, so Matra was virtually unopposed apart from their own fragility and poor pit work. Although the Beltoise/Amon car blew its engine just after the start, and Jabouille/Hobbs retired with gearbox trouble, Pescarolo/Hill and Cevert/Ganley took the first two places.

*This view of the second-place car in the pits with Ganley at the wheel emphasizes the twin-boom styling of the tail.* (Nigel Snowdon)

## The MS670B, 1973

With victory at Le Mans under their belt, Matra withdrew from Formula 1 and concentrated on Endurance racing. Although the engine department remained at Vélizy, the main racing department was transferred to the Ricard-Castellet circuit and engine development work resulted in power rising to over 500 bhp, but the engines were still far from reliable and often would break unexpectedly. Steady development work on the cars continued throughout the year and the team used both ZF and Hewland DG300 gearboxes.

Throughout the year the main opposition came from the flat-12 Ferraris, but Ferrari's greatest year had been 1972 and the pace of Matra development was such that Matra now had the edge. At the beginning of the season only a single MS670 was sent to Daytona for Beltoise/Cevert/Pescarolo, but it retired with engine problems. Victories followed at Vallelunga, where Pescarolo/Larrousse were the winners, and at Dijon, where Pescarolo/Larrousse won again. Ferrari won at Monza, Spa (where Pescarolo/Larrousse were third) and the Nürburgring.

At Le Mans Matra again entered four cars. Three of these were new MS670Bs with long tails, an endplate and rear wings supported by centre posts. The fourth car was an earlier MS670. Although two of the Matra entries retired, Pescarolo/Larrousse won with one of the new 670B cars, with Jabouille/Jaussaud in third place. Further victories followed in the Österreichring 1000 km race by Larrousse/Pescarolo, who also won the Watkins Glen 6 Hours race. There remained one round in the Championship, at Buenos Aires, but this race was cancelled, and so Matra-Simca won the Championship.

At long last French motor racing was regaining its self-respect and both Larrousse and Pescarolo were awarded the *Legion d'Honneur* by the French President.

## MS670B and MS680, 1974

For 1974, the high cost of racing resulted in Matra Sports accepting sponsorship from Gitanes cigarettes. The task ahead was now much easier, because Ferrari had withdrawn from Prototype racing at the end of 1973. The result was complete domination by Matra, and it must be recognized that under the control of Ducarouge the team was now very well organized and efficient. Although retirements occurred, particularly at Le Mans, where two cars retired right at the start of the race because of badly fitted gudgeon pin circlips, Matra's strength was reliability in the face of much weakened opposition.

The first race of the year was the Monza 1000 km, in which the Matras retired with engine problems and victory went to the Alfa Romeo team. From then on it was a Matra-dominated year, starting with a win by Jacky Ickx/Jarier at Spa with the new revised MS670C car, powered by the new and more powerful MS73 V-12 engine, the Hewland TL200 gearbox/final drive unit, revised suspension and modified body with slit nose air intake. Beltoise had declined to drive at the Spa circuit, but he returned to the team at the Nürburgring and scored another Matra win, partnered by Jarier. At Imola the Matra 670C of Pescarolo/Larrousse was the winner and this pair also won at Le Mans with the newly built MS670B, chassis number 06, built for this race and not used again. At this race there also appeared the new MS680, with side-mounted radiators replacing the radiators in the nose, but it retired with engine failure at midnight. Pescarolo/Larrousse also won the Österreichring 1000 km race at the end of June, whilst Beltoise/Jarier were the winners at Watkins Glen. The victory parade rolled on with a win by Beltoise/Ja-

*The winning Matra-Simca MS670C of Beltoise/Jarier in the 1974 British Airways 1000 Km race at Brands Hatch. Matra withdrew from racing at the end of that year.* (Nigel Snowdon)

rier, with Pescarolo/Larrousse second, in the Paul Ricard 1000 km race, the same pair winning from the same team-mates in the British Airways 1000 km race at Brands Hatch at the end of September and, finally, Pescarolo/Larrousse winning the Kyalami 9 Hours race in November from Beltoise/Jarier.

In the Championship Matra-Simca scored an overwhelming victory with 140 points, way ahead of their nearest rivals, Gulf-Ford, with 81 points. It had been an impressive succession of wins for Matra, not always in the face of the strongest opposition, but there is no better time to withdraw from racing than when enjoying a winning streak. Matra no longer has any involvement with motor racing in any form.

# Mirage (United Kingdom)

In late 1966 John Wyer lost control of the development of the works competition Fords and, in partnership with John Willment, formed a new company known as JW Automotive Engineering Ltd. This company took over from Ford Advance Vehicles the works at Slough and the responsibility for the manufacture of the road-going and Group 4 versions of the GT40. However, Wyer also entered a very successful arrangement with the Gulf Oil concern that was to last for many years. It initially consisted of building improved versions of the GT40 for endurance racing, but there followed firstly 3-litre Mirage Prototypes, then the works Porsche 917s and later a further range of Mirage Sports Cars. In addition, as described in an earlier section of this book, Wyer enjoyed an immense run of success with Gulf-sponsored GT40s in 1968–69 after the works had withdrawn from racing. In a sense everything that Wyer achieved, and the achievement was considerable, between 1967 and 1971 more than balanced the many failures that he had suffered as racing manager and later technical director of Aston Martin, when his efforts to run a serious world-beating team of sports cars was so often frustrated by the whims and wishes of David Brown.

## M1, 1967

The Mirage M1, a name apparently chosen because it could be pronounced in so many different languages and with a designation that was only applied later, was a modified version of the standard GT40. The cars were finished in the distinctive Gulf colours of pale blue with an orange stripe down the centre. Gulf had been encouraged by Wyer's success in running a team of Group 4 GT40s for the Essex Wire Corporation in 1966, managed by former Vanwall team manager David Yorke.

Early in the season the team had fielded a standard GT40, but the new Mirage first appeared at the Le Mans Test Weekend. The Mirage retained the lower steel structure of the GT40, but the upper part of the body in aluminium had a reduced frontal area and a different cockpit of more rounded shape with sloping side windows. Wyer continued to use the ZF 5-speed gearbox as on the production cars, very large disc brakes were fitted and the front ones had large, flexible air hoses which led to aluminium 'muffs' over the braking surface. At Le Mans the cars had the standard Ford 4.7-litre engines. By the Monza 1000 km race at the end of April two cars appeared with 5-litre engines and the following weekend at Spa Jacky Ickx/Dick Thompson won the 1000 km race with a Mirage fitted with a 5.7-litre

*The B.R.M.-powered Mirage in the pits before its race debut in the 1969 BOAC 500 Miles race.* (Nigel Snowdon)

engine, fully modified by American engine developers Holman and Moody. Later in the year the Mirages scored outright wins in the Paris 1000 km race at Montlhéry and in the Kyalami 9 Hours race. Neither of these events were rounds in the Championship, but because the Commission Sportive Internationale regarded the Mirage as a separate make, the team's victory at Spa could not count towards Ford's total in the Championship and as a result the Championship winners were Ferrari.

## M2/300, 1969

John Wyer had raced his very successful GT40 cars throughout 1968 and retained them for 1969, running them in the first three rounds of the Championship and, because of their reliability, fielding them at Le Mans in June. However, work had been proceeding since 1967, when it first became known that there would be a 3-litre capacity limit for Prototypes in 1968, on a new Mirage designated the M2/300. This was the work of Len Terry and featured an aluminium-alloy central monocoque section with extensions running to the rear to carry the engine. The fuel, with a capacity of 26.5 gallons, was carried in tanks in the side pontoons of the monocoque. Front suspension was by double wishbones and coil spring/damper units, while at the rear there were single top links, lower parallel links, twin radius arms and coil spring/damper units. Transmission was by a ZF 5-speed all-synchromesh gearbox in unit with the final drive. To power the new car, Wyer chose the B.R.M. 60-degree V-12 engine with a capacity of 2999.5 cc (73.81 × 57.15 mm). This design featured chain-driven twin overhead camshafts per bank of cylinders and, in its original form, two valves per cylinder. With Lucas fuel injection power output was around 375 bhp.

The new Mirage had been designed to comply with the 1968 Prototype regulations, which imposed minimum windscreen height, ground clearance, cockpit width, and all-up weight. Accordingly by the time that the new car was raced in

*In the BOAC race the Mirage was driven by Jacky Ickx/Jack Oliver, but it retired because of a broken drive-shaft.* (Nigel Snowdon)

*Jacky Ickx with the Mirage M3 accelerates away at the start of the 1969 Austrian 1000 Km race. To his right is Bonnier's Lola. The Mirage retired because of a broken steering column bracket. (LAT)*

1969, with its rather bulky coupé body, distinguished by radiators mounted either side ahead of the rear wheels, and the usual Gulf blue and orange colours, it was already outdated.

Initial testing had taken place as long ago as the summer of 1968, but development was slowed after Robin Widdows crashed heavily with the first car. It was tested again at Daytona in January 1969, but it was not raced until the BOAC 500 Race at Brands Hatch in April. It was driven by Jacky Ickx/Jack Oliver and retired because of a broken drive-shaft. The team next appeared at Spa, where two of the new Mirages were entered, and whilst Ickx/Oliver retired, the slower car of Hobbs/Hailwood finished seventh. At the Nürburgring 1000 km race, Wyer produced two new variants of the Mirage. One of these, with redesigned rear chassis strengthened by riveted box-section members and with a new space-frame extension, housed a Cosworth-Ford DFV V-8 Formula 1 engine driving through a Hewland 5-speed gearbox. The second car was fitted with the latest and rather more powerful 48-valve version of the B.R.M. engine said to develop around 450 bhp. The engine had been loaned by B.R.M. and was used only in this one race. Once again both cars retired.

By Watkins Glen, Wyer had produced the new M3/300 car, basically similar to the earlier model, but with the combined roof and tail-section removed to produce a neat-looking Spyder of lower weight and with reduced frontal area, Ford-Cosworth engine and Hewland gearbox. In the American race it was obvious that its handling needed sorting very badly, and after a slow race it was retired with loss of oil pressure. By the Austrian 1000 km race Wyer had sorted the handling of the M3 and Ickx led the race until forced to retire with a broken steering column bracket. Later in the year Ickx scored the Mirage-Cosworth's only race victory in the non-Championship Imola 500 km event.

In late 1969, John Wyer received an approach to run the works Porsche 917s in 1970–71 and so the Mirage M2s and M3s were not again raced by the works.

## M6, 1972

By late 1971, when Wyer's contract with Porsche had terminated, and development work was well advanced on a new Mirage, the M6, entered under the banner of the Gulf Research Racing concern and designed by Len Bailey. There was no M4, and the designation M5 had been used on a proposed production single-seater for Formula Ford.

The M6 was based on a monocoque chassis constructed from 18- and 20-gauge aluminium alloy skinning, with reinforced mild steel sub-structures. The monocoque terminated at the rear of the cockpit, there were large side pontoons carrying the ancillary equipment and a 160-litre fuel tank each side. Although the team had hoped to use the new Weslake-designed Ford V-12 engine, this failed to materialize in 1972 and so the team relied on the Ford-Cosworth DFV unit. This acted as a stressed member and was bolted to the steel rear bulkhead. Because the team was still hoping to use the V-12 engine when it became available, there was a 6.125 in. spacer between the clutch and the Hewland DG300 5-speed gearbox. Front suspension was by lower wishbones, fabricated top links and outboard coil spring/damper units. At the rear there were twin parallel lower links, single top links, twin trailing and outboard coil spring/damper units. Girling disc brakes were hub-mounted front and rear and the water radiator was also front-mounted. A very short nose curving upwards to deflect air over the cockpit area was fitted and there was an engine cover designed to deflect non-turbulent air under the large, raised, fully adjustable rear wing.

*In the 1972 Spa 1000 Km race Derek Bell/Gijs van Lennep finished fourth, despite a misfiring engine in the closing laps of the race.* (Nigel Snowdon)

The new car first appeared at Sebring, but both here and at Brands Hatch it was plagued by teething problems. The team missed the Monza race, but at Spa, Derek Bell/Gijs van Lennep finished fourth, despite a misfiring engine in the closing stages of the race. The team next ran at the Nürburgring, where Bell/van Lennep gained another fourth place, although they were not running at the finish because the engine had blown. Mirage missed Le Mans and next ran at the Austrian race, where Bell/van Lennep were eliminated by an engine misfire. By the Watkins Glen 6 Hours race the team was able to field two cars, both fitted with larger radiators. Bell/Pace finished third, but the other car was eliminated by gearbox failure. All in all it had been an encouraging season for a team working on a very small budget.

## M6, 1973

The team continued to race the M6 in 1973, but there were hopes that the Weslake-Ford WRP190 engine would be available. This was a V-12 with a capacity of 2995 cc (75 × 56.5 mm) with twin gear-driven overhead camshafts per bank of cylinders, four valves per cylinder, Lucas fuel injection, transistor ignition and a claimed power output of 460 bhp at 10,600 rpm. It had been planned to run one of these cars at Daytona, but although there had been no problems in pre-race testing, once at the circuit there were gearbox troubles, caused apparently by the oil pump location. Accordingly two V-8 Ford-powered cars were run, but both retired. At the Le Mans Test Weekend the Gulf team produced a dramatically styled coupé, with long tail surmounted by twin tail fins bridged by a fixed aerofoil, and powered by the V-12 engine. Unfortunately during both days' testing the car was plagued by problems, fuel feed on the Saturday and electrical on the Sunday. As a result of

*At Le Mans in 1973 this M6 Mirage driven by Hailwood/Watson/Schuppan was eliminated when young Vern Schuppan crashed.* (Nigel Snowdon)

these tests and tests elsewhere, Wyer decided that the car had no future and it was not raced.

By the Dijon race in April the team had realised that the V-12 engine was unlikely to prove satisfactory that year and concentrated their efforts on the V-8. In France Mike Hailwood/Vern Schuppan (replacing John Watson, who had broken a leg in a Formula 1 accident) finished fifth overall, nine laps in arrears of the winning Matra. At long last at Spa-Francorchamps in the 1000 km race the following month good fortune shone on the Gulf team. Mainly because of the shortcomings of the Ferrari and Matra teams, the Mirage M6s of Bell/Hailwood and Schuppan/Ganley took the first two places. Gulf missed the Nürburgring 1000 km race to concentrate on preparations for Le Mans, but the team was again out of luck in the 24 Hours race. Although the car of Hailwood/Watson/Schuppan held third place at one time, it dropped back and was eliminated when Schuppan crashed. The other car, shared by Bell/Ganley, later retired with gearbox failure. Later in the year Hailwood/Watson and Bell/Ganley finished fourth and fifth in the Austrian 1000 km race at the Österreichring and these placings were repeated at Watkins Glen, where Bell/Ganley were fourth and Hailwood/Watson were fifth. Gulf-Mirage took fourth place in the World Championship of Makes. It could hardly be regarded as a successful season, despite the win at Spa, because the cars were certainly no match for either Ferrari or Matra, mainly because they were overweight, and the Gulf team really lacked the resources to take on this strength of opposition.

## The GR7, 1974

Throughout 1974 the Gulf team raced the improved Gulf GR7 (formerly the Gulf-Mirage M6). Weight had been reduced by some 140 lb due to the use of many titanium components. The drive-shafts had been changed to permit greater suspension movement, the suspension pick-up points had been redesigned and there was a low-drag air-box. On the slower circuits the cars were completely outclassed

*James Hunt 'yumping' at the Nürburgring in 1974 with the Gulf GR7 that he, Vern Schuppan and Derek Bell drove into fourth place.* (Nigel Snowdon)

by the Matras, but provided a reasonable degree of opposition on the very fast circuits such as Spa and the Österreichring. Throughout the year Derek Bell proved a tower of strength to the team, but all his hard work did them little good. During the year a new car appeared at Brands Hatch in September, and this featured revised rear suspension and the engine moved more to the centre of the car. The sum total of the team's successes were fourth place at Monza by Hailwood/Bell, a very encouraging second place by Hailwood/Bell at Spa, a circuit well suited to the car, fourth by James Hunt/Schuppan/Bell at the Nürburgring, fourth at Le Mans by Hailwood/Bell, fourth again by these drivers at the Österreichring, third at the Paul Ricard circuit in August, third by Bell/Hobbs at Brands Hatch and to round off the year a third place by Bell/Hobbs at Kyalami. The season had been completely dominated by Matra, who had won nine of the year's ten races, but Gulf-Ford finished second in the Championship, but with little more than half the points accumulated by the winners.

## The GR8, 1975

In 1975 the Gulf team contested Le Mans only, that year a race in which the organizers set their own regulations concerning fuel consumption, and as a result the race was excluded from the World Championship of Makes. For Le Mans Gulf prepared two GR8 cars powered by Cosworth-Ford V-8 DFV engines prepared by and detuned specifically by the team itself. This meant that the drivers were only using around 8000–8400 rpm compared with the 10,400 rpm the previous year. Although the basic design of the chassis was retained, the wheelbase was lengthened and there was a completely new body shape openly cribbed from the success-

*In 1975 Gulf entered only the Le Mans 24 Hours race and, in the face of negligible opposition, took first and third places with their GR8 cars. This is the winning GR8 of Derek Bell/Jacky Ickx. (Nigel Snowdon)*

ful turbocharged Alpine, and this resulted in a much reduced drag coefficiency. Because the race was not a round in the Championship, the entry was not so competitive and Derek Bell/Jacky Ickx won the race by a lap from a Ligier-Ford. The second Gulf driven by Jaussaud/Schuppan finished third, after delays caused by an inexplicable vibration.

## Postscript

At the end of the year Gulf Oil withdrew its support from the team, which was acquired by American Harley Cluxton, a lawyer and Ferrari dealer. He concentrated the team's efforts on Le Mans. Mirage ran the GR8 at Le Mans in 1976 and this Cosworth-powered car driven by Lafosse/Migault took second place. In 1977 the car was revised as the M9 and was now powered by a Renault V-6 turbocharged engine. This was driven to second place at Le Mans by Schuppan/Jarier behind the Porsche 936 of Ickx/Barth/Haywood. Two Renault-powered Mirages ran at Le Mans again in 1978, with lower, short and narrower chassis. The car driven by Leclerc/Posey retired with a broken alternator early in the race, while Laffite/Schuppan, despite many problems, eventually finished tenth. Harley Cluxton returned to Le Mans in 1979 with his Mirage team, now having reverted to Cosworth-Ford DFV power. Again the team was out of luck; one of the revised M10 cars retired because of failure of its new ZF gearbox and the other car, driven by Schuppan/Bell, struggled on to shortly before the finish of the race, leading the field, despite electrical problems. Schuppan crashed into a guard-rail when the engine failed shortly before the finish and the car was not classified. Mirage missed the Le Mans race in 1980, although it had been planned to run cars with Cosworth DFX turbocharged engines. The team returned to Le Mans for the final time in 1982. There had been a flat-out race to prepare two new M12 coupés of superb aerodynamic appearance, with monocoque constructed by Tiga Cars, Kevlar and

173

glass-fibre bodywork designed by team manager John Horsman, Cosworth DFL V-8 engine and Hewland DG 5-speed gearbox. Only one car could be made ready in time for the race and this was to be driven by Mario Andretti, together with his son Michael. Unfortunately Horsman had made the most enormous blunder and the scrutineers discovered during a random check that the gearbox oil cooler was located, illegally, behind the gearbox. Apparently the Mirage team was only told an hour before the race, and although the oil cooler was hurriedly repositioned, the M12 was not allowed to start. It was a sad end to a long racing history.

# Morgan Plus-4 Super Sports (United Kingdom)

The Morgan Company of Malvern in Worcestershire had a long history of building 3-wheelers and it was not until 1936 that 4-wheelers were also built. Morgans had run at Le Mans before the war, but although they were, and still are, fine traditional sports cars, they have not been fast enough for international long-distance racing. There was, however, a major exception to this, in 1962, when Chris Lawrence ran at Le Mans with his Plus-4.

Lawrence had been racing Plus-4s, as did many other drivers, in British events for a number of years, but he persuaded the Morgan factory that they should build a higher-performance version of their Plus-4, normally powered by the Triumph TR4, 2138 cc 4-cylinder engine, developing 100 bhp at 4600 rpm. The result was the Super Sports announced in March 1961. This featured light-alloy body and wings as standard, together with the Lawrencetune engine modified by Westerham Motors, Lawrence's business, with polished and gas-flowed cylinder head, raised compression ratio, high-lift camshaft, cast-iron inlet manifold, four-branch exhaust manifold and two 42 or 45 Weber DCOE carburettors. In this form engine capacity was 2196 cc and power output was boosted to 125 bhp at 5500 rpm. As

*A typical racing Lawrencetune Plus-4 of the 1960s – said to be the spare car at the Nürburgring in 1963.* (The Author's Collection)

*Gordon Spice at the wheel of a Morgan Plus-4 SLR at the European Grand Prix meeting at Brands Hatch in 1964. He is leading a Lotus Elan.* (T. C. March)

raced by many private owners, the cars were extensively modified, with further engine modifications, a Daimler SP250 clutch housing, sometimes Jaguar E-type suspension uprights and, occasionally, a hard top manufactured by Lawrence in glass-fibre with perspex rear window and flock lining.

During 1962 the Plus-4s enjoyed a good run of success. In the Spa Grand Prix Richard Shepherd-Barron finished second with his Super Sports to a Porsche in the Class for GT cars over 1300 cc and below 2000 cc. At Le Mans Chris Lawrence, partnered by Richard Shepherd-Barron with Lawrence's old car TOK 258, but with full Super Sports modifications plus, finished 13th overall and won the 2-litre class at an average of 93.97 mph, having covered a total distance of 2255 miles. In the Tourist Trophy at Goodwood, Chris Lawrence finished eighth overall and second in his class.

In 1963 Morgan successes continued. In the Spa 500 km race Lawrence entered a team of three cars and Lawrence himself and Arnold took the first two places in the 2500 cc class. The team then moved on to the Nürburgring for the 1000 km race and again three cars were entered. The team also had a spare car at this race and mention of this will be made later. Although well down the field at the finish, the Morgans of Slotemaker/Braithwaite and Arnold/Carnegie took the first two places in the 2500 cc GT class. Despite their success in 1962, the Morgans did not run at Le Mans and they were completely out of the picture in the Tourist Trophy at Goodwood. Although the Super Sports was available until January 1968, its days as a competition car in international racing were over. At a national level, in Britain and elsewhere, Morgans of all types have continued to be raced widely, and they still form a sound, relatively inexpensive and easy-to-maintain car for the club driver.

During the years 1965–1967 the writer competed in club events with a Plus-4

Super Sports, said to be the Lawrence spare car at the Nürburgring. For its basically simple concept, it was amazingly quick, but at a price. The normal very stiff, very uncomfortable ride of the Morgan suspension was made even more extreme by competition dampers, and the 4-cylinder Triumph engine was so highly tuned that the most prominent features were its sheer noise and vibration. High noise level was exaggerated by the reverberance from the hard top and the level of vibration was such that the normal Morgan tendency to self-destruct its wood-framed body was greatly increased. For financial reasons it was always driven to meetings on the road, but it was a totally unsuitable car for road use and in reality should have gone everywhere on a trailer. This Super Sports, 208 FOJ, is one of the few of the type to remain in the United Kingdom and is owned by an enthusiast in Shropshire, albeit now minus its hard top, and is likely to be seen in Classic events during 1988.

Alongside his racing programme with Morgans, Chris Lawrence had developed his own car, the Deep Sanderson Prototype, which was to prove unsuccessful, but he was still keen to go on racing Morgans and was seeking something more competitive for international racing. One of the real problems with the Morgan was that its aerodynamics were little better than those of a brick wall and it was in this direction that improvement was sought. In collaboration with John Sprinzel, Lawrence undertook the construction of the Morgan S.L.R. (Sprinzel Lawrence-tune Racing), an aerodynamic coupé version of the Super Sports designed jointly by Sprinzel and Lawrence and constructed in aluminium by Williams and Pritch-ard. The cars remained eligible for Grand Touring racing because the regulations permitted a change in the bodywork of the original car, provided that weight was not reduced by more than 15 per cent. In all four of these cars were built, three on Morgan chassis and one on a Triumph TR4 chassis. Although these cars were widely raced, they achieved very little in the way of success.

# Nomad (United Kingdom)

Motor racing is a difficult business for any small team to break into, but the Nomad financed and driven by Mark Konig, a former Lotus driver, came close to achieving success. The design was the work of Konig's mechanic Bob Curl and was designed specifically for Group 6 Prototype racing. It was a mid-engine design, with a multi-tubular space-frame chassis built from 1 and 1.5 in. 16- and 18-gauge round tubing, front suspension by wide-base double wishbones and coil spring/damper units, with at the rear single top links, wide-based lower wishbones, twin radius arms and coil spring/damper units. Girling disc brakes were mounted front and rear. The maximum fuel capacity permitted under the regulations of 90 litres was carried in two glass-fibre-clad aluminium side tanks. In its original form the engine was a Ford 1600 cc twin-cam developed and modified by engine tuner Chris Steele, with a Hewland 5-speed gear box and final drive. The radiator was mounted in the nose of the car. Whilst Bob Curl designed the body, an elegant, handsome coupé, it was built in aluminium panelling by Williams & Pritchard.

The new car made its debut at the Crystal Palace at the end of May 1967, driven by Konig, but this was merely a shakedown race and it finished well down the field. Shortly afterwards, in June, Konig finished seventh in the Auvergne 300 km race at Clermont-Ferrand and won the 1600 cc class. With Rollo Fielding as co-driver, Konig was holding a class second in the Reims 12 Hours race when the clutch failed only 45 minutes before the finish. Later in the year, the car ran in the Mugello 4 Hours road race, finishing 12th, and third in the 1600 cc Prototype class, the

*The Mk 1 Nomad-B.R.M. of Jackson/Crabtree in the 1969 BOAC 500 Miles race at Brands Hatch. This Nomad finished at the tail of the field in 22nd place.* (Guy Griffiths)

Nürburgring 500 km race, where it retired, and, with Lanfranchi as co-driver in the Paris 1000 km race at Montlhéry in which it won its class. All this was quite promising for a new car's first season, especially when it was in effect an amateur project rather than the product of a professional racing team. There were, however, basic problems with the design, for it was too big and too heavy.

For 1968 Konig concentrated on the reduction of weight, and the Nomad was fitted with glass-fibre nose, tail and doors, and wider rear wheels were now adopted. The small team started the year with an entry in the Daytona 24 Hours race and although, with Konig partnered by Lanfranchi, the car finished the race, it was well down the field. By the BOAC 500 Miles race at Brands Hatch in April, the Nomad had been fitted with the lighter Hewland FT gearbox and an 1800 cc engine. It ran strongly in the 2-litre class until the crankshaft broke after an hour's racing. The team then tackled the Targa Florio road race, but again finished well down the field. Retirements followed in two other international races, on both occasions because of engine trouble. Accordingly the team decided to adopt a B.R.M. V-8 1498 cc engine and 6-speed gearbox. Both reliability and performance were much improved. Konig finished sixth overall and second in his class in August at the Jyllandsring in Denmark; in the Nürburgring 500 km race, where the car was fitted with a larger radiator and oil cooler to cure overheating problems, he took a good fifth place; and shortly afterwards he was seventh (and third in his class) in the Imola 500 km race. He rounded off the season with 14th place, with Lanfranchi as co-driver, in the Paris 1000 km race.

Konig persevered with the Nomad in 1969 and built a new Mk 2 version, selling the existing car. Although the new car followed the basic chassis design of the Mk 1, Bob Curl took full advantage of the relaxation in the Prototype rules so far as weight and windscreen height were concerned. The new car was an open *Spyder*, with ultra-light glass-fibre body. The chassis incorporated a number of B.R.M. components, including suspension uprights and wheels, and the engine was the 2-litre B.R.M. V-8 developing 250 bhp at 9500 rpm, used in conjunction with a Hewland FT400 gearbox. At the start of the season the car had a long, sweeping tail and in this form it was raced in the Targa Florio (where Konig was partnered by his wife, Gabrielle), but they were eliminated by suspension damage following a puncture. Other failures followed at the Martini International meeting at Silverstone and at Le Mans. At this point in the season it was decided to abandon the long, sweeping tail, and the Nomad now appeared with new rear bodywork cut off immediately behind the rear wheels and was also fitted with wider rims. Very little success was

*At Le Mans in 1969 the Nomad Mk 2 of Konig/Lanfranchi holds up the Ferrari 312P of Rodriguez/Piper, with its headlamps ablaze, through the Esses.* (Nigel Snowdon)

enjoyed during the remainder of the year, but Konig and Lanfranchi finished fifth overall (and first 2000 cc car across the line) in the Madrid 6 Hours race.

In 1970 Konig was offering the Mk 2 as a rolling chassis at £3188 or £5900 with a B.R.M. 2-litre engine, but there were no takers. Although he retained his Mk 2, he had built for himself a new Mk 3 car, with smaller chassis tubes, much lighter glass-fibre body, modified suspension, Hewland FG400 gearbox and Brabham wheels.

In the BOAC 500 km race at Brands Hatch the Mk 2 Nomad was leading its class when Lanfranchi crashed during the final hour of the race. The Mk 3 appeared at the Martini International meeting at Silverstone, but Lanfranchi was eliminated by a misfiring engine. Konig reappeared with the Mk 2 in the Vila Real 500 km race in Portugal and finished fourth. Several other continental outings were made during the year and in the winter Konig competed in the Springbok series of races in South Africa with the Mk 3, but without success.

By 1971 Konig had decided to give up the uphill struggle and the Nomad project was abandoned.

# *Porsche (Germany)*

Almost from the appearance of the first aluminium-bodied 356 coupé built at Gmünd in Austria in 1948, Porsches have been raced. The first real competition sports car built by the factory, following the appearance of prototype cars in 1953, was the 550 *Spyder*, which was introduced in 1954 and from the end of that year became available to private owners. Throughout the years of the Sports Car Championship, 1953–61, Porsche entries, both works and from private owners, achieved immense racing success in their class, and sometimes, when the larger-capacity opposition fell by the wayside, scored outright victories. The 550 and it successors were not only extremely competitive in, initially, the 1500 cc class and later with enlarged engines, but they were superbly reliable, they handled well and they were perfect endurance racers. When they appeared in short-circuit British events against the Cooper and Lotus opposition they were outclassed, but they were built for a different sort of racing from these British lightweights. It was after the introduction of the Prototype Championship in 1962 that Porsche competition activities really flourished and since then there has been an unbroken epoch of competition entries by the Zuffenhausen factory and it is now without doubt that Porsche is the most successful of all entrants in post-war sports car and endurance racing. During 1962 Porsche raced a development of the RS 61 model, based on the earlier *Typ* 718, itself a successor to the original 550 *Spyder*. In their original form these cars were powered by the usual mid-mounted 4-cylinder *Typ* 547 engine of 1587 cc or 1498 cc. By 1962 the cars had been modified to take the new 8-cylinder horizontally opposed engine developed by Porsche for Formula 1 in 1494 cc form, but enlarged for Prototype racing to 2 litres. This engine featured four twin-choke Weber carburettors, twin plugs per cylinder fired by four Bosch coils and transmission by a 6-speed gearbox mounted behind the final drive.

## The RS61, 1962

The new 8-cylinder cars first appeared in the 1962 Targa Florio, but were plagued by problems with their new disc brakes; Dan Gurney crashed the open model, and Vaccarella/Bonnier could manage no better than third place with a coupé, behind two Ferraris. Another third place followed at the Nürburgring, where Graham Hill/Hans Herrmann finished third. Because of the company's preoccupation with its Formula 1 programme, there were no 8-cylinder entries at Le Mans. At the end of the year the cars appeared on the western side of the Atlantic and a few places were taken, including sixth by Bonnier in the Canadian Sports Car Grand Prix and fourth in the North-Western Grand Prix at Pacific Raceway, Gurney was third in the Puerto Rican Grand Prix and Holbert finished second in the Governor's Trophy race at Nassau.

*In 1962 this 2-litre 8-cylinder Porsche coupé painted Italian red and entered by the Scuderia Serenissima Republica di Venezia was driven into third place in the Targa Florio by Nino Vaccarella and Joakim Bonnier. (LAT)*

*The start at Le Mans in 1962 with the Abarth-Carreras of Pon/de Beaufort (30) and Buchet/Schiller (35) well to the fore. Other cars to be seen are the Sunbeam Alpine of Harper/Procter (32), the Ferrari 250GTO of 'Elde'/'Beurlys' (22), the Jaguar E-type of Cunningham/Salvadori (10) and the A.C. Ace-Bristol of Magne/Martin (60).* (David Phipps)

## The RS61, 1963

At the end of 1962, Porsche had withdrawn from Formula 1 racing, disappointed after a season during which the team had won only one Championship Grand Prix and one minor race, at Solitude. This resulted in greater efforts and facilities being available for the 1963 Prototype season, and rather more success was enjoyed. With a coupé 8-cylinder car, Bonnier/Abate won the difficult Targa Florio from the Dino Ferrari shared by Bandini/Scarfiotti/Mairesse. Two 8-cylinder cars were entered at the Nürburgring, and although the coupé of Bonnier/Phil Hill took the lead, Hill crashed; the other 8-cylinder entry was already out of the race with rear axle failure. The same two 8-cylinder cars appeared at Le Mans and although Linge/Barth finished eighth and won their class with the open car, Bonnier went off the road with the coupé.

## The RS61 and 904, 1964

When the new *Typ* 904 Carrera GTS first appeared in the 1964 Sebring 12 Hours race, it represented a major turning point in Porsche competition history, and was the model from which the long line of successful race winning cars of the later 60s and early 70s flowed. The chassis was a simple pressed steel frame formed from rectangular-section longitudinal and cross-members. Suspension at the front was

*The 8-cylinder Porsche that was driven to victory in the 1963 Targa Florio by Bonnier/Abate, but here at the Nürburgring Phil Hill rolled it on the first lap.* (LAT)

*Barth/Linge drove this 8-cylinder* Spyder *into eighth place at Le Mans in 1963.* (Nigel Snowden)

by unequal-length wishbones, with, at the rear, wishbones, twin forward-facing radius rods and coil springs. The engine was the familiar 587 Carrera, but, in the 904, installed ahead of the rear-axle line and with a new 5-speed gearbox behind the axle line. There was a single-plate clutch and ZF limited slip differential. In racing form power output of the 1966 cc flat-four engine was 180 bhp at 7000 rpm. For this model Porsche adopted a glass-fibre reinforced plastic coupé body, built for the company by Heinkel.

In the Sebring 12 Hours race, the private 904 of Underwood/Briggs Cunningham finished ninth overall and won its class. At the Le Mans Test Weekend in April the works produced a 904, unchanged externally, but fitted with the flat-eight 2-litre engine. Very shortly afterwards two 4-cylinder 904s driven by Pucci/Davis and Linge/Balzarini finished first and second in the Targa Florio, whilst a 904 with the 8-cylinder engine, driven by Barth/Maglioli, took sixth place. In this race the team also entered the 1963 8-cylinder open car for Bonnier/Graham Hill, but this broke a drive-shaft coupling. This was the last occasion on which the 1963 8-cylinder cars were raced, but they continued to enjoy a limited career in the European Hill Climb Championship. As more and more of the 904 cars were delivered to private owners, so they enjoyed an immense run of success, and performances during the year included a fifth place by Barth (works car) in the 2000 cc class at Spa, third place by Pon/Koch at the Nürburgring (with a works 8-cylinder 904 fifth after throttle problems), seventh place and a class win at Le Mans (there were five 904 starters and five finishers in this race, but both 8-cylinder works 904s retired), fifth, sixth and seventh places in the Reims 12 Hours race and third place in October in the Paris 1000 km race by Barth/Davis with the 8-cylinder car.

*What seems to have been the coupé crashed by Hill at the Nürburgring was driven at Le Mans in 1963 by Bonnier/Maggs, but was again eliminated in an accident.* (Nigel Snowdon)

## The 904, 1965

At the beginning of the year the 904 achieved a remarkable performance; in the Monte Carlo Rally a 904 driven by Böhringer/Wutherich finished second overall. Fifth places and class wins were gained by private owners both in the Daytona 2000 km and Sebring races. By the Targa Florio, the works Porsche team were not only

*The Targa Florio in 1964 was won by this 4-cylinder 904 Porsche driven by Colin Davis/Antonio Pucci. (LAT)*

*At Le Mans in 1964 this 904 driven by 'Franc'/Kerguen finished 12th, a typical, stolid performance by private owners. (LAT)*

running the 904 with flat-eight 2-litre engine, but had also entered for the first time a 904 powered by the flat-six 1991 cc engine as used in the new production 911 model. This car had been seen briefly at Montlhéry in October 1964 and had run at the Le Mans Test Weekend. Another new Porsche development seen at this race was an 8-cylinder *Spyder*, developed for the European Hill Climb Championship and driven in the Sicilian race by Mitter/Davis. Ferrari won the race, but despite major handling problems the new hill climb car finished second, with the 6-cylinder 904 third and the 8-cylinder fourth. Shortly afterwards Ben Pon finished third in the Spa 500 km race with his own 904.

At the Nürburgring Bonnier/Rindt finished third with a 904 8-cylinder car, but for much of the race they had trailed the new Ferrari Dino and it was quite clear that the 904s were losing their competitive edge. They were raced until the end of the year, but already Porsche had a new and more advanced car under development. At Le Mans the Porsche entries were overshadowed by the battle between Ford and Ferrari; Ferraris took the first three places (all were privately entered cars), but Linge/Nöcker finished fourth and won the Index of Performance and their class with a 6-cylinder 904.

## The 906, 1966

The new Porsche model, of which Porsche laid down a production run of fifty to comply with the new category of Competition Sports Cars known as Group 4, was advanced in almost every way over its predecessor. There was a completely new multi-tubular space-frame chassis with gull-wing doors, a very low nose and the whole of the rear of the body hinged so that it could be raised to uncover the engine and transmission. Suspension and braking were very similar to the 904, mainly because Porsche had large stocks of these parts, with unequal-length wishbones and coil spring/damper units at the front, wishbones, twin forward-facing radius

*The 906 was a very consistent performer. This car driven by Koch/Poirot finished eighth at Le Mans in 1967.* (The Author's Collection)

*Typical privately owned car – the 906 of Jeff Edmonds in the 1968 Tourist Trophy at Oulton Park.* (Guy Griffiths)

arms and coil spring/damper units at the rear and ATE-Dunlop disc brakes front and rear. The engine was a much developed 6-cylinder 911 production engine, with a magnesium instead of aluminium crankcase, together with new pistons, con-rods, cylinders and valve gear. Three twin-choke Weber carburettors were fitted, there was dry sump lubrication as on the production car and power output was 210 bhp at 8000 rpm. Transmission was by a dry single-plate clutch and 5-speed all-synchromesh gearbox.

During the year the 906s enjoyed an immense run of success, both in the hands of works drivers and private entrants. In the Daytona 2000 km race Herrmann/Linge finished sixth and won their class, Herrmann/Buzzetta finished fourth at Sebring, winning their class, Mitter/Herrmann were fourth and class winners at Monza and then came the Targa Florio, in which Porsche scored an outright victory; the winning car was a 906 prepared at the works, but entered by Scuderia Filipinetti and driven by Mairesse/Müller. Also entered in this race was a new version of the 906 with an 8-cylinder engine driven by Klass/Davis, but this retired with suspension failure. The team had also entered two 906s with fuel injection (which meant that they ran in the Prototype class), but both of these were crashed. Other successes during the year were gained at the Nürburgring, where Bondurant/Hawkins finished fourth and won their class, Le Mans, where Davis/Siffert were fourth and won their class, and in the Circuit of Mugello, where Koch/Neerpasch were the outright winners. 906s also took the first three places at Zeltweg and second place and a class win in the Paris 1000 km race at Montlhéry in October.

## The 910 and 907, 1967

Whereas the 904 had been an interim design, incorporating a simple and inexpensive chassis together with an existing engine, the 906 represented for Porsche a major leap forward, with a completely new multi-tubular chassis and incorporating the new 6-cylinder engine. From the 906, there sprang the whole line of Prototypes and competition sports cars that were to come to dominate racing. For 1967, Porsche produced two different variants of this basic theme.

The first of these was the *Typ* 910, again a coupé, with the glass-fibre body bonded to the tubular multi-space frame. The first 910 was a *Spyder*, built for international hill climbs, and this was powered by an 8-cylinder 1981 cc engine developing 270 bhp at 9000 rpm. The examples built for endurance racing were

*At Le Mans in 1967 the Porsche 907 of Siffert/Herrmann which finished fifth leads the sixth-place 910 of Stommelen/Neerpasch. (Nigel Snowdon)*

powered either by the 1991 cc (80 × 66 mm) flat-six engine developing 220 bhp at 8000 rpm or, from the 1967 Targa Florio, an improved version of the flat-eight engine, with a capacity of 2195 cc (80 × 54.6 mm) developing 270 bhp at 8000 rpm. Although it had never been the intention of Porsche to sell the 910 to private owners, many cars were sold after they had been raced by the team during 1967, and as 28 cars were built during the year, when the FIA reduced the number required for homologation in the Sports Car category for 1968 from 50 to 25, the 910 qualified as a Competition Sports Car. Later in 1967, there appeared the *Typ* 907, which was basically a slightly developed version of the 910, with an aero-dynamically much improved body. Just as the 910, it was raced with both the 2-litre flat-six and 2.2-litre flat-eight engines. Unlike the 910, the 907 was fitted with right-hand drive.

This meant that Porsche had now almost complete domination in the 2-litre class, whilst the battle for outright victory on faster circuits was waged between Ford and Ferrari, and for the slower circuits, such as the Targa Florio and the Nürburgring, Porsche had the 2.2-litre cars and a real chance of outright victory. For Porsche the season was exceptional, but only a foretaste of even better things to come. In the Daytona race, now extended to 24 hours, Siffert/Herrmann were fourth overall and won their class with a 2-litre 910, at the Sebring 12-Hours Mitter/Patrick were third with a 910 and won their class, whilst at Monza Rindt/Mitter were again third with a 910 and won the class. A second place for Siffert/Herrmann with a 910 at Spa in the 1000 km race was followed by complete domination by Porsche in the Targa Florio; Paul Hawkins/Ralph Stommelen with a 2.2.-litre 910 were the winners from other 910s driven by Cella/Biscaldi and Neerpasch/Elford. Yet another outright win followed at the Nürburgring, where 910s took the first four places, and the winners were Schütz/Buzzetta with a 6-cylinder 910. For the Le Mans 24 Hours race Porsche concentrated on security in the 2-litre class and did not enter any cars of larger capacity. Fifth place overall and

*The 8-cylinder Porsche 907s of Elford/Neerpasch and Siffert/Mitter lined up in front of the pits before the start of the 1968 BOAC 500 Miles race.* (Nigel Snowdon)

a class win went to Siffert/Herrmann with a 2-litre 907 with long-tail bodywork. At the end of July Mitter/Schütz were first across the line with an 8-cylinder 910 with 2.2-litre engine in the Circuit of Mugello. In the newly inaugurated BOAC 500 race, Siffert/McLaren were third overall and class winners with their 2-litre 8-cylinder 910. In the Prototype Championship, Porsche was only narrowly beaten by Ferrari. This was the last time the works raced the 910.

## The 907 and 908, 1968

Porsche had been aware 'on the grapevine' that the FIA would set a maximum engine capacity for Prototypes of 3 litres for 1968 and, by the time the official announcement was made in October 1967, work on a completely new 3-litre engine was well advanced. In the early part of the year the works Porsche team relied on the 2195 cc 907, both in its ultra-light form of 600 kg, with short-tail bodywork, and also in *Langheck* (long-tail) form, whilst the 910 continued to be raced by works-assisted private owners. The new 908 first appeared at the Le Mans Test Weekend in April 1968 with a 2924 cc (84 × 66 mm) engine developing, when it first raced, around 335 bhp. This power unit, incorporating in its original form the cylinder dimensions of the 6-cylinder engine and with two valves per cylinder and chain-driven camshafts, was given a greater bore of 85 mm by Le Mans; this increased engine capacity to 2997 cc, and by the end of the season power output had risen to 370 bhp at 8400 rpm.

Throughout the 1968 season, Porsche encountered very little in the way of opposition, apart from John Wyer's Ford GT40s, and these achieved during the year far more success than might reasonably have been expected. Porsche started

*The Porsche 908 of Siffert/Herrmann which retired with transmission problems at Le Mans in 1968.* (Nigel Snowdon)

the season with wins in the Daytona 24 Hours and Sebring 12 Hours races, but had a nasty shock in the BOAC 500 race at Brands Hatch, where the 907s were plagued by brake problems. The Ford GT40 entered by Wyer and driven by Ickx/Redman won from the 907s of Scarfiotti/Mitter and ElfordNeerpasch. The new 908s first appeared at the Monza 1000 km race, where two were entered along with a 907 *Langheck*. Both the brand-new 908s ran into problems and Hawkins/Hobbs won with a GT40 from a 907 Porsche driven by Stommelen/Neerpasch. Porsche won the Targa Florio (with the 907 2.2-litre of Elford/Maglioli) and the Nürburgring 1000 km race (with the 908 of Siffert/Elford). At Spa the Porsche entries failed again and whilst the Wyer-entered GT40s took first and fourth places, Porsche had to be satisfied with second and third. All the 908s had problems at Watkins Glen, mainly with wheel bearing failure, possibly caused by a bump in the middle of one of the fastest corners that threw an excessive strain on the left-hand front wheel, and so once again the race was a Ford benefit, with the GT40s in first and second places, and the highest placed 908 finisher sixth. John Wyer had decided to concentrate all his resources on Le Mans and missed the Austrian Grand Prix at Zeltweg run over 500 km. The result was Porsche 908s driven by Siffert and Herrmann/Ahrens first and second, ahead of the private Ford of Paul Hawkins.

The highlight of the 1968 season was the Le Mans 24 Hours race postponed until the end of September. Here Porsche entered four 908 *Lang* coupés with twin fixed vertical rear fins, a fixed aerofoil and suspension-operated rear flaps (a device first seen at Watkins Glen), whilst John Wyer entered three GT40s. In addition there were three 2.2-litre 907s prepared at the works for private owners. They were very much back-up cars, should the 908s fail. And the 908s did fail, with the result that the race was won by the Ford GT40 of Rodriguez/Bianchi with the 907 of Steinemann/Spoerry second and the only surviving 908 of Stommelen/Neerpasch in third place.

Porsche had put an immense effort into the 1968 racing season, both in terms of expense and personnel, and although they had on balance taken the greater share of wins during the season, the now elderly 5-litre Ford GT40 Competition Sports Cars of the Wyer team had provided unexpected and surprisingly strong opposition. It was a situation that Porsche were not prepared to accept and even greater efforts were made for 1969.

## The 908 and 917, 1969

By December 1968 Porsche had completed a total of sixteen 908 coupés and they originally planned to race these in *Normal* and *Lang* forms. The *Normal* short-tail car was claimed to have a speed of 185 mph and was intended to be used on medium-speed circuits, but the new *Spyder* (referred to below) was so successful that the *Normal* was not raced at all during the year. Porsche claimed that the *Lang* coupé which was raced on all the faster circuits in 1969 had a maximum speed of 200 mph. Although the cars were usually fitted with 6-speed gearboxes, just as in 1968, a 5-speed gearbox was used at Daytona. A new version of the 908 was the *Spyder*, with lightweight open body to take advantage of the relaxation in the Prototype regulations which had dispensed with minimum ground clearance, windscreen height, interior dimensions, etc. The claimed maximum speed of the *Spyder* was 175 mph.

The most significant development from Porsche was first seen at the Le Mans Test Weekend. This was the new 917, a 4.5-litre car, which Porsche built at vast expense to exploit the loophole in the regulations that allowed Group 4 Competition Sports Cars (minimum production of 25) to compete alongside the Prototypes.

*With this 908* Spyder *painted in the colours of Porsche's Austrian subsidiary Jo Siffert (seen here at the wheel) and Brian Redman won the 1969 Nürburgring 1000 Km race.* (Nigel Snowdon)

*The Elford/Attwood 917, which was allowed to run with fully moveable rear spoilers, seen before the 1969 Le Mans race. It retired with engine trouble.* (Nigel Snowdon)

The 917 was not in fact a remarkably sophisticated design, but a clear development of existing Porsche practice. The engine was based on that of the flat-eight 908, but with four additional cylinders so as to give a capacity of 4494 cc. The air-cooled engine featured a magnesium-alloy crankcase split along the centre-line, with the crankshaft having a pinion in the middle to provide drive to the twin overhead camshafts per cylinder bank by a train of gears. This central train of gears also drove the usual Porsche horizontal cooling fan. There were two valves and two plugs per cylinder fired by twin distributors. Bosch fuel injection was fitted. When the 917 first appeared, it was claimed that it had a power output of 520 bhp at 8000 rpm, but by the end of the season this has risen to 560 bhp at 8300 rpm. Transmission was by a dry triple-plate clutch and a 5-speed all-synchromesh gearbox in unit with the final drive.

Whilst the general layout of the chassis followed that of the 908, the space-frame was constructed from aluminium-alloy tubing, and the driving position was very much to the front of the car. There were 60-litre fuel tanks in the side members, but this was sufficient for less than an hour's racing. Front suspension was by double wishbones and coil spring/damper units at the front and wishbones, radius arms and coil spring/damper units at the rear, very similar to the layout of the 908. The glass-fibre coupé body had an overall length of 15 ft 6 in *Lang* form and in 1969 form had rear spoilers forming an integral part of the body and actuated by rods from the rear suspension.

Certainly the FIA, when it had permitted 5-litre Competition Sports Cars to compete, had never reckoned that either Porsche would build the 917 or that Ferrari would join in the following year with the 512S. However much these designs may have frustrated the ideas of racing's governing body, they brought the standard and speed of racing to a level never previously seen. As these 220 mph cars screamed through the curves of Spa or thrashed through the rain at Le Mans, they

*The Porsche 908 of Herrmann/Larrousse which finished second at Le Mans in 1969 leads the similar car of Schütz/Mitter which crashed. (Nigel Snowdon)*

provided a motor racing spectacle that had never been previously witnessed and at the time completely overshadowed Grand Prix racing.

Despite these efforts by Porsche to dominate the year's racing, not every race went Stuttgart's way. In the Daytona 24 Hours race, the 908s were plagued by cracked exhausts and were eventually eliminated by a broken gear between the crankshaft and the camshaft. The result was an unexpected victory for the Penske-entered Lola of Donohue/Parsons. The 908s failed again at Sebring, where the winner was the Ford GT40 of Ickx/Oliver with the highest placed Porsche, the 908 *Spyder* of Stommelen/Buzzetta, in third place. It was only with the start of the European season that Porsche seemed to get their house in order and the team won

*At Le Mans in 1969 Jo Siffert and Brian Redman opted to drive this 908 Spyder, which proved very fast, but was eliminated by gearbox trouble.* (Nigel Snowdon)

the next five races in succession; 908 *Spyders* took the first three places in the BOAC 500 race at Brands Hatch, Siffert/Redmond won with a *Lang* 908 at Monza, 908 *Spyders* took the first four places in the Targa Florio, Siffert/Redmond won at Spa with a 908 *Lang* and the 908 *Spyder* took the first two places at the Nürburgring. At the Nürburgring Porsche had introduced a new version of the *Spyder*, that became known in due course as the 908/02, with a much smoother body and a slightly raised glass-fibre panel round the cockpit instead of a windscreen and faired-in cockpit. As originally designed, this 908 was intended to have fully operative flippers, but at Monaco in 1969 all movable aerodynamic devices had become banned and so small fixed spoilers were substituted. The 908/02 of Stommelen/Herrmann finished second at the Nürburgring.

In the meantime, the 917 had run at the Le Mans Test Weekend at the end of March and was homologated as a Competition Sports Car with effect from 1 May. Two 917s were entered at Spa, but their handling was so appalling, snaking badly on the straight and using much of the road through the corners, that it was decided to run only one car for Mitter/Schütz. This was a long-tail car. It retired after only a single lap with engine trouble. Again a single car was entered at the Nürburgring, driven by David Piper/Frank Gardner, and after a slow race it finished eighth.

At Le Mans Porsche made a massive six-car entry, with two 917s and four 908s, of which three were the *Lang* coupés and one was a *Spyder*, which the fastest of the team's drivers, Siffert and Redman, considered preferable because of its superior handling, braking and good acceleration. Both 917s arrived at Le Mans with fully operative rear flippers, the form in which they had been homologated, and after a great deal of argument they were allowed to race with these operative flaps. It did look as though the race would prove a complete Porsche benefit, but events turned out very differently. The 917 of Stommelen/Ahrens retired early in the race, the 908 *Spyder* was eliminated by gearbox trouble, and on the Sunday morning Schütz rolled his 908. At this stage in the race the 917 of Elford/Attwood had a clear lead, five laps ahead of the 908 of Lins/Kauhsen and the John Wyer-entered Ford of Ickx/Oliver, with the other 908 of Herrmann/Larrousse in fourth place. Then the whole face of the race changed, the 917 retired with transmission problems after long delays in the pits, the 908 of Lins/Kauhsen was abandoned on the circuit with clutch failure and the Ford of Ickx/Oliver took the lead from the surviving 908 of Herrmann/Larrousse. Although the Porsche was the faster car, it was mechanically sick and off-tune, whilst the Ford had been driven with great restraint and a strict rev limit. For the remaining one and a half hours of the race the two drivers,

Herrmann and Ickx, waged a furious battle, constantly swapping places, but at the chequered flag, after 24 hours' racing, the Ford led by a matter of 100 yards.

Porsche was bitterly disappointed by the results at Le Mans, after so much effort and expense had been put into the entry, and announced that it was withdrawing from racing for the remainder of the year. But in fact what this meant was that for the remainder of the year the name of Porsche System Engineering did not appear on entry forms. At Watkins Glen, where the team ran 908 *Spyders*, they were entered in the name of Porsche Saltzburg, the company's Austrian subsidiary, and they took the first three places. The final round of the Championship was at the Österreichring, where two short-tail 917s were entered for Siffert/Ahrens and Attwood/Redmond, entered in the names of David Piper and Karl von Wendt, both of whom were potential 917 Porsche buyers. In addition three 908 *Spyders* ran in the name of Porsche Saltzburg. The race was to provide the 917 with its first victory and Siffert/Ahrens won, with the 908 of Attwood/Redman third. Despite the failures at Daytona, Sebring and Le Mans, Porsche were the clear winners of the Championship.

## The 917 and 908/03, 1970

During the latter part of 1969, negotiations had been taking place between Porsche and John Wyer which resulted in Wyer operating the works Porsche team in 1970 in Gulf Oil Corporation colours and with their sponsorship. Working with Wyer, were David Yorke, former Vanwall Grand Prix team manager, who acted as team manager for the Wyer team, and John Horsman, who had worked with Wyer at Aston Martin and was now deputy managing director of J. W. Automotive Engineering Limited.

Wyer's first problem was to resolve the handling problems of the 917. He substantially cured them during a test session at Zeltweg in October, with temporary modifications to the bodywork, which transformed the handling and was refined to the short, cutaway, uplifted tail seen throughout 1970. This version, which became known as the 917 *Kurz*, first appeared on David Piper's private 917 raced in the Kyalami 9 Hours race in November 1969. However, whilst Wyer was running what was supposed to be the works cars, with the chassis prepared at Slough, but the engines supplied by Porsche, the works were also running cars under the name of Porsche Konstruktionen KG, their Austrian subsidiary, and one of the main areas of complaint was that much of the benefit of factory development work was being supplied to their subsidiary in the first instance, rather than to Wyer.

In addition, Porsche developed the new, lightweight 908/03 car, inspired by the *Typ* 909 *Bergspyder*, with polyurethene body, many titanium components and intended only for use on the very tortuous circuits – the Targa Florio and Nürburgring. When these cars were raced, all preparation work was carried out at the factory and not by Wyer.

In 1969 the only real opposition to the 908s had been the obsolescent Ford GT40s of the Wyer team, but the face of racing had been transformed. The massive 917s now faced formidable opposition from the new Ferrari 512S 5-litre Competition Sports Cars raced both by the works and by private teams. Generally, however, the Porsche 917s were slightly lighter than the Ferraris, had better air penetration at speed, matched the Maranello cars in terms of power, but were not so reliable. The Ferraris were heavy, not so well developed or prepared, and generally Ferrari lacked drivers of the calibre of the Porsche entries; with the

*The 917 driven by Rodriguez/Kinnunen which won the rain-soaked 1970 BOAC 500 Miles race at Brands Hatch.* (Nigel Snowdon)

notable exception of Jacky Ickx. Another problem faced by Ferrari was the fact that Maranello was trying to compete in both Formula 1 and endurance racing at the same time and it was only too obvious that the demands made on the team were too excessive for them to do well in both categories. The result was that Porsche dominated the year, not always with cars entered by Wyer, and Ferrari was to achieve only one Championship win.

The Wyer team with the Gulf 917s took the first two places at Daytona in the 24 Hours race at the end of January, but failed at Sebring, where Ferrari scored its sole victory. Another Porsche victory for Wyer followed at the BOAC 1000 km race at Brands Hatch in April, with the Wyer car of Rodriguez/Kinnunen leading home two Porsche Salzburg entries; Rodriguez/Kinnunen were again the winners at Monza. Ferrari was well aware that the 512S was not a suitable car for the Targa Florio, but had nothing else to enter and so fielded a single car. The result was that, apart from the Alfa Romeo Tipo 33/3 cars, the Porsche 908/03s were unopposed and Siffert/Redman and Rodriguez/Kinnunen took the first two places. Although an enlarged engine of 4907 cc (86 × 70.4 mm) developing around 575/590 bhp at 8400 rpm had appeared in one of Wyer's 917s in practice at Monza, these engines were not raced until Spa, where both Wyer cars and one Salzburg car used the enlarged unit. In this case Siffert/Redman again won for Wyer. At the Nürburgring there were 908/03s for both the Wyer team and for Porsche Konstruktionen. Although the Gulf-sponsored cars led the race, Kinnunen crashed and Siffert was eliminated by a seized engine. The result was a victory for Porsche Salzburg, with

*The 917s in the Gulf workshops at Slough in 1970.* (Nigel Snowdon)

Elford/Ahrens leading across the line, five minutes ahead of team-mates Herrmann/Attwood.

Le Mans was to prove very much a three-sided battle, for the Gulf team faced opposition not only from Ferrari but also from other works-supported Porsche entries. Wyer entered three 917s, two of which were powered by 5-litre engines and one with a 4.5-litre, all with the short-tail body, now fitted with small angled spoiler, that Wyer had raced all season. From Porsche Konstrucktionen there were three 917s, two with 5-litre engines and one with a 4.5-litre. Two of the cars were the short-tail cars, as raced by Wyer, one of which was withdrawn after practice; the third Porsche Salzburg entry was a long-tail car of the type first seen at the Le Mans Test Weekend earlier in the year and with a maximum speed of around 220 mph. In addition a 917 *Lang* had also been made available to the Martini Inter-

*For the Targa Florio and the Nürburgring, Porsche produced the 908/03s which were prepared at the factory. Siffert is at the wheel of a Gulf-entered car at the Nürburgring, but both Slough entries were eliminated.* (Nigel Snowdon)

national Racing Team. From Ferrari and Ferrari entrants came a total of ten 512S cars.

It proved a disastrous race for John Wyer's team; Rodriguez/Kinnunen retired out on the circuit early in the race with a broken fan drive-shaft; in the wet, Mike Hailwood crashed the 4.5-litre 917 into Facetti's Alfa, which had spun, and during the night hours Siffert missed a gear-change and broke the engine. The Ferraris too had a host of problems and the race was won by the Porsche Salzburg entry of Attwood/Herrmann from the 917 *Lang* of Larrousse/Kauhsen. This latter, long-tail car was finished in a striking psychedelic mauve and green. There were two remaining rounds in the Championship, at Watkins Glen and in Austria, and both were won by the Wyer team.

*Le Mans in 1970 was won by this Porsche Salzburg-entered 917 driven by Hans Herrmann and Dickie Attwood.* (Nigel Snowdon)

*At Le Mans in 1970 the Martini team entered this long-tail 917 painted in psychedelic mauve and green and driven by Larrousse and Kauhsen. It finished second behind the short tail 917 of Attwood/Herrmann entered by Porsche Salzburg.* (Nigel Snowdon)

*Third place at Le Mans in 1970 was taken by this older Porsche 908* Spyder *entered by the Martini team and driven by Marko/Lins.* (Nigel Snowdon)

## The 917 and 908/03, 1971

The same two models continued to be raced, but a number of modifications had been made to both. From the BOAC 1000 km onwards, Porsche had available a 4999 cc (86.8 × 70.4 mm) engine with increased power output of 620 bhp; for Le Mans, however, the factory favoured the 4907 cc unit. Much effort had been expended on aerodynamic development and at Daytona there first appeared a new and slightly longer tail-section, surmounted by twin tail fins. Two further developments were seen at the Le Mans Test Weekend. The first of these was what might be described as the definitive *Lang* version, with wider body, long and very smooth tail, rear wheels partially enclosed and twin tail fins bridged by an aerofoil. This bodywork was only used at Le Mans. The second development was an experimental body produced in collaboration with the French SERA concern, and featured rotund, stubby lines, with a short tail surmounted by twin fins and enormous louvres in the tops of the front wings. This new car, because of its shape, was nicknamed 'the Pig' and it won the 3 Hours race at the Le Mans Test Weekend driven by Kauhsen/van Lennep.

Few changes were made to the 908/03s, save for steps to reduce weight and the addition of tail fins.

Although Ferrari had abandoned development of his 5-litre Competition Sports

Cars for use by the works, and built cars only for private owners, while concentrating on the development of a new 3-litre Prototype for 1972, the Gulf team faced severe opposition from another team entering Porsche cars. This was the Martini Racing Team, successor to the Porsche Salzburg team of 1970. The Martini team was very closely linked to the works in its racing activities. It depended heavily on works advice and support and whilst John Wyer tended to go his own way and make his own decisions, he sometimes strongly felt that the Martini team was receiving favourable treatment. For their part Martini drivers constantly complained that their cars were down on power compared with the Gulf entries. There was one other serious rival in 1971, Autodelta, who had now got their V-8 3-litre Prototypes well sorted, and stood poised to take class win after class win and snatch outright victory when the Porsche 917s failed.

A new addition to the World Championship was the Buenos Aires 1000 km race in January, and here the Gulf 917s took the first two places. Another victory followed for the Gulf team at Daytona, but at Sebring the Gulf cars ran into problems and victory went to the Martini entry of Elford/Larrousse. Of the Gulf cars, Siffert's had run out of fuel on the circuit and lost 19 laps while fuel was brought on a motorcycle (and there were four penalty laps in addition because the motorcycle was used!) and Rodriguez lost time following a collision with Donohue's Ferrari. There were more problems for the 917s at Brands Hatch, and victory, unexpectedly, went to the Autodelta-entered Alfa Romeo of de Adamich/Pescarolo. Then the Gulf team found its form again and took the first two places at both Monza and Spa, high-speed circuits on which the 3-litre Prototypes of Autodelta were outpaced.

Originally it had been planned to run four 908/03s in the Targa Florio, but only three could be prepared in time; two ran in the blue and orange colours of John Wyer's Gulf Team and one ran in the distinctive silver and blue colours of the Martini team. Both Gulf cars were eliminated by accidents on the first lap, but

*The winning Wyer-entered 917K if Rodriguez/Oliver at Spa in 1971.* (Nigel Snowdon)

*The Martini-entered 917 Lang of Marko/van Lennep leads Pescarolo in the third-place Alfa Romeo 33/3 up the hill from the pits at Spa in 1971. Behind is the Kauhsen/Jöst 917.*
(Nigel Snowdon)

Larrousse pulled out a strong lead with the Martini car, lost time through punctures and then wrecked the suspension on a kerb. The result was an Alfa Romeo landslide with the Autodelta entries taking the first two places. The 908/03s were also entered in the next race, the Nürburgring 1000 km, and here there were four of the cars. Although one of the Gulf cars retired, the other 908/03s took the first three places with Martini first and third, and this was in fact the only race during the year in which Alfa Romeo did not win the 3-litre Prototype class.

At Le Mans there was a total of six 917 entries from the Wyer and Martini teams. John Wyer entered two of the 1971 *Lang* cars, together with a standard 917 with the swept-up tail used at Monza. From the Martini team came a 917 *Lang*, a standard short-tail 917 with the swept-up tail, but also the car with SERA body that had run at the Le Mans Practice Weekend. Because of its nickname, this car had now been painted a porcine pink with dotted lines to indicate the 'cuts' formed by a pig's anatomy. After the first six hours the Gulf-entered cars occupied the first three places, but mechanical troubles intervened, Jöst crashed 'the Pig' and the Martini-entered short-tail 917 of Marko/van Lennep took a lead during the early hours of Sunday morning that it was never to lose. The standard Gulf-entered 917 of Attwood/Müller finished second. Two races remained to round off the Championship year. Rodriguez/Attwood won at the Österreichring for the Gulf team, but at Watkins Glen the 917s again ran into problems and victory went to an Autodelta-entered Alfa Romeo driven by Peterson/de Adamich, with the Gulf-entered 917 of

*In 1971 Porsche continued to field the 908/03, but they were all crashed in the Targa Florio. This Martini-entered car driven by Elford/Larrousse wrecked its front suspension on a kerb. (Nigel Snowdon)*

*Seen on the Saturday evening at Le Mans in 1971 is the 917 Lang of Larrousse/Elford entered by the Martini team. It retired with engine problems caused by overheating.* (Nigel Snowdon)

Siffert/van Lennep in second place. Porsche again won the Championship by a comfortable margin, 72 points to the 51 of Alfa Romeo.

With the ban on 5-litre Competition Sports Cars at the end of 1971, the 917s were no longer seen in international long-distance racing. It has been stated that the 917 programme cost around DM15 million and so the actual cost of the 43 cars completed (parts for 50 were laid down) was DM350,000 each. These figures include the cars that were built for Can-Am racing and Interserie racing. As early as the summer of 1969 a *Spyder* version of the 917 had been built for Jo Siffert to race in the Can-Am series. The cars did not appear in Can-Am racing in 1970, but Siffert raced an unblown car in 1971 from the fourth round onwards, but died in a

*The Gulf team failed again at Le Mans in 1971. This is the long-tail car of Siffert/Bell laying a trail of oil smoke shortly before it retired with engine failure.* (Nigel Snowdon)

crash at Brands Hatch prior to the last round at the end of October. Nevertheless, on his performances in just five races, he took a posthumous fourth place in the Can-Am Challenge Cup. By 1972 Porsche had developed a turbocharged version of the 5-litre, and this was said to have a power output of around 1000 bhp and Porsche signed a three-year contract with Roger Penske Racing with the intention that the turbocharged 917-10 should be driven by Mark Donohue. Donohue finished second in the first round, but was then badly injured in a testing accident and his place was taken by George Follmer. Follmer won the Can-Am Challenge Cup that year and Donohue was the winner in 1973, by when the engine capacity of the 917 had been increased to 5.5 litres. A change in the rules, imposing a fuel consumption restriction on turbocharged cars, effectively ruled out Porsche's chances of success in 1974, and so the cars were withdrawn from the series. Nevertheless 917-10 turbos with 4.5-litre engines were still raced in Europe until the end of 1975, when, again, large-engined turbocharged cars were excluded from Interserie racing.

So far as the 908/03 cars are concerned, at the end of 1971 most were sold to private entrants. Some continued to appear in Sports Car racing, but because there was now a minimum weight of 650 kg (1433 lb) it was necessary to ballast the cars by over 100 kg to comply with the Sports Car regulations, and as a result they lost their competitive edge.

## The 908, 1972

Porsche did not develop a new model for the 1972 season, but left racing to private owners with their now elderly 908 cars. Despite the domination by Ferrari, a measure of success was gained, including second place by Jöst/Schüller in the Monza 1000 km race, and fourth place by Tony Dean/Brown with a very early 908 *Spyder* at Watkins Glen. However, the highlight of the season was Le Mans, where a 908 *Lang* coupé, prepared at the works and looked after by works mechanics 'on holiday', was driven by Jöst/Weber/Casoni and finished third, 19 laps behind the winning Matra.

*Although Porsche temporarily withdrew from racing at the end of 1971, this four-year-old 908 Lang was prepared for the 1972 Le Mans race and driven into third place by Jöst/Weber/Casoni. (Nigel Snowdon)*

## Carrera RSR, 1973

Throughout the years of Prototype and Grand Touring racing covered in this book, Porsche 911s were always well to the fore in their class, scoring success after success, but the factory had always been content to leave these entries to private owners, who raced with support and encouragement from Zuffenhausen. With the 908/03 effectively outlawed from endurance racing (and before long also the 917-10 and 917-30 from Can-Am racing), the factory decided to implement a racing programme based on the 911 and this seemed a particularly wise course of action as there was under discussion a new formula which would require the cars running in World Championship long-distance races to be production-derived. The new Carrera RSR Prototype was closely based, so far as the body and chassis were concerned, on the standard 2.7-litre Carrera RS, but with the engine increased in capacity to 2806 cc (92 × 70.4 mm) and developing 300 bhp at 8000 rpm. Throughout, however, there had been substantial detail changes and for a full account of these the reader is referred to *Porsche Racing Cars of the 70s* by Paul Frère (Patrick Stephens Limited, 1980).

The new cars first appeared in the Daytona 24 Hours race in February 1973 and Gregg/Haywood won the race outright from a Ferrari Daytona driven by Minter/Migault. At this point the factory decided to take over the entry of the cars itself and these were run in the colours of Martini, who were sponsoring the team. With these production-derived cars, Porsche won outright the Targa Florio (by which race engine capacity had been increased to 2993 cc, 95 × 70.4 mm, and power increased to 315 bhp) with a car driven by van Lennep/Müller and, taking into account points gained by the 908/03, the make finished third in the Endurance Championship. It also won the Grand Touring Cup by a very substantial margin.

*In 1973 the Targa Florio was won by this Martini-entered Porsche Carrera RS driven by van Lennep/Müller.* (Nigel Snowdon)

### Carrera RSR, 1974

Porsche continued the line of 911 development by producing a turbocharged version of the 911. Because of the equivalency formula whereby turbocharged cars were regarded as having a capacity of 1.4 times the actual, the new engines had a capacity of 2142 cc (83 × 66 mm) and developed close to 500 bhp. Although the year in Championship racing was dominated by the Matras, the new Porsche RSRs took second place at Le Mans (van Lennep/Müller) and Watkins Glen (the same driver pairing) and in fact during the year, out of nine races entered, van Lennep/Müller retired only twice.

Porsche stayed out of racing in 1975, but reappeared in 1976. That was the first year of the new World Championship for Makes and Porsche embarked once again upon an era of domination, unbroken to the present day, apart form Jaguar's World Championship victory in 1987.

# Rover-B.R.M. (United Kingdom)

In 1963 the Rover Company, a long-time pioneer of gas-turbine cars and Formula 1 constructor B.R.M, collaborated with a car aimed at winning the special prize of £2,000 for the first gas-turbine car to average 150 kph for the 24 hours of the Le Mans race. The car was based on the P25 B.R.M. Formula 1 multi-tubular space-frame chassis, cut down the middle and widened to make a 2-seater. As on the Formula 1 car, front suspension was by double wishbones and inclined coil spring/damper units, with, at the rear, a de Dion axle located by a Watts linkage, and twin radius arms with coil spring/dampers. The Rover gas-turbine was a two-shaft, free-power unit, in fact built for industrial purposes. It consisted of a gasifier section, with turbine and compressor, and a power output section. The

*In 1963 the gas-turbine Rover-B.R.M. ran at Le Mans in a category of its own and carried the number '00'. It had a completely trouble-free race.* (Nigel Snowdon)

compressor turbine turned at 65,000 rpm, the power turbine at 43,000 rpm and developed around 150 bhp. Drive was through two pairs of helical reduction gears to the B.R.M. final drive with a forward-reverse lever whereby the driving dogs could be withdrawn and an idler gear for reverse picked up. Because of the braking problems with a gas-turbine car, larger and thicker brake discs were fitted. There were knock-on light-alloy Dunlop disc wheels. A total of 48.5 gallons of paraffin was carried in two light-alloy side tanks, considered to be sufficient for two and a half to three hours of racing. There was a very simple open light alloy body.

At the Test Weekend Ginther lapped in 4 mins 35.3 sec, 176.02 kph, and so the prospects of the car achieving its target in the race were excellent. The Le Mans Weekend did reveal a number of problems. Firstly the body admitted water just about everywhere and secondly the tail tended to lift at speed. By the race itself a number of modifications had been carried out, including the fitting of a spoiler in the tail, lowered front wings to improve aerodynamics and the windscreen set in a wide perspex surround sweeping back slightly over the cockpit and with partially enveloping sides.

So far as the official results at Le Mans were concerned, the Rover-B.R.M. was not a contender, but ran in its own category with the number 00 and started 30 seconds after the rest of the field. Driven by Graham Hill and Richie Ginther, the Rover-B.R.M. whistled round the circuit, in almost complete silence, completely trouble free, covering the race with only brake pad changes to the front wheels, some oil added to the transmission and without a tyre change. The car covered 4,172.91 kilometres at an average of over 173 kph, and although not officially classified, it would have in fact been in seventh place just ahead of the A.C. Cobra of Bolton/Sanderson.

In 1964, Rover-B.R.M. returned to the Sarthe circuit for the Test Weekend, but now the car had neat and stylish coupé bodywork, the work of Rover stylists, and the engine was fitted with a heat-exchanger which was said to increase the power and vastly improve the fuel consumption. Now the Rover-B.R.M. was eligible to run in the 2000 cc class. The car was withdrawn from the race however for further development. When it reappeared at the Le Mans Test Weekend in 1965 it was suffering from brake problems, but was otherwise trouble-free. In the 24 Hours race itself in June it proved less than trouble-free, mainly because of overheating, and with Graham Hill/Jackie Stewart at the wheel it was classified tenth overall, having covered 3,815.36 km, and finished third in its class. Although the distance covered was lower than in 1963, because of the overheating problems, fuel consumption had vastly improved and it had averaged around 13 mpg compared with 7 mpg in 1963. The Rover-B.R.M. was purely an experiment and it did not again appear in Prototype racing.

# Serenissima (Italy)

Towards the end of 1961, there was a major disagreement between Enzo Ferrari and some of his senior staff, who left the company, and a few of them set up a new organisation known as A.T.S. (Automobile Turismo y Sport). The designer was Carlo Chiti, whilst the organisation was sponsored by Count Volpi. Volpi had been running a team known as the Scuderia Serenissima di Republica Venezia, mainly entering sports Ferraris. Under Chiti's direction, the company had two main aims, the development of a Formula 1 car and the production of a Grand Touring Prototype. The Formula 1 car featured a 90-degree V-8 engine of 1,494 cc (66 × 5.46 mm), allegedly developing, with four twin-choke Weber carburettors, 190

*Racing appearances by the Serenissima were rare, but this 3.5-litre Spyder was driven in the 1966 Le Mans race by Sauer/de Mortemart. It retired because of gearbox failure.* (Nigel Snowdon)

bhp at 10,000 rpm. This was used in conjunction with a 6-speed Colotti Type 35 gearbox. The chassis was a multi-tubular space-frame with front and rear suspension by double wishbones and coil springs. Because of the dissension at Ferrari, A.T.S. had succeeded in signing Ferrari drivers Phil Hill and Giancarlo Baghetti. The new Formula 1 car was an abysmal disaster, badly designed, appallingly prepared, and, when it did race, hopelessly unreliable. During the year the team ran in only three Grands Prix, retiring in two events, but in the Italian Grand Prix, Hill and Baghetti finished in 11th and 15th places. Mainly because Volpi had withdrawn his financial support, the team face severe financial difficulties, but their reason for withdrawing at the end of the season was primarily the sheer loss of will to continue with the hopeless project.

When Volpi withdrew his support, he took with him the 2500GT car, which had reached a reasonable state of development. General design principles followed that of the Formula 1 car, but the rear-mounted 90-degree V-8 engine with twin overhead camshafts had a capacity of 2,467 cc (76 × 68 mm) and with four Weber carburettors was claimed to develop 245 bhp at 7,700 rpm. There was a 5-speed fully-synchromesh gearbox. As with the Formula 1 car, the chassis was a multi-tubular space-frame with front and rear suspension by double wishbones and coil spring/damper units. Originally A.T.S. had planned to build the car either as a lightweight competition model with alloy body, and as a road-equipped car with steel body by Allemano. More than anything else Volpi was an enthusiast for motor racing and once he had his hands on the future of the GT model, he decided to concentrate only on the competition version, which he called the Serenissima.

Development work was carried out by former Ferrari technician Alberto Massimino and by de Tomaso, and when tested at Monza very early in 1965 the car

207

*The 1969 Mk 168 Serenissima* Spyder *which appeared at the Norisring.*

featured a 2996 cc (91.5 × 57 mm) engine with three valves per cylinder and claimed to develop 300 bhp at 8500 rpm. There was also to be a 3.5-litre version of this engine with a claimed power output of 340 bhp at 8000 rpm. The body was a very neat and stylish coupé with gull-wing doors, sloping bonnet line and broad air intake at the front. Like so many other projects since the dawn of motor racing, conception was far easier than development, and the car made no impression in 1965. Volpi, however, was determined to press on with the development of the car and, apart from coming to an arrangement with Bruce McLaren to supply the Serenissima engine in 3-litre form to power the McLaren Formula 1 car in 1966, he had built a very attractive 3.5-litre Prototype with stylish Spyder bodywork by Fantuzzi, which was entered at Le Mans in 1966. At Le Mans the car was driven by Sauer/de Mortemart, but it retired during the fourth hour of the race with gearbox problems. For a while nothing further was heard of the Serenissima, but in 1968 a new coupé Prototype appeared based on an old McLaren M1B Group 7 (sports car) chassis. Jonathan Williams drove this car in the Enna Cup Race in Sicily and finished second to a Porsche 910 driven by Jo Siffert. For 1969 the Prototype regulations had been relaxed with many of the requirements as to minimum dimensions and weight done away with, and so the Serenissima was rebuilt with an open roadster body. Williams drove the car at the Norisring in Germany, but achieved no success. Not long afterwards Serenissima went into liquidation and in 1970 Moreno Baldi purchased some of the components of the original company and tried to revive the A.T.S. name. Morena built an open Spyder A.T.S. with Cosworth 1-litre engine which he raced during 1970, but this effort soon evaporated.

# Sunbeam Tiger (United Kingdom)

In 1961 a Sunbeam Alpine with Harrington coupé body had won the Index of Thermal Efficiency at Le Mans and in 1964 the team returned to Le Mans with two special Tiger cars. The Tiger, which had been introduced at the New York Automobile Show in the spring of 1964, was basically the Alpine 1.7-litre car, appropriately strengthened and modified and fitted with the Ford V-8 4.2-litre engine. It did not achieve great success as a production sports car, although over the years it has attracted an enthusiastic following. The two Le Mans cars were built by Lister of Cambridge, a concern that had a famous reputation as a builder of sports-racing cars in the 1950s, but who were now somewhat out of touch with racing. Lister, however, wanted to fit aluminium bodies, but the Rootes Group insisted on steel bodies so that the cars should retain a closer affinity with the production models. The body of the Le Mans Tiger was a very smooth coupé designed by Ron Wisdom of the Rootes Group, with Kamm cut-off tail. The 4.2-litre engines had been modified by Shelby and featured special camshafts, cylinder heads and four-barrel carburettors; power output was 275 bhp.

The first of the cars appeared at the Le Mans Test Weekend in April, very shortly after the announcement of the production car, and it was driven by Peter Procter and Mike Parkes. On the Mulsanne straight, the Sunbeam achieved 149 mph compared with the 168 mph of Peter Sargent's E-type Jaguar.

It was obvious that the Tiger still needed a great deal of development work, but there was no real time for this before the 24 Hours race in June. Rootes seriously considered pulling the cars out of the race, but so much money had been expended that there seemed little alternative but to carry on. In practice the cars were handling badly and in addition there were bearing and piston problems. In the race neither car was as fast as expected, both ran well down the field, the Ballisat/Dubois car retired in the fourth hour of the race with a blown engine and the second car, driven by Blumer/Procter, retired in the early hours of Sunday morning with no oil pressure. The cars were not again raced by the works, but did make one or two appearances in private hands. They represented the nadir of Rootes competition efforts, after many years of successful rallying with the Alpine and its predecessors.

*Two Sunbeam Tigers built by Lister ran at Le Mans in 1964. This car, driven by Blumer/Procter, is seen with Blumer hanging out the tail at Mulsaune, but both entries were eliminated by engine failure.*

# Tojeiro (United Kingdom)

From 1952 John Tojeiro had been building a very small number of sports-racing cars, based on a twin-tubular chassis, with independent suspension front and rear. These cars were supplied to a number of private entrants and the best known was

Cliff Davis's Bristol-powered car, which he raced with considerable success during 1953–54. This chassis formed the basis of the production A.C. Ace. From 1955 onwards Tojeiro built a number of more advanced cars with multi-tubular space-frame chassis, front suspension by unequal-length wishbones and coil spring/damper units and rear suspension by a de Dion axle suspended on coil spring/damper units. The first of these cars, again Bristol-powered, was supplied to Percy Crabbe and from this there was developed the Tojeiro-Jaguar, two examples of which were supplied to Ecurie Ecosse and a small number of cars were also built powered by 1098 cc Coventry Climax engines.

David Murray's Ecurie Ecosse team had raced Jaguars since 1952, graduating to C-type and D-type cars, winning at Le Mans in both 1956 and 1957, and from 1958 onwards turning to proprietary chassis, both Lister and Tojeiro, which they raced with Jaguar engines. By 1961 the traditional Jaguar-powered sports car was obsolete, no match in British races for the lightweight breed of Coopers and Lotuses, and both outclassed and, when powered by the 3-litre version of the Jaguar engine, insufficiently reliable for endurance racing. Accordingly Murray commissioned John Tojeiro to design and build for the team a new Prototype coupé to comply with the regulations of 1962 onwards.

Tojeiro, in accordance with contemporary practice, decided on a mid-mounted engine and a multi-tubular space-frame chassis; this chassis was constructed from 1 in. and ³/₄ in. round- and square-section steel tubing. Front suspension was by wide-based, unequal-length wishbones, coil spring/damper units and anti-roll bar. Again, at the rear, there were, initially, double wishbones and coil spring/damper units. The steering was rack and pinion, the brakes were Dunlop discs and there were 15 in. magnesium-alloy wheels. The power unit was the 2495 cc 4-cylinder Coventry Climax engine with transmission by a Cooper-Knight 5-speed gearbox. The light alloy coupé body, with strikingly handsome lines, was the work of

*At the European Grand Prix meeting at Brands Hatch in July 1964 the Mk 2 Tojeiro-Buick was driven into eighth place in the Guards Trophy race by Jackie Stewart.* (Nigel Snowdon)

*The Tojeiro-Buick photographed at Ecurie Ecosse's premises at Merchiston Mews, Edinburgh in about October 1964.* (The Author)

Williams & Pritchard Ltd. Whilst the cars, typed the EE, were constructed by Tojeiro in his works at Barkway, Essex, they were finished and subsequently repaired and rebuilt at Ecurie Ecosse's famous premises in Merchiston Mews, Edinburgh.

Ecurie Ecosse had hoped to field two cars at Le Mans in 1962, but only the one could be prepared in time. This was driven by Dickson/Fairman, and after running steadily in mid-field, gearbox problems developed and these caused its eventual retirement.

Although this was a debut of some promise, the reality was that Tojeiro's concept was not sufficiently advanced to achieve any real success and the development of such a new car was beyond the resources of the Ecurie Ecosse team. It had also become obvious that the 2.5-litre Climax engine, originally designed for use in Formula 1, was simply not a suitable power unit for Prototype racing, and Murray hastily looked for a substitute. For 1963 Murray re-worked the cars into the Mk 2 version, which were powered by a Buick V-8 3.5-litre engine and with a 4-speed Chevrolet Corvair gearbox. Originally it was intended to reduce the stroke of the Buick engine to a capacity of under 3 litres. If this was not done, then the complicated weight/capacity requirements of the regulations would have meant that the car would have been below the minimum weight limit.

Ecurie Ecosse indicated that they would be running in a full season of races during 1963, but in fact they could not even secure an entry at Le Mans. This was a sad blow for a team that had won the race only six years previously, but their own shortcomings were the real problem. The Automobile Club de l'Ouest were hardly able to accept an entry from a team that did not know whether it would be able to field one or two cars and was not even sure what engine capacity they would have. As it was Ecurie Ecosse had to content themselves with running the cars in a few minor British events, in the main with Jackie Stewart at the wheel. Murray had recognized the young Scotsman's talent at a very early stage. Ecurie Ecosse pressed on with the cars in 1964, but they were not sufficiently reliable for endurance racing (and the team could not afford a full season) and they were not sufficiently competitive in British short-circuit events. The best performances of the year were a sixth place by Stewart at the Sports Car race at Silverstone in May and an eighth in the Sports Car race at the British Grand Prix meeting at Brands Hatch in July.

For 1965 Ecurie Ecosse were planning a Mk 3 version of the Tojeiro EE with a Shelby-modified Ford 4.7-litre V-8 engine and Hewland gearbox. One of the cars was rebuilt as a Group 7 open sports-racing car and this form was known as the Ecosse-Ford.

By this stage the cars were completely obsolescent and lacked the potential to do well in the face of the might of the American-powered opposition, be it at an international endurance level or in Group 7 Sports Car racing. Both cars were offered for sale in 1966, and the Ecosse-Ford was badly crashed by Bill Stein at the British Grand Prix meeting at Brands Hatch in July 1966. It also marked the end for Ecurie Ecosse, a sad finale for a team that had achieved so much in international Sports Car racing.